The BIG SCRUM

The BIG SCRUM

How Teddy Roosevelt
Saved Football

JOHN J. MILLER

HARPER ● PERENNIAL

NEW YORK ● LONDON ● TORONTO ● SYDNEY ● NEW DELHI ● AUCKLAND

HARPER ● PERENNIAL

A hardcover edition of this book was published in 2011 by HarperCollins Publishers.

HarperCollins books may be purchased for educational, business, or sales promotional use. For information please write: Special Markets Department, Harper-Collins Publishers, 10 East 53rd Street, New York, NY 10022.

FIRST HARPER PERENNIAL EDITION PUBLISHED 2012.

Designed by Renato Stanisic

Library of Congress Cataloging-in-Publication Data has been applied for.

ISBN 978-0-06-174452-5 (pbk.)

HB 10.04.2021

TO BRENDAN, JOSIE, AND PATRICK,

my favorite athletes

Contents

Introduction: America's Game

I met my wife on the way to a football game. At least that's my first clear memory of her—our walk from Mary Markley Hall, across the Diag, down State Street, and finally to Michigan Stadium. We didn't start dating until basketball season. Yet long before we were joined in matrimony, we shared a love for the maize and blue. It's what got us started.

My romance with college football goes back farther than my romance with her. It begins in my early boyhood—a period of indoctrination orchestrated by my father, who had attended the University of Michigan in the 1950s. When most other kids were learning their letters, he made sure that I could sing "Hail to the Victors." For us, the "Carter era" isn't a reference to a troubled presidency in the late 1970s, but rather to a glorious era in which wide receiver Anthony Carter wore a winged helmet and caught touchdown passes under the watch of coach Bo Schembechler (of sainted memory). Our family celebrated Christmas, Easter, and all the other usual holidays. Then there was one more, on what was always the biggest game day of the year: the Saturday in November when Michigan played Ohio State.

When I first began to attend Michigan football games as a student, along with my future bride and more than one hundred thousand of our closest friends, I came to realize that these contests are more than athletic competitions. They are cultural rituals of deep significance. They not only unite a diverse campus of engineering students and English majors, but they also create a community of fans across a region and beyond. Michigan's boosters can be young or old, black or white, alumni or high school dropouts. They can be well-groomed auto executives or lunchbucket union guys. They can be flannel-wearing Yoopers from the Upper Peninsula or suburban trolls from metro Detroit. They can meet on the other side of the world. Conversations about the team are social icebreakers—a way to form bonds between fathers and sons, colleagues at work, and strangers at parties. My marriage is not the only one that owes a debt to the game.

Love for a college football team, whether it's the Tennessee Volunteers or the Texas Longhorns, is almost tribal. In some cases, such as my own, the affiliation is practically inherited. In others, it's chosen. Whatever the origin, it has the power to form lifelong loyalties and passions. I still get chills thinking about the sound of the marching band when it plays our fight song and the roar of the crowd when our squad runs onto the field. The sensation is a close cousin of patriotism. On brisk autumn afternoons, my three main allegiances are to God, family, and football.

I didn't play football except as a pickup game in the backyards of my neighborhood or on the fields by school—never under the glare of Friday night lights. I know the sport primarily as a spectator. No other game has such a combination of brute force and pure grace, the crashing bodies at the line of scrimmage and the careful choreography of a well-executed play involving eleven men, and the infantry combat of a rushing attack as well as the air war of a passing assault. There's a strong intellectual dimension as well. Baseball may bask in its reputation as a cerebral pastime, but no sport demands more meticulous planning or quick calculation than football. This is a pursuit not just for players and the fans who cheer them on, but also for coaches and the armchair generals who second-guess their every move. Little wonder that football has become the most popular sport in the United States, with millions of kids who play in youth leagues or high schools, millions of adults who fill stadiums on weekends and Monday nights, and millions of others who watch broadcasts from the comfort of home. Americans are probably more likely to know the name of their favorite team's starting quarterback than the name of their congressman. A good case can be made that they have their priorities straight.

Football has become such a central part of our national identity that we almost take it for granted. We expect the season to kick off around Labor Day, enjoy games as the air cools and trees shed their leaves, and anticipate college bowl matchups on New Year's Day and the professional championship on Super Bowl Sunday. The sport has earned a permanent place in the rhythm of our lives. If we didn't have football, a lot of us wouldn't know what to do with ourselves.

Yet there was a moment when football almost was taken away from us—a time when its very existence was in mortal peril as a collection of Progressive Era prohibitionists tried to ban the sport. They objected to its violence, and their favorite solution was to smother a newborn sport in its cradle. It took the remarkable efforts of one of America's most extraordinary men to thwart them.

Had the enemies of football gotten their way, they would have erased one of America's greatest pastimes from our cultural life.

And maybe I'd still be a bachelor.

The BIG
SCRUM

Frederic Remington became a famous artist of the American West, but football was also a common subject of his work, as in this 1893 illustration. *(© North Wind Picture Archives)*

Chapter One

THE KILLING FIELDS

On an autumn afternoon in 1876, Theodore Roosevelt attended his first football game. He was a college freshman who had just turned eighteen. This young man who was destined for great things was enthusiastic about athletics and keen on seeing the newfangled sport of football in person. The previous afternoon, he and about seventy or eighty classmates had traveled from Cambridge, Massachusetts, to New Haven, Connecticut. They wanted to watch Harvard play Yale, in the second-ever football game between two of the greatest rivals in college sports.[1]

Roosevelt spent the morning of Saturday, November 18, touring the local sights with a Yale student he knew from his days of growing up in New York City. "I am very glad I am not a Yale freshman," wrote Roosevelt. "The hazing there is pretty bad. The fellows too seem to be a much more scrubby set than ours."[2]

The weather was scrubby as well, with overcast skies and gusting winds. Ships jammed the nearby harbor, driven in by gale-force blasts of cold air from the sea. By early afternoon, Roosevelt and his friends started to assemble for the game in Hamilton Park, where patches of mud would cause the players to slip and slide as they battled up and down the field.[3]

Before play began, the two teams met to discuss the rules. Football was in its infancy, still a work in progress, and only remotely like the sport into which it would evolve. There was no common agreement about many of its most basic elements. What number of men would participate? What would count for a score? How long would the game last? Teams had to make these decisions prior to the kickoff, like 21st-century schoolchildren who must set up boundaries, choose between a game of touch or tackle, and figure out how to count blitzes.

Harvard was confident of victory. Its players were more experienced than Yale's and they had recently tasted success. Three weeks earlier, they had defeated a pair of Canadian teams in Montreal, shutting out both in the span of three days. Against Yale, Harvard was favored by odds of five-to-one.[4] The previous year, the first time the two schools ever met to play football, Harvard had beaten Yale by a score of four goals to none. The game was even more lopsided than the score would seem to indicate. Harvard had dominated just about every aspect of the play. Yale's men had looked tentative, as if they were confused about the most basic elements of the sport. In the sequel, many expected a repeat performance. "Everybody accepted it as a foregone conclusion that Yale was destined to defeat," wrote the *New York Sun*.[5]

When it came to football, Harvard was the teacher and Yale the student—so much so, in fact, that just a few days before the 1876 contest that Roosevelt would watch, Harvard had sent Yale an elongated, rugby-style ball. Up to that point, Yale had trained for the Harvard game with a spherical ball. When the new one showed up, Yale's players had to figure out how to play with it. They experimented with the best ways of holding it and tried to make sense of its unpredictable bounces. They did not agree on everything and wound up debating fundamentals such as whether it was most effective to punt the ball on its side or on its end.[6]

Harvard may have felt some pity for its opponent. As the school's veterans prepared for the rematch, they agreed to a couple of suggestions proposed by Yale. The first would carry with it a lasting legacy: Rather than playing with fifteen men to a side, as was the current custom, the teams would play with eleven men apiece. This was to become the first football game featuring eleven players on the field per team, giving rise to the habit of referring to a football squad as "the eleven." The second suggestion would not have quite the same impact on the future of the sport, but it would affect the outcome of the upcoming contest: Touchdowns would not count for points, and only goals kicked after touchdowns or from the field would contribute to the final score.

Shortly after two o'clock on that unpleasant afternoon of soggy turf and wintry wind, the teams took the field. It measured 140 yards in length and seventy yards in width.[7] Harvard wore red and Yale wore blue. The players warmed up for about half an hour. They flipped a coin. Harvard won the toss and called for Yale to defend the north end of the park. The game began a little before three o'clock.

If Harvard's players thought they were going to demolish Yale once more, they soon learned their error. A year earlier, they had scored almost immediately against Yale. This time, most of the forty-five-minute first half would tick away before F. A. Houston escaped from the clutches of Yale's tacklers and ran for a long touchdown. Under the rules agreed upon that very afternoon, touchdowns did not earn points. Yet they did lead to goal-scoring opportunities: A kicker had to boot the ball over a clothesline stretched between a pair of posts set about twenty feet apart, from a distance of a hundred feet. Harvard set up for the attempt—and missed. At halftime, the game remained scoreless.

Even so, many observers thought that Harvard looked like the stronger team. It was more organized and better disciplined. If Yale's players were bigger and faster, they were also raw and prone to mistakes. Harvard's men knew the essentials of how to play the game. Over time, the battle-tested experience of well-practiced teams often trumps the raw abilities of individual athletes. Roosevelt and his classmates must have liked their team's chances going into the second half.

After the break, loud chants of "Ya-Ya-Yale" erupted from the fans—and the men in blue soon pushed their way into Harvard territory. A lanky Yale freshman named Walter Camp tried to shovel the ball to his teammate, Oliver D. Thompson. It was a poor lateral pass that failed to reach Thompson's outstretched arms. Instead, it hit the ground. The ball bounced upward, taking one of those odd hops that can befuddle the most skilled players. Thompson sensed an opportunity. In a split second, he decided to take a chance. From about thirty-five yards away and at a wide angle, he put his foot to the ball. It soared into the air. Remarkably, it sailed over the rope and through the uprights. The improbable kick gave Yale a lead of 1–0.[8]

The game still had about fifteen minutes left on the clock, but Yale students celebrated the point as if they had triumphed in sudden-death overtime. They tossed their hats into the air and stormed the field, hoisting players onto their shoulders and marching them around in delight. Rather than watch these celebrations, or even wait for them to conclude, Harvard tried to put the ball back in play and quickly ran for a touchdown. Yet a referee disallowed it. He reasoned that Yale might have stopped Harvard if only its players had enjoyed a better understanding of the rules, which called for the game to go on after a score—even a score by a rambunctious underdog against a heavily favored opponent. Harvard complained about the decision, but the official refused to change his mind. The game would go on when Yale was ready.[9]

When play finally resumed, Harvard took the ball and forced it into Yale's end. The clock became Harvard's enemy, almost as much as the opposing players. With just seconds to go, E. H. Herrick, a senior, grabbed the ball, rushed forward, and crossed the goal line for a touchdown. Then the referee ruled that time had expired. The touchdown counted, but there would be no try for a goal kick. The game was over. Yale had won.

Harvard's loss frustrated Roosevelt and the crowd from Cambridge. They felt their team was better than Yale's, no matter what the final score indicated. The *Boston Daily Globe* grumbled that Yale's players were "so ignorant of the rules that they persisted in a course of play which throughout the game was very productive of 'fouls.'" In particular, Yale displayed a "reckless disregard of the rules concerning 'off side.'" Moreover, sniffed the anonymous writer of the article, the referees did not call nearly enough penalties: "The Harvard team bore with these mischances with creditable patience under the circumstances."[10]

Roosevelt shared this view. In a letter to his mother the next day, written from Cambridge, he did not say whether he had enjoyed himself as he shivered among his fellow students and watched a game of football for the first time. The future president certainly had no inkling of football's eventual popularity. Neither could he have anticipated the crucial role that he would play in the sport's development, as it changed from a rugby-like activity into the game that millions of Americans know and love in the 21st century.

On the day after Harvard suffered its loss to Yale, the young Roosevelt simply gave voice to the frustrations that so often accompany the agony of defeat. "I am sorry to say we were beaten," he wrote, "principally because our opponents played very foul."[11]

. . . .

IN 1876, ROOSEVELT turned eighteen—and the United States celebrated its one hundredth birthday. Millions flocked to the Centennial Exhibition in Philadelphia, where the Declaration of Independence had been signed. Gruesome memories of the Civil War remained fresh, but Americans tried to orient themselves toward the future. They preferred to look upon their nation's history with a sense of satisfaction and approval. They had come a long way in just a century.

The years ahead were full of bright possibility. During the 1870s, the population of the United States surged from about 38 million to more than 50 million. Cities burst with people, thanks to healthy birthrates among natives and immigration from Europe. Both the interior of the continent and its west coast, full of elbow room, beckoned for settlers.

The pace of technology picked up speed. Early in 1876, Alexander Graham Bell received a patent for the telephone. An express train traveled from coast to coast for the first time, chugging from New York to San Francisco in three and a half days. Colorado gained admission to the Union as the thirty-eighth state. Budweiser beer and Heinz ketchup made their commercial debuts. Professional baseball's National League organized itself, with eight participating clubs. *The Adventures of Tom Sawyer*, by Mark Twain, appeared in print. The book's initial sales were disappointing, but in time, Twain's tale of boyhood adventure would become recognized as a popular classic of American literature.

Several years would pass before another of Twain's famous characters, Huck Finn, promised to light out for the territory. In 1876, there was still time to escape from civilization. The West remained wild. In a Deadwood saloon, Jack McCall murdered Wild Bill Hickok. Just a few weeks earlier, near the Little Bighorn River in the Montana Territory, Sitting Bull and Crazy Horse had led a combined force of Lakota and Northern Cheyenne warriors against the 7th Cavalry Regiment, commanded by the flamboyant General George Armstrong Custer. According to most accounts, the crushing defeat of Custer and his men took about as long as the first half of the Harvard-Yale football game.

In truth, the era of the frontier was coming to a close. Custer's last stand was a last gasp of Indian resistance—it marked a temporary setback in the permanent settlement of the West, rather than a reversal of fortune for tribes that soon found themselves confined to reservations. For years, men in search of challenge and excitement had sensed the promise of the region. Theodore Roosevelt would feel its pull in the 1880s, when his student days were over. Yet its allure began to shift, however subtly. The days of exploring a vast and untamed wilderness transitioned into a period of agricultural development and community building.

On the east coast, sports boomed in popularity. Prior to the Civil War, organized athletics were almost unknown. Afterward, they became ubiquitous. Baseball started to assume its position as a national pastime. A huge and diverse range of activities—croquet, lawn tennis, archery, bicycling, and roller skating—spread from city to city. "This phenomenal expansion in the field of sports was the most significant development in the nation's recreational life that had yet taken place," wrote Foster Rhea Dulles, a historian (and a cousin of Secretary of State John Foster Dulles). "The traditions of pioneer life had influenced [Americans] along very definite lines, and the restrictions of urban living warred against a feeling for the outdoors which was in their blood. With the gradual passing of so much of what the frontier had always stood for, sports provided a new outlet for an inherently restless people."[12]

Into this environment, football was born. Several early commentators thought the sport was preposterous. In 1873, the University of Michigan tried to arrange a contest against Cornell, to be played in Cleveland. The president of Cornell, Andrew D.

White, refused the invitation: "I will not permit thirty men to travel four hundred miles merely to agitate a bag of wind."[13] Soon enough, Cornell and just about every other institution of higher learning would have a team and strive to fill a schedule with challenging games.

As much as the young Theodore Roosevelt wanted Harvard to beat Yale in 1876, he was almost certainly more interested in seeing Hayes beat Tilden. A couple of weeks before the game in New Haven, the United States had conducted one of the closest and most controversial presidential elections in its history. Roosevelt was for Rutherford B. Hayes, a Republican from Ohio, and opposed to Samuel Tilden, a Democrat from New York. He had rallied for Hayes on the streets of Cambridge. On the night of October 26, his gang raised the hackles of a Harvard senior, who leaned out a second-story window and yelled, "Hush up, you blooming freshmen!" The order stirred the crowd. "Every student there was profoundly indignant," recalled one of the marchers. "I noticed one little man, small but firmly knit. He had slammed his torch to the street. His fists quivered like steel springs and swished through the air as if plunging a hole through a mattress: I had never seen a man so angry before."[14] The little man was Roosevelt, participating in his first known political activity.

After the election on November 7, it looked as though Tilden had won. A slight majority of Americans had voted for him, but nobody knew the outcome for sure. The states still had to confirm their totals. The results in Florida, Louisiana, and South Carolina remained unclear. As election officials counted votes, partisans wrangled for advantage.

The *New York Times*, which was a Republican paper, assured its readers in almost every edition that Hayes would prevail. On November 19—the day after the Harvard-Yale football game— the front page reported a late-breaking development: "Our news this morning is of the highest importance." South Carolina had gone Republican, which meant that Hayes, beyond almost any reasonable doubt, would become the nineteenth president. He lost the popular vote but carried the electoral college by the slimmest of margins, 185 votes to 184. Bitter Democrats would nickname him Rutherfraud B. Hayes.

ON THE DAY this article appeared in print, a copy of the *Times* cost a nickel. It did not have a separate sports section. That invention of journalism would have to wait for another two decades, when it first appeared in William Randolph Hearst's *New York Journal*.[15] Even so, readers were treated to reports on college football games. In the edition of the *Times* that included the article on South Carolina's presidential choice, the seventh page carried a three-sentence, matter-of-fact account of the previous day's Harvard-Yale game:

> NEW HAVEN, NOV. 18.—A foot-ball match here to-day between the Yale and Harvard elevens resulted in a victory for the Yales, who won one goal, Harvard scoring none. In the first three quarters of an hour Harvard scored one touch-down, and in the second three-quarters of an hour Yale scored a goal, Thompson of the University crew, being credited with the play. After this goal Harvard scored another touch-down, and in this way the game stood at the close.[16]

This was the entirety of the article. Many casual readers were certain to miss it.

The newspaper provided much more prominent and extensive coverage of another game. It took place at the same time and held more local interest. Across the Hudson River from Manhattan, in Hoboken, New Jersey, Columbia took on Princeton. As with the Harvard-Yale contest, the teams negotiated rules before-hand. Princeton's captain proposed stretching a rope between the goalposts, ten feet off the ground—only kicked balls that sailed between the uprights and over the rope would count for goals. Columbia agreed, just as Harvard had agreed to a similar suggestion from Yale. The game began with Princeton's kickoff, received by the son of George Francis Train, whose globe-trotting travels were said to have inspired Jules Verne to write *Around the World in Eighty Days*. In Verne's novel, Phileas Fogg circumnavigates the planet by locomotive and steamship; in Hoboken, young Train was quickly tackled. Columbia squandered a scoring chance when a goal kick hit an upright. Then Princeton's bigger and stronger squad took control of the game, which was played almost entirely on Columbia's half of the field. When it was over, Princeton had prevailed, three goals to none.

Almost as notable as the score, judging from the detailed coverage of the game in the *New York Times*, were the injuries. E. S. McCalmont of Princeton took a shot to the knee and limped to the sidelines. A teammate was booted in the abdomen during what the *Times* called a "melee." Columbia's Lindley fared the worst. Kicked in the ribs, he lay on the grass, unable to move. The game halted so that his fellow players could carry him from the field. They put Lindley on a table, where he remained prone. He "eventually recovered and was taken home," reported the newspaper. The game continued until darkness made further play impossible.[17]

These injuries foreshadowed a problem that would come to haunt football as it matured over the next three decades: violence. In 1876 and the years that followed, Roosevelt and his contemporaries watched a game that resembled rugby more than the sport on display in the 21st century. There were no quarterbacks, wide receivers, or dazzling end-zone receptions. Football always has prized size, strength, and power, but this was especially true in its early years. Quirks in the rules compressed the game's action into a small space, rather than spread it across a large field. Big men pushed and shoved their way through and around masses of bodies that clashed and grappled for the ball without the benefit of protective gear. The era of the leatherheads lay in the future: Nobody wore helmets, face masks, or shoulder pads. During the frequent pileups, hidden from the view of referees, players would wrestle for advantage by throwing punches and jabbing elbows. The most unsporting participants would even attempt to gouge the eyes of their opponents. Bruises, sprains, and other minor injuries were taken for granted. More serious impairments, such as cracked bones and concussions, were causes of greater concern but also generally accepted as the unfortunate by-products of a demanding and entertaining sport.

In just about any activity, a certain amount of collateral damage is unavoidable. Some of it is sad but acceptable. Cars and streets make deadly accidents unavoidable. The value of efficient transportation, however, outweighs the costs. Football provides its own benefits. Participants engage in a physical activity that improves their fitness. Spectators derive enjoyment from watching well-played games. Yet in the last years of the 19th century, as football grew in popularity and young men played at every level from the neighborhood sandlot to the college gridiron, the high incidence of on-field injuries became impossible to ignore.

Worst of all were the deaths. They were not freak accidents as much as the inevitable toll of an activity that encouraged strong men to crash into each other, again and again, over the course of a long afternoon. An ordinary tackle can become a life-threatening calamity if the hard-thrusting knee of a ball carrier strikes the head of a defenseman. In 1905, a year of momentous importance for football and its future, eighteen people died playing the sport.[18]

Horrified by the slaughter, a group of activists crusaded against football. They wanted not merely to remove violence from the sport, but to ban it as an activity. At the dawn of the Progressive

Era, the prohibition of football became a social and political movement whose most outspoken proponents recoiled from the sport. Their ranks included the renowned Harvard president Charles W. Eliot, frontier scholar Frederick Jackson Turner, aging Confederate general John Singleton Mosby, and muckraking journalists. The *Nation*, an influential magazine of news and opinion, worried that colleges were becoming "huge training grounds for young gladiators, around whom as many spectators roar as roared in the [Roman] amphitheatre."[19] After watching a Yale-Harvard match in 1903, one writer condemned the game: "The dirty players in football are the thugs of society, and the disgrace of the university that tolerates their presence on the team."[20] The *New York Times*, which played a role in the sport's rising popularity, worried about football's trend toward "mayhem and homicide."[21] About two weeks after printing these words, the *Times* ran a new editorial. The headline was "Two Curable Evils." The first evil it addressed was the lynching of blacks. The second was football.[22]

If football was going to survive, it would have to change. The tale of how it evolved into America's most popular sport features a colorful cast of characters from the turn of the 20th century. Many were football's founding fathers. Legendary coach Walter Camp, who was a player in the 1876 Harvard-Yale game that Roosevelt watched, began to turn the game away from its rugby-like origins and popularized it for the masses. When Camp's influence waned, Notre Dame's Knute Rockne perfected innovations that allowed football to take full advantage of its untapped potential. John Heisman, Amos Alonzo Stagg, Pop Warner, and Fielding Yost contributed as well. Other figures less associated with the sport also helped shape it, or at least were witnesses to its shaping: professor-turned-president Woodrow Wilson, the jurist Oliver Wendell Holmes, Jr., the writer Charles Francis Adams, the editor E. L. Godkin, the economist Thorstein Veblen, the grand-nephew of Edgar Allan Poe, the artist Frederic Remington, the war hero

Leonard Wood, the front-line correspondent Richard Harding Davis, and West Point cadet Dwight Eisenhower.

Theodore Roosevelt was not as important to the development of football as Camp or several other men of that generation. He never played on its fields or coached from its sidelines. Instead, he enjoyed the sport as a spectator. Yet he also played a vital role during its greatest crisis. Due in part to his encouragement, football took steps to correct its violent excesses while also preserving its physical demands and competitive spirit. It is possible to believe that without his presidential intervention, football might not even exist today. Even if it had survived this period, it might look quite different from the game that now packs millions of fans into stadiums and draws tens of millions more who watch the sport on television.

The drive to prohibit football failed, of course. At the time, however, its failure was anything but foreordained. Even if the movement had come short of outlawing the sport, it might have succeeded in marginalizing the game—and condemning it to a future of limited appeal, along the lines of a second-tier pastime such as hockey or lacrosse. The story of what happened is a unique tale of American culture, politics, and sports. It is also virtually untold. A few old and scattered articles, warehoused in research libraries, discuss what happened. Several accounts of the history of football include obligatory and often erroneous coverage.[23] Before now, no book has focused on these events in exclusive detail. Even the most comprehensive biographies of Theodore Roosevelt— including Edmund Morris's multivolume narrative—overlook this episode completely.

THE DISPUTE OVER football and its future marked not only a turning point for the development of sports in the United States, but a crisis for what was becoming the most dominant force in American politics. In the 1890s, just as football was growing into a popular sensation, the Progressive movement was gaining irresistible momentum. A broad-based drive for social reform, it blossomed during Roosevelt's presidency and never has released its grip on American life. Its fundamental achievement was to recast the relationship between citizens and their government. Whether this was for good or ill remains a bitter argument a century later among partisans on the left and the right. Liberals tend to view the Progressive Era as a missed opportunity—a series of reforms that delivered modest benefits to middle-class voters anxious about economic instability and demographic shifts, but also an accommodation with Christian morality and market capitalism that put off a more radical rearrangement of the social contract. Conservatives view Progressivism as a quixotic effort based on an unfounded faith in human perfectibility that led directly to the rise of the welfare state and the erosion of individual freedom and personal responsibility. Whatever the merits of these warring claims, the diverse accomplishments of the Progressive movement include trust-busting, railroad regulation, the passage of food and drug laws, restrictions on child labor, the prohibition of alcohol, and the implementation of a federal income tax.

When the Progressives turned their eyes to football, many saw nothing but the violence. If their first impulse was to wince at the brutality, their next urge was to protect boys and young men from what they considered a frivolous and fatal activity. Why pass laws to get children out of urban factories and coal mines if they were simply going to maim themselves on football's killing fields? So the Progressives tried to address the problem of football by turning to their favorite solution: They sought to regulate it out of existence. They saw the sport as an unacceptable risk and believed that its participants were not capable of making their own judgments about the costs and benefits of the game. Instead, elites would relieve them of the burden of choosing to play or not to play. They would ban the sport for the sake of its players.

The supporters of football took a different view. They appreciated the game's organic development and valued the place of athletic competition in American culture. Although some relished football's violence and were content to ignore its occasional corruption, most wanted to refine the rules and broaden the appeal of the game, even though they could not always agree on the particulars of how to do this. They recognized that one of the chief goals of sports—especially a rough sport such as football—was to socialize young men by helping them learn how to channel their masculine impulses toward productive ends. Shortly before he was president, Theodore Roosevelt became well-known for the promotion of what he called "the doctrine of the strenuous life." In a speech in 1899, he hailed "that highest form of success which comes, not to the man who desires mere easy peace, but to the man who does not shrink from danger, from hardship, or from bitter toil, and who out of these wins the splendid ultimate triumph."[24] In Roosevelt's estimation, the foes of football were wrongheaded idealists who simply refused to accept the risks that are attached to virtually any human endeavor. They threatened to feminize an entire generation. At stake was nothing less than the future of the United States: On the threshold of a new century, would the country seize its historic destiny and grow into a world power or would it stop short of this accomplishment because it had turned out, in Roosevelt's words, "mollycoddles instead of vigorous men"?[25]

SPORTS BEGAN TO occupy a central place in American culture during Roosevelt's life. They have become even more important since. In the United States today, parents not only encourage but often expect their children to participate in athletics. They will cite many motives, starting with the obvious fact that sports are good for health and fitness. They will also discuss the intangible benefits of learning about teamwork and building individual character. These factors can be tricky to measure, though several academics have found evidence that kids who play sports stay in school longer. As adults, they vote more often and earn more money. Explaining this phenomenon is difficult, but it may have something to do with developing a competitive instinct and a desire for achievement. Parents rarely talk about sports as a patriotic duty the way Roosevelt did, but athletic participation almost certainly influences the character of a nation. Americans are much more likely than Europeans to play sports. They are also more likely to attribute economic success to hard work, as opposed to luck.[26] This may be another source of American exceptionalism.

For all of his flamboyant chest-thumping, Roosevelt did not wholly discount the concerns of football's prohibitionists. Their complaints about violence were the products of a genuine problem. Other pastimes shared many of football's virtues without the same dangers. Would it be possible to balance a desire for safety with a proper understanding of the social value of a rugged sport? This was the challenge—an age-old concern that remains alive today whenever debates erupt over zero-tolerance policies in public schools, the use of aluminum bats in Little League baseball games, and the frequency of concussions in youth athletics. At what point do the risks of play become unacceptably great? Quite often, there are no easy answers.

Violence in football remains a subject of occasional controversy—and so does the Progressive instinct to impose regulations on it. In 2010, *Time* put a deflated ball on its cover and called the sport "too dangerous for its own good."[27] Players of all ages are vulnerable to pulled muscles and twisted ankles. In rare cases, they may suffer catastrophic injuries, such as broken necks. Some debilities become obvious only with the passage of time. A 2009 study sponsored by the National Football League found that retired professional football players who were at least fifty years old were five times more likely to suffer from dementia than members of the general population. The problem was worse with younger veterans.[28] Data such as these inspire questions about how the game is played and how it might be improved for the benefit of its participants. It has also prompted outrage. In 2009, popular author Malcolm Gladwell compared the "suffering and destruction" in dogfighting to injuries from football. He suggested that both activities were "morally unacceptable."[29] Congresswoman Linda Sanchez, a California Democrat, said that the NFL's research could not be trusted. "Hey, why don't we let tobacco companies determine whether smoking is bad for your health or not?" she asked. "It's a very appropriate metaphor."[30]

And still we watch and play, urging our children to do the same. Nobody speaks of prohibiting football anymore. At a time when many influential people did, however, Theodore Roosevelt stepped in and played an unheralded but critical role in the sport's development. It is probably too much to call him football's savior. Yet he may very well have been its most indispensable fan.

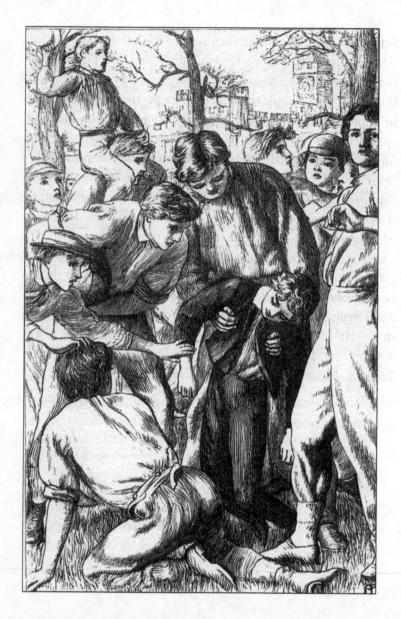

The 1857 novel *Tom Brown's Schooldays* was one of Theodore Roosevelt's favorite books. It describes the experiences of a British schoolboy who learns to play rugby football—and suffers a few hard knocks along the way.

Chapter Two

CREATION STORIES

Theodore Roosevelt's early life is a chronicle of sickness. He was born at home, in a New York City brownstone on East Twentieth Street, early in the evening on Wednesday, October 27, 1858. At about eight and a half pounds, he was above average in size and apparently healthy. He took his father's name, though he quickly acquired a nickname that would stick with him for years, at least in family circles: "Teedie." During his infancy, he suffered from a scalp rash that his parents called "milk crust." The problem vanished well before his second birthday. Contemporary accounts, which are few, also note a teething problem—a normal travail of babyhood. Overall, the existing records suggest a lively and intelligent boy. "He is almost a little beauty," boasted his grandmother.[1] Yet a severe affliction soon took hold of him and it would not let go.

"Wednesday's child is full of woe," says the old nursery rhyme. By the time Teedie had reached the age of three, he was woefully unwell. His illnesses assumed many forms—colds, fevers, coughs, and diarrhea. "I feel badly," he complained one morning. "I have a toothache in my stomach."[2] Teedie's parents, Theodore Roosevelt, Sr., and Martha Bulloch Roosevelt, also known as "Mittie," lost sleep caring for their son. Mr. Roosevelt wondered if there was something wrong with the house, perhaps in the furnace. The source of the problem, however, lay in Teedie's own fragile constitution: He had chronic asthma.

One of Roosevelt's first recollections involved his poor health. "I was a sickly, delicate boy, suffered much from asthma, and frequently had to be taken away on trips to find a place where I could breathe," he wrote in his autobiography. "One of my memories is of my father walking up and down the room with me in his arms at night when I was a very small person, and of sitting up in bed gasping, with my father and mother trying to help me."[3]

Learning to cope with this condition would become the major challenge of Roosevelt's youth. The experience shaped his activities and gave rise to lifelong beliefs about the value of fitness and athletics. His views were so strong that when he was president, they helped shape the evolution of football. Roosevelt's unique character and determination made much of this possible, but his ideas did not develop in the isolated forge of his personal history. Large social forces were also at work, as Americans changed their thinking about the nature of individual health and the importance of sports.

WHEN ASTHMA STRUCK, Roosevelt often looked to his father for relief: "The thought of him now and always has been a sense of comfort. I could breathe, I could sleep, when he had me in his arms. My father—he got me breath, he got me lungs, strength—life."[4] When these simple measures failed, Mr. Roosevelt sometimes would wrap the boy in blankets, call for his carriage, and ride into the night. The hope was that a change in the air would help Teedie respire. It seems to have worked often enough that the practice became a habit. Even so, in an age when many children failed to reach adulthood, some of little Theodore's relatives feared that he would not survive his early years.

Teedie was not the family's only challenge with health. His older sister, Anna—born in 1855 and known to all as "Bamie," which was short for *bambina*—suffered from a spinal disease that would cause her a lifetime of pain. The family blamed her ailment on a nurse who had dropped her as a baby, but that was almost certainly not the source of Bamie's problems. She may have had Pott's disease, a form of tuberculosis that causes the spine to curve. For her parents, treatment was an enigma. A doctor once put Bamie in a steel contraption that seemed to succeed merely at giving her the additional aggravation of rashes. Eventually another doctor recommended a form of physical therapy. It did not cure Bamie, but it allowed her to live a fairly normal life, at least by outward appearances. Even so, she frequently had to lie down and often had difficulty with routine activities, such as sitting upright in a chair.

After Bamie and Teedie, the Roosevelts had two more children. It was not until the birth of their third, Elliott, in 1860, that they could enjoy the experience of raising a child who did not have unusual problems with health. Corinne, born in 1861, had to deal with asthma, though nothing on the scale of what afflicted her brother.

Teedie's first decade became a study of extremes—periods of great vigor punctuated by terrible weakness. He grew up as a small and skinny boy, a condition that was accentuated in the presence of his healthy younger brother, who many assumed was the senior member of the pair. Teedie came to love the outdoors, where he could run, ride, and swim. Oftentimes, however, what he called "the Asmer" would strike and leave him incapacitated. The family became accustomed to making plans around his needs, always worrying about whether the quality of the air in one place or another would strain his breathing.

In 1869, the Roosevelts embarked on a yearlong tour of Europe, in part so that Mrs. Roosevelt could visit relatives in England and also for the sake of the children's education. In his diary, Teedie wrote about extensive hikes, some upwards of twenty miles in length. Yet the asthma always lurked nearby, ready to incapacitate. After an attack in London, his father whisked him off to the coast. On the continent, Teedie wheezed and hacked his way up the Rhine, was bedridden in Lucerne, and had a rotten time in Vienna. "Teedie," wrote his mother, "seems hardly to have three or four days complete exemption and keeps us constantly uneasy and on the stretch."[5]

In desperate attempts at alleviation, his parents resorted to every conceivable remedy. They even gave him cigars to smoke and black coffee to drink. For many children, a tour of Europe would have represented the journey of a lifetime. Roosevelt, however, always remembered it as a joyless ordeal. If his parents had hoped the trip would make their oldest son more robust, they were mistaken. On his way back home, in the spring of 1870, a fellow traveler on the steamship recalled "a tall thin lad and legs like pipestems."[6] The fresh air of the ocean provided no relief: Teedie was seasick.

The following summer was little better. Roosevelt's parents sent him from place to place—Philadelphia, Saratoga, Oyster Bay—in search of a climate that would agree with him. He tramped outdoors whenever possible, riding ponies or hunting for bird nests. Yet the illness always resurfaced. The boy simply could not defeat it. He enjoyed the periods when his asthma let him alone, but he and his family knew that it could seize him at almost any moment and with little warning.

AROUND THIS TIME—PROBABLY in the fall of 1870, after the family had returned from its various summer retreats to New York City—came an event that would go down in Roosevelt lore. In the story that his mother loved to tell and that his sister Corinne recorded for posterity, Teedie would have been eleven or twelve years old. Some historians have regarded the tale as embellished, and perhaps it was. But there can be no doubt of its essential truth. One day, Theodore Roosevelt, Sr., summoned his boy for a conversation. "Theodore," said the father, "you have the mind but you have not the body, and without the help of the body the mind cannot go as far as it should. You must make your body. It is hard drudgery to make one's body, but I know you will do it." Upon hearing this, Teedie threw back his head and grinned with determination. "I'll make my body!" he declared. Corinne called it "his first important promise to himself."[7]

The boy was soon going on daily visits to Wood's Gymnasium, a few blocks from his home. Since 1856, John Wood, the gym's proprietor, had hosted some of New York's most prominent families: Goulds, Sloanes, and Vanderbilts. Athletes from Columbia also exercised there. Wood, a wiry man with a raspy voice, was well-known for the dedication he showed to the young men who walked through his doors. According to one account, he was an ever-present fixture at his gym, constantly there unless it was time to eat or sleep. Some three decades after Teedie's visits, Wood recalled the boy as "a sturdy, self-reliant little chap."[8]

Roosevelt stuck to a rigid schedule, coming to the gym even in foul weather and always with his mother and brother in tow. Mrs. Roosevelt would sit at one end of the gym and watch her sons sweat through their workouts. Wood remembered one time when Teedie was learning to use a chest weights machine that Wood had invented. The device required its user to grip a pair of wooden handles and pull them forward, thereby lifting cast-iron weights attached to a rope-and-pulley mechanism. "The machine was new then," wrote Wood, "and I had just given little Theodore his first lesson, how to stand, with the left foot well advanced, body forward, weight evenly divided upon both legs, head and chest well up and arms fully extended, as he pulled the weights up and let them subside. The boy took to the work bravely and kept the weights going steadily for many minutes." Mrs. Roosevelt summoned the instructor. "Mr. Wood," she asked from her seat, "how many horse-power do you suppose Theodore will have used by the time he gets through with that machine?"[9]

Roosevelt's parents must have been satisfied with their son's progress, because they hired Wood to outfit their home. He transformed a second-floor porch into an open-air gymnasium. It was stocked with horizontal bars, swings, seesaws, and other devices—a workshop for the building of bodies. The Roosevelts had tapped into an emerging social trend. Gymnasia were growing in popularity, both as commercial enterprises operated by the likes of Wood and in private homes of well-off families such as the Roosevelts. Facilities dedicated to exercise could trace their heritage back to ancient Greece, but in the United States they had remained rare up to that point.

This new arrangement marked the end of Theodore's visits to Wood's Gymnasium, but not his devotion to exercise. The private gym quickly became a playground for Teedie as well as a neighborhood attraction for friends and relatives. A door in the hallway led to the porch, but Teedie preferred to scramble through a bedroom window. Corinne recalled an incident of daredevilry, when her brother and a cousin placed a wooden seesaw on a rail that was supposed to prevent gymnasts from falling from the porch to the ground, a full level below. The boys, wrote Corinne, "thought they would add a tinge of excitement to the merriment by balancing the seesaw in such a manner as to have one boy always in the thrilling position of hanging on the farther side of the top rail, with the possibility (unless the equilibrium were kept to perfection) of seesaw, boys, and all descending unexpectedly into the back yard."[10] When Mrs. Roosevelt observed their recklessness, she put a quick stop to it. Yet she and her husband continued to encourage and support Teedie's new habit of exercise.

From the start, Roosevelt's parents saw their boy's physical development as important but also subservient to his intellectual growth. As Theodore Sr. had told him, "without the help of the body the mind cannot go as far as it should." Before Teedie embarked on his project of bodybuilding—back when people in his family wondered how long he would live—he had set off on a different kind of journey.

POOR HEALTH OFTEN had kept Roosevelt shuttered indoors. When he was old enough to attend school, he went for a few months and then stopped. He switched to taking lessons at home. Early on, he demonstrated a precocious intelligence. He loved books even before he could read them. A boy confined to his home will make many discoveries within its walls, and it did not take Teedie long to encounter the wonders of his parents' well-stocked library. One family story tells of his coming across *Missionary Travels and Researches in Southern Africa*, by David Livingstone, the medic and explorer whose name would achieve lasting fame when Henry Morton Stanley greeted him in what is now Tanzania: "Dr. Livingstone, I presume?" The Livingstone book in the Roosevelt home was a bulky volume, full of words and pictures. The words meant nothing to young Roosevelt. Yet he carried the book around, even though it rivaled him in size, and demanded that adults explain its engrossing contents.[11] Years later, Jacob A. Riis, his friend and biographer—as well as the author of *How the Other Half Lives*—conjured "the picture of a little lad, in stiff white petticoats, with a curl right on top of his head, toiling laboriously along with a big fat volume under his arm."[12]

The pictures of animals fired his vivid imagination. So did many other activities. One day, as he played tag at a park near his home, the sexton of a church invited Roosevelt to have a look inside the building. The boy hesitated, glanced into the church nervously, and then dashed away. His mother asked him why he had refused to go in. Roosevelt said he was afraid of "the zeal." Confused, his mother asked: "What on earth do you mean by the zeal?" Roosevelt replied: "I suppose it is some big animal like a dragon or an alligator." He had heard about it at a recent church service, he said. His mother looked up "zeal" in a concordance and read aloud from Psalms 69:9. "That's it," exclaimed Roosevelt. It was the passage he had heard in church: "For the zeal of thy house hath eaten me up."[13]

As this attentive churchgoer learned to decipher letters and words, tales of adventure and the outdoors enthralled him. One of his favorite authors was Mayne Reid, an Irish-born writer who had immigrated to the United States, served in the Mexican-American War, and finally settled in England, where he began pumping out novels of derring-do. Later in life, when Roosevelt reexamined the books of his boyhood, he said that he found Reid unreadable—but his passion for exciting stories nevertheless had been born in large part because of "Captain" Reid. His parents indulged this pursuit and did not try to channel their son's interest in any particular direction. "There was very little effort made to compel me to read books, my father and mother having the good sense not to try to get me to read anything I did not like, unless it was in the way of study," recalled Roosevelt. "I was given the chance to read books that they thought I ought to read, but if I did not like them I was then given some other good book that I did like."[14] A few books were ruled off-limits, such as dime novels. Roosevelt read several in secret, but found that the experience led more to guilt than pleasure. He delved into *Robinson Crusoe* (enjoying the second part, but not the first), *The Swiss Family Robinson* (which he criticized for its "wholly impossible collection of animals"), and the poetry of Henry Wadsworth Longfellow (especially "The Saga of King Olaf"). He also admitted, "at the cost of being deemed effeminate," to a fondness for the books of Louisa May Alcott, the author of *Little Women*.[15] In all, he was a voracious reader and hard to interrupt when he was in the middle of a story he enjoyed. He would read both sitting down and standing up. Sometimes he balanced on one leg, birdlike, and propped open a book on his lifted thigh.[16]

AT SOME POINT, Roosevelt discovered a novel called *Tom Brown's Schooldays*. Shortly before becoming president, he singled it out as one of two "delightful books . . . which I hope every boy still reads."[17] It was published in London in 1857, a year before Roosevelt's birth. *Tom Brown's Schooldays* soon became a popular sensation on both sides of the Atlantic and planted the seed for what has become a vast subgenre of children's literature that mixes stories of school and athletics.[18] It was by no means the first book aimed at children, but it was one of the very first that understood its audience to be primarily male—that is, boys, rather than boys and girls together.

The author was Thomas Hughes, a social reformer who was the father of nine children. In the 1850s, he helped found the Working Men's College in London, where he made a troubling observation: "The first thing we found out was, that the young men who came to us were in very poor health. They lived in a great city, in considerable poverty, and were very tight about the shoulders." He taught them to play cricket as well as to row and box. Soon enough, the college turned out "healthy young men."[19]

When his oldest son, Maurice, reached the age of eight, Hughes resolved to write a story that would explain English schooling to the boy—and encourage a lifestyle that would make him more fit than the young men he was encountering at the college. Tragically, Maurice died in 1859, before he could receive the full benefit of his father's insights.[20] Yet the book that he inspired would live on: Within five years of its appearance, *Tom Brown's Schooldays* had sold twenty-eight thousand copies, which was a large number for its day.[21]

It begins with a portrait of Tom Brown, an ordinary boy with an ordinary name, at home in rural England. Tom roams about the countryside and watches grown-ups play games such as "back-sword," which involves combatants who hit each other over the head with sticks. His parents eventually ship him off to Rugby, the famous school in Warwickshire. Their goal is for the boy to gain an education, but they expect him to receive much of it away from his books and assignments. "Shall I tell him to mind his work, and say he's sent to school to make himself a good scholar?" asks Tom's father. "He isn't sent to school for that—at any rate, not for that mainly. I don't care a straw for Greek particles, or the digamma; no more does his mother. What is he sent to school for? Well, partly because he wanted so to go. If he'll only turn out a brave, helpful, truth-telling Englishman, and a gentleman, and a Christian, that's all I want."[22] Tom's father—and by extension Hughes, for whom the character is a mouthpiece—believes that the value of school lies primarily in its ability to socialize young people.

As Tom approaches Rugby for the first time, he does not initially see its gray buildings. Instead, his eyes settle on its playing fields, flanked by towering elms, where "several games at football were going on."[23] By "football," the author meant "rugby," or at least a primitive version of the sport that took its name from the school. Within hours of his arrival, Tom begins to learn its rules as well as the importance it holds in the academy's culture. He puzzles over "the mysteries of 'off your side,' 'drop-kicks,' 'punts,' 'places,' and the other intricacies of the great science of football." In addition, one of Tom's new friends, Harry "Scud" East, warns him about the "break-neck" quality of the game: "It's no joke playing up in a match, I can tell you," says East. "Why, there's been two collar-bones broken this half, and a dozen fellows lamed. And last year a fellow had his leg broken."[24]

Within a few pages, Hughes defends this level of brutality—he slips out of his narrative voice in a passage that speaks directly from author to reader: "You say, you don't see much in it all; nothing but a struggling mass of boys, and a leather ball, which seems to excite them all to great fury, as a red rag does a bull," he writes. "My dear sir, a battle would look much the same to you, except that the boys would be men, and the balls iron; but a battle would be worth your looking at for all that, and so is a football match."[25]

Hughes was not the first to link the athletic training of boys with their performance on the battlefield as men. "The battle of Waterloo was won on the playing fields of Eton," said the Duke of Wellington, in reference to the school he had attended in the 1780s.[26] His point was that many English soldiers and sailors had learned to do their duty because they had grown up clutching and kicking balls on the lawns of respected academies.

Tom Brown's school, Rugby, was so connected to sports that it gave its name to one of them. If football has a creation myth, it may be this: In 1823, a group of boys were engaged in a kicking game at Rugby—something that they would have called "football" because it relied primarily on footwork, but which Americans would recognize as soccer. (The word *soccer* was a slang term derived from "association football.") A plaque at the school commemorates "the exploit of William Webb Ellis who, with a fine disregard for the rules of football as played in his time, first took the ball in his arms and ran with it, thus originating the distinctive feature of the rugby game."

Ellis would have been about sixteen years old at the time. His father had died a dozen years earlier, serving his country at the Battle of Albuera in Spain. Owing to his mother's destitution, Ellis became a charity case at Rugby. He received a tuition-free education and was seemingly a bit of an outsider among his classmates, due to his special status. After graduating from Rugby, he attended Oxford, where he was known for playing cricket and writing a poem on beer (which is, alas, lost to time). He became a clergyman of minor repute. A London newspaper printed his picture in 1854, revealing a man with a formidable nose and a receding hairline. It is the only known image of him from life.[27]

When Ellis died in 1872, he was apparently unaware of his role in the history of football—or at least the role that others soon would assign to him. His posthumous fame as the inventor of rugby comes from a claim first advanced in 1876 by an antiquarian researcher. As the esteem of rugby grew in the 1880s and 1890s—at a time when its American cousin, football, was surging in popularity as well—the story of Ellis and his decision to pick up the ball and run became a part of the game's lore. Skeptics have questioned the authenticity of the tale, and the full truth of what happened at Rugby in 1823 is probably unknowable. One thing is certain: Webb has become a figure of legend.

BALL GAMES THEMSELVES have an ancient pedigree. Parke Davis, an early historian of football, points to an Old Testament verse: "He will surely violently turn and toss thee like a ball" (Isaiah 22:18). This allusion may be "slight," wrote Parke, but it "is sufficient unto the antiquary to indicate that some form of a game with a ball existed as early as 750 years before the Christian era."[28]

The Greeks were of course famous for the Olympian Games, which they played every four years for centuries. Yet these were a series of individual competitions. Athletes ran, jumped, and wrestled. They did not form teams or play with balls. The concept, however, was not alien to them. In the *Odyssey*, Homer describes Nausicaa as playing a ball game on a beach with her handmaidens when Odysseus discovers them. In fact, the Greeks and Romans played a team sport that featured a ball about the size of a modern-day softball. They called it *phaininda* (in Greek) and *harpastum* (in Latin). The exact rules remain something of a mystery, and they probably varied across time and from place to place. A handful of contemporary writers have provided brief glimpses of the game.

Athenaeus, a native of Egypt who lived around the turn of the second century, offered an account that may make him one of the world's first play-by-play commentators:

The player takes the ball elate,
And give it safely to his mate,
Avoids the blows of th' other side,
And shouts to see them hitting wide;
List to the cries, "Hit here," "hit there,"
"Too far," "too high," "that is not fair,"—
See every man with ardor burns
To make good strokes and quick returns.[29]

This description might fit a modern football play, at least in a broad sense: It seems to involve a pair of teams, a handoff or a pass, an effort to stop the ballcarrier with blows and tackles, and a concept of penalties.

A contemporary of Athenaeus provided another look at the game. Galen was a doctor in Asia Minor who looked after the health of gladiators. He eventually became the personal physician of the Roman emperor Marcus Aurelius. He also wrote extensively. In one essay, he described *harpastum* as "better than wrestling or running because it exercises every part of the body, takes up little time, and costs nothing." He noted that it could be "played with varying degrees of strenuousness" and observed its aggressively physical aspects: "When, for example, people face each other, vigorously attempting to prevent each other from taking the space between, this exercise is a very heavy, vigorous one, involving much use of the hold by the neck, and many wrestling holds."[30]

Other cultures have their own ball games, including American Indians, Mayans, Australian Aborigines, and even Eskimos. The ancient Chinese, according to a 2,500-year-old military text, played a sport that involved kicking a ball through a hole. Versions of it spread to Japan and Korea, and some of the rules required goalposts that are reminiscent of the big yellow ones seen on football fields today.

It would seem that lining up two teams of opposing players who battle over a ball is an almost universal phenomenon. In the winter of 1913–14, after his presidential years, Theodore Roosevelt searched for the River of Doubt in the Amazon wilderness, where he encountered the Pareci Indians. Even this tribe, cut off from much of the rest of the world, had its peculiar version of the sport. It involved a pair of teams that would drive a ball back and forth by butting it with their heads. The spectacle amazed Roosevelt:

> They have developed "Association football"—what you call "Soccer football"—but they play it with their heads. The two sides are ranged as in soccer football. The round, hollow rubber ball is placed on the ground between them. A man runs towards it, throws himself flat on the ground, and butts it. It rolls towards a man on the other side, who flings himself on the ground and butts it back. Usually he catches it so as to make the ball rise, and then the men on each side in turn run, catch it on their heads, and send it to and fro without throwing themselves on the ground. The ball is only touched with the head, and it travels almost as if from a drop-kick or punt. It is really an interesting game, and they are absorbed in it.[31]

Europeans invented their own variations on the theme. In medieval England, neighboring towns participated in games known as "mob football" or "folk football." Large crowds would descend upon an inflated pig's bladder and try to deliver it to certain demarcated points. The term "pigskin," in reference to the ball, comes from this period. Some versions of the game required the ball to be kicked onto the balcony of a rival village's church. Violence and drunkenness were often a part of the action. The tradition survives in Derbyshire, where the town of Ashbourne still holds the Shrovetide Football Match on Shrove Tuesday and Ash Wednesday of each year. Storekeepers board up their windows and locals move their cars off the streets so that two teams of residents can play a game that involves goalposts and millstones set three miles apart. The competition usually leads to large groups of clashing adversaries. One of the game's few rules states that murder is prohibited, apparently because this would not have been obvious otherwise. Since 1928, the event has been formally known as the Royal Shrovetide Football Match because that was the year the Prince of Wales turned up. The future King Edward VIII left with a bloody nose.

Shakespeare made a couple of references to football, neither of them favorable. In *King Lear*, Kent angrily blurts out, "you base foot-ball player!"[32] In *The Comedy of Errors*, Dromio bemoans his plight:

> *Am I so round with you as you with me,*
> *That like a football you do spurn me thus?*
> *You spurn me hence, and he will spurn me hither:*
> *If I last in this service, you must case me in leather.*[33]

Sir Walter Scott was more bemused in the 19th century. He once likened a game of football to "riot, revelry, and rout." On another occasion, he wrote of a match between the men of Ettrick and Yarrow, near Selkirk in Scotland:

> *Then strip lads, and to it, though sharp be weather;*
> *And if, by mischance, you should happen to fall,*
> *There are worse things in life than a tumble on heather,*
> *And life is itself but a game at foot-ball!*[34]

Before long, football would become a metaphor in politics. In 1857, an American newspaper introduced the term "political football," which has gone on to achieve the ubiquity of cliché.[35]

By the middle of the 19th century, after Ellis allegedly had carried the ball at Rugby, the rules of the various English games that might fit broadly under the category of "football" were diverse and often incompatible. Yet, the rise of public schooling promoted the games' popularity as well as their standardization. Improved transportation, especially by railroad, made it easier for teams from different areas to meet and play. Participants exchanged ideas about which rules made the sport most competitive and enjoyable. At this point, the game's development was entirely organic: It did not involve organizing bodies or rulebooks. The ball took on a distinct shape that is best described as a prolate spheroid—technically, a spheroid whose polar diameter is longer than its equatorial diameter. The major objective involved carrying the ball over a goal line. Several types of kicks over crossbars and through posts also generated points. Teams put about a dozen players on the field at a time. There were handoffs, tackles, sidelines, end zones, game clocks, and so on.

The game placed a premium on personal strength and cooperative play. Small boys found themselves at a natural disadvantage. Players learned that practice improved performance. Some observers have described football as a reflection of the industrial age—an athletic version of labor-intensive factory work, in which players perform specialized, manual tasks in order to achieve a common goal, set to the relentless ticking of a clock. The best teams operated like efficient machinery.

YOUNG THEODORE ROOSEVELT would not have known any of this deep history when he encountered *Tom Brown's Schooldays*. He simply responded to the adventurous spirit of a book for boys, appreciating the way it embraced his impulses and addressed his concerns. *Tom Brown's Schooldays* not only recognized but positively affirmed what even the best-behaved boys come to realize in their rough-and-tumble schoolyards: No matter what the grownups say, sometimes fights are unavoidable. In one significant scene, Tom bests a bully called Flashman—not by tattling to teachers or parents, but by taking matters into his own hands. (This character, who is disgraced in *Tom Brown's Schooldays*, went on to inspire a series of popular novels by George MacDonald Fraser more than a century later.) "The world might be a better world without fighting, for anything I know, but it wouldn't be our world; and therefore I am dead against crying peace when there is no peace, and isn't meant to be," wrote Hughes in his book. Yet he did not think that fighting was a regrettable if necessary evil. Hughes believed it could actually make the world a better place, especially when it involved the defeat of menaces such as Flashman: "From the cradle to the grave, fighting, rightly understood, is the business, the real, highest, honestest business of every son of man. Every one who is worth his salt has his enemies, who must be beaten, be they evil thoughts and habits in himself or spiritual wickedness in high places, or Russians, or Border-ruffians, or Bill, Tom, or Harry, who will not let him live his life in quiet till he has thrashed them."[36]

If Teedie enjoyed the sports and fisticuffs, the book's attraction for adults was different. For them, as for Hughes, it had a didactic purpose. One of its main characters is patterned after Thomas Arnold, a highly regarded and devout schoolmaster at Rugby when Hughes was a student. (Arnold was also the father of the poet Matthew Arnold and the great-grandfather of the author Aldous Huxley.) Hughes wanted to propel his readers toward a life of Christian dynamism that recognized the religious and social benefits of athletics. In *Tom Brown at Oxford*, an 1861 sequel, Hughes wrote that "a man's body is given him to be trained and brought into subjection and then used for the protection of the weak, the advancement of righteous causes."[37] Tom Brown was not just an entertaining fictional character, but an evangelist for a certain kind of living. In the 1880s, Hughes himself became involved in the creation of a short-lived utopian community in east Tennessee: He called it Rugby Colony, and he meant for it to reflect the ideals he had outlined in his books.[38]

In one respect, Hughes prophesied the success of *Tom Brown's Schooldays* in the United States. As the book's first paragraph observes, "For centuries, in their quiet, dogged, home-spun way, [the Browns] have been subduing the earth in most English counties, and leaving their mark in American forests."[39] Even so, the book's seed very well could have fallen on rocky soil in the United States. The book's depictions of school life are quintessentially English. Moreover, American schools had not emphasized athletics. "Sport as a pursuit was unknown," wrote Henry Adams of his Boston upbringing in the 1840s and 1850s.[40] Many academies, especially in the Northeast, were the inheritors of a Calvinist tradition imported to the New World by strict Pilgrims. They stressed the importance of labor over loafing. For them, spare time was not an opportunity for self-improvement through athletics or other means. Instead, it created an opening for temptation and wickedness. Although 19th-century New Englanders had given up their hat buckles and ruffled collars, they remained obedient to the moral habits of their forebears. In the New York City of Theodore Roosevelt's boyhood, church steeples dominated the skyline, serving as ever-present spiritual reminders. Much of American culture frowned on sports and games.

This was by no means a monolithic view. The competitive instinct runs deep, and Americans found ways to express it. Dutch Calvinists in New York—Roosevelt's paternal ancestors—bowled on lawns and skated on ice. Among the aristocratic class in the South—Roosevelt's ancestors on his mother's side—horse racing and fox hunting were popular activities. Slaves and poor whites occasionally watched or participated in these events. Benjamin Franklin outlined his ideas for schooling: "To keep them in health, and to strengthen and render active their bodies," he wrote, children should be "frequently exercised in running, leaping, wrestling, and swimming." At Valley Forge, the soldiers of the American Revolution left records of playing a ball game called "base." Around 1830, a medical journal published by doctors in Philadelphia claimed that gymnastics provided a treatment for hypochondria and that golfers in Scotland lived a decade longer than nongolfers.[41]

By the time *Tom Brown's Schooldays* appeared in the United States, Americans were ready to take up organized sports. Yet they still required a cultural imprimatur that would allow a full embrace of athletics.

In England, a commentator called *Tom Brown's Schooldays* an example of "Muscular Christianity." The label first had been applied to a novel by the clergyman Charles Kingsley, a friend of Hughes who espoused "a healthful and manful Christianity; one which does not exalt the feminine virtues to the exclusion of the masculine."[42] Kingsley apparently lacked a mind for marketing: He found the term *Muscular Christianity* irritating. Hughes, however, did not object. In the wake of *Tom Brown's Schooldays*, references to Muscular Christianity became common. The main accomplishment of Hughes was to take the ideas of Kingsley and insert them into a book for boys—one that their elders were more than happy to pass along.[43]

As a movement, Muscular Christianity sought to combine Christian spirit with physical vigor. Bodies existed for a divine purpose. They were not to be abused or neglected. In fact, they should be developed. In emphasizing the importance of bodies, not just souls, Muscular Christianity took some of its inspiration from the Bible: "Your body is the temple of the Holy Ghost" (I Corinthians 6:19). It also built upon scientific and economic trends. New ideas about medicine, nutrition, and sanitation supported the growing belief that the quality of human health was not a consequence of an indifferent or preordained fate but rather the result of behavior. Meanwhile, industrialization and urbanization were beginning to replace manual labor with automation, and the open spaces of rural life with the confinement of factories. The advocates of Muscular Christianity welcomed new technologies and increased productivity but worried that they would lead to withered bodies and the erosion of national strength. Most important, from the Christian perspective, was the threat of a different kind of deterioration. Would inactivity at work and more leisure time at home contribute not only to a physical and imperial softening, but to a moral softening as well? The period's central scientific revelation—the theory of natural selection, as proposed by Charles Darwin—made concerns about social decline seem even more pressing.

Born in 1809, Darwin began his life with a pair of false starts. In Edinburgh, he studied medicine but decided that he could not stomach surgery. In Cambridge, he prepared to become a parson but found himself drawn to wildlife and the outdoors. A professor who understood this passion recommended the young man for the position of naturalist aboard the H.M.S. *Beagle*, which was bound for South America and the Pacific Ocean. Darwin got the job and sailed in 1831. He examined fossils in Argentina, experienced an earthquake in Chile, and observed finches on the Galapagos Islands. Upon his return to Britain five years later, he had amassed the knowledge that would shape the rest of his life—and go on to transform the understanding of life itself.

Based on his investigations abroad, Darwin had come to believe in the concept of natural selection—the notion that plants and animals produce more offspring than necessary and that only those with the best adaptations for survival will reproduce and transfer these traits to the next generation. Over time, gradual changes possessed the power to alter species in fundamental ways. Earlier naturalists, including Darwin's own grandfather, had hinted at theories like this. Yet Charles Darwin was to become the idea's great synthesizer and popularizer. He spent more than two decades amassing evidence but kept most of his work in this area secret until 1859, when he finally published *On the Origin of Species*.

Darwin's book inaugurated biology as a fully modern science and built the foundation for insights into everything from animal behavior to genetics. Nobody was immune to its broad influence. As an adult, Theodore Roosevelt occasionally packed *On the Origin of Species* in his saddlebags while he hunted.[44] The book had a profound social and political effect. Although its author avoided a discussion of whether evolutionary rules also applied to people, others were eager to extrapolate. They hypothesized that if natural selection governed human behavior, then perhaps Darwin's laws could explain everything from racial success to the fates of empires. In 1864, Herbert Spencer introduced the catchphrase "survival of the fittest" and gave birth to the doctrine known as Social Darwinism. While some of its adherents pushed racist ideologies, others merely believed in a connection between the health of a society and the physical and mental well-being of the individuals who constitute it.

For at least a generation, many Americans had agonized over the fitness of their countrymen. "A healthy man in New York would be a curiosity," complained the *New York Mirror* in 1833. The newspaper called upon schools, colleges, and seminaries to promote exercise.[45] Others worried about the decline of physical culture. In 1843, Ralph Waldo Emerson worried about physical health in the United States and contrasted it unfavorably with what he perceived in England. He returned to the theme almost fifteen years later. Just as *Tom Brown's Schooldays* was starting to find its audience, Emerson wrote his book *English Traits*. He praised his subjects as "broadchested" and believed they were destined to rule the world.[46] Edward Everett—a Massachusetts politician who holds the distinction of orating for two hours at Gettysburg immediately before Abraham Lincoln delivered the two-minute Gettysburg Address—shared these concerns. "Noble, athletic sports, manly outdoor exercises . . . which strengthen the mind by strengthening the body," he said, "are too little cultivated in town or country." *Harper's Weekly* was vexed as well: It pondered the possibility of Americans turning into "a pale, pasty-faced, narrow chested, spindled-shanked, dwarfed race."[47]

THE GENIUS OF Muscular Christianity was in how it appealed to the spiritual value of athletics, answered Calvinist reservations about sports, and addressed Darwinist concerns about the survival of the fittest. It took Thomas Wentworth Higginson, an abolitionist minister and failed congressional candidate, to unite faith and physicality in the United States. He did it by writing Muscular Christianity's American manifesto. A tall and fiery graduate of Harvard, Higginson was the son of his father's second wife. Louisa Storrow had been the family governess who, Jane Eyre–like, married her employer after he had become a widower. Thomas was their tenth and last child.[48] He developed an interest in physical activity, performing calisthenics and playing a game akin to touch football. He also swam across the Charles River in Boston—an exploit he concealed from his parents and once described as the proudest moment of his life.[49] As he grew older, he became increasingly involved in the abolitionist movement. A sense of Christian justice motivated him. So did a profound admiration for the vigor of runaway slaves: "These men and women, who have tested their courage in the lonely swamp against the alligator and the bloodhound, who have starved on prairies, hidden in holds, clung to locomotives, ridden hundreds of miles cramped in boxes, head downward, equally near to death if discovered or deserted—and who have then, after enduring all this, gone voluntarily back to risk it over again, for the sake of wife or child—what are we pale faces, that we should claim a rival capacity with theirs for heroic deeds?"[50]

As the 1850s unfolded, Higginson became a member of the "Secret Six," a covert group that offered financial support to John Brown, the militant antislavery crusader. When federal soldiers under Robert E. Lee captured Brown in 1859 during his attempt to ignite an insurrection at Harpers Ferry, many of his erstwhile compatriots abandoned him. They burned correspondence and denied knowing him. Some even fled the country. Higginson, however, refused to distance himself from Brown. ("Only the tough, swart-minded Higginson / Kept a grim decency, would not deny," wrote Stephen Vincent Benét in his long poem *John Brown's Body*.) Higginson even pondered the idea of helping Brown break free from jail. In the end, he merely provided counsel to the imprisoned radical, possibly because he had come to believe Brown was more useful as a martyr than a fugitive. Brown was hung for treason and Higginson remained true to the cause of abolition. During the Civil War, he led a regiment of black soldiers. Later he made a significant contribution to American literature by publicizing the poetry of the reclusive Emily Dickinson.[51]

Before all of that, however, Higginson came across a copy of *Tom Brown's Schooldays* and helped make it popular in the United States. After its publication in the United States, he praised the book in a brand-new literary magazine called the *Atlantic Monthly*. "There is in the community an impression that physical vigor and spiritual sanctity are incompatible," he wrote. He noted the influence of Calvin and observed, mischievously, that Calvin "was an invalid for his whole lifetime." Like Emerson and others before him, Higginson lamented the health of Americans. He said it was the one area in which his country was losing ground internationally: "Guaranty us against physical degeneracy, and we can risk all other perils—financial crises, Slavery, Romanism, Mormonism, Border Ruffians, and New York Assassins." He described the English as "robust" and Canadians as "a more athletic race of people than our own." The solution, he believed, was a regime of exercise for adults and physical fitness training for children. Higginson specifically praised the example of *Tom Brown's Schooldays* for its display of "the healthy boy's-life . . . which is so novel to Americans." If more play resulted in less study, he would not complain: The advantages of fitness far outweighed the loss in scholarship. He commended "a recent match at football between the boys of the Fall River and New Bedford High Schools." What Higginson had written was a plea for Muscular Christianity in the United States.[52]

A social movement may owe its initial potency to thinkers and their writings, but its lasting success depends upon organizations that can influence the masses. Muscular Christianity manifested itself most obviously in the rise of the Young Men's Christian Association, better known by its abbreviation, YMCA. Founded in London in 1844 and spreading to Boston in 1851, the YMCA at first sought merely to promote prayer and biblical study. By the time of the Civil War, it boasted more than two hundred chapters in the United States. After the war, it became a major vehicle for putting the theory of Muscular Christianity into practice.

Americans were ready for it. The Civil War had transformed attitudes toward sports, most notably baseball. The game was gaining popularity during the 1850s, but the war effectively nationalized it. Soldiers in both the North and the South adopted uniform rules that had varied from region to region. One game, played on Christmas in 1862, drew an estimated forty thousand spectators.[53] As the troops marched home from the battlefields, many of them had sports on their minds. More than ever before, however, they returned to cities, especially in the Northeast, where about half the population was urban. Many veterans held deskbound jobs or engaged in monotonous manufacturing work. Some of the very problems identified in the antebellum years were growing worse, not better. Into this breach stepped the YMCA. It opened its first gym in New York in 1869—a development that the *New York Times* described as a "concession to the muscular Christianity of the time."[54]

Sports exploded in popularity. Professional baseball was born with the advent of the Cincinnati Red Stockings in 1869. Over the next decade and a half, Americans took up everything from croquet to roller skating. Endurance walking enjoyed a brief heyday: Edward Payson Weston—"Weston the Pedestrian"—won prizes in long-distance events. Along his courses, which included a trek from Maine to Chicago, he paused to deliver talks on the health benefits of physical activity. Around the same time, the word *coach* evolved into its modern form. Previously, it had referred to private tutors who prepared students for academic tests, but that definition was suddenly eclipsed by its new meaning in athletics. Railroads and telegraphs encouraged competition between communities, the adoption of fads, and the nationalization of leisure activities. "We may divide the whole struggle of the human race into two chapters," observed James A. Garfield in 1880, shortly before he became president. "First, the fight to get leisure; and then the second fight of civilization—what shall we do with our leisure when we get it?"[55]

Muscular Christianity strived to make leisure productive, both spiritually and physically. YMCAs converted prayer rooms into gymnasia, seeing their mission as one of saving souls by building character through physical fitness. An activist in the Boston chapter, Robert J. Roberts, invented the term *body building*. When the YMCA in Springfield, Massachusetts, sought an indoor sport for wintertime in 1891, James Naismith invented basketball. Five years later, the same chapter drew up the rules for a less demanding alternative for older members. It was called volleyball.[56]

THE CIVIL WAR transformed American life, and sports were only a small part of it. The conflict shaped Theodore Roosevelt, too. He grew up in a divided house. His father was a Union man. His mother, a native of the South, harbored Confederate sympathies—she is sometimes described as a model for Scarlett O'Hara in Margaret Mitchell's novel *Gone with the Wind*. Yet she did nothing to contradict or embarrass her husband in public. A story claims that she once flew the Stars and Bars from their New York home, but this account appears not to be true.

Theodore Sr. was twenty-nine when Fort Sumter fell. He was also in good health. In other words, he was precisely the sort of able-bodied young man who might have been expected to join the Union army as an officer. Yet he chose to avoid it. Instead, he hired a substitute to go in his place—a legal maneuver that permanently exempted him from conscription. Essentially he bought his way out of the draft, an option that was available only to men of means. As the war advanced, he became a vigorous advocate of an allotment system that allowed soldiers to deduct a portion of their salaries to support their families back home. Roosevelt not only pushed for the federal legislation to make this possible, but he also visited New York regiments and persuaded many soldiers to participate. It could be argued that in this capacity, Roosevelt did more for the troops and thereby the war effort than he would have accomplished by putting on a blue uniform. Even so, his decision not to take up arms against the South, a choice perhaps motivated by loyalty to his wife and her views, haunted him for the rest of his life.

It haunted his son as well. Theodore Jr. revered his father, but the older man's refusal to serve in an all-consuming war was a blemish on his reputation that could not be wiped clean. There is no record of father and son having discussed the matter. It would have been an uncomfortable conversation for both of them. Everything in Teedie's nature suggests that had he been old enough, he would have volunteered for the military at his first opportunity. During the war, he loved to reenact combat scenes with his siblings in the park—and he always played the part of a brave Union soldier. Yet the example of his namesake may have taken a mere inclination and turned it into something that bordered on obsession. Young Theodore would spend the rest of his life creating his own example of manhood, in everything from his love for fitness and athletics to his own wartime heroics.

That was all in the future when Theodore promised his father that he would make his body. In time, the doctrine of Muscular Christianity would come to influence his thinking about physical activity: "I do not like to see young Christians with shoulders that slope like a champagne bottle," he wrote in his autobiography, after retiring from public life. As a boy, however, his mind did not churn with deep thoughts about cultural trends. At most, it was full of the tales of Tom Brown. Yet his desire to overcome his debilities probably was even more basic. He just wanted to get rid of the asthma that bedeviled him. In the gym that John Wood built for him on the porch at the home on East Twentieth Street, Teedie spent hour after hour sucking in the fresh air and building his body through grueling workouts and sheer determination. "For many years," wrote Corinne, "one of my most vivid recollections is seeing him between horizontal bars, widening his chest by regular, monotonous motion—drudgery indeed."[57]

Corinne was a sharp observer of her brother, but she was wrong about this. "I rarely took exercise merely as exercise," Roosevelt recalled. "Primarily I took it because I liked it."[58] For the young Theodore Roosevelt, exercise was not a chore of mind-numbing toil. It was an act of personal liberation.

Chapter Three

GAME TIME

In the summer of 1872, Theodore Roosevelt left his family and departed on a trip to a faraway place. His destination was Moosehead Lake, in the hinterlands of Maine. Roosevelt's father thought the journey would do him good. Despite the thirteen-year-old boy's commitment to exercise in the family gym, his asthma showed no signs of going away. An especially bad episode compelled Mr. Roosevelt to send Theodore to camp, alone. He hoped that the crisp air of the northern woods would rejuvenate his son, or at least give the poor kid a break from his illness.

Theodore had not spent much time away from his family. The trek to Moosehead Lake separated him even from Elliott, the little brother who was in fact bigger. Elliott's presence usually offered a measure of security. Roosevelt soon learned what life could be like without the protection of his brother or his other guardians. The experience would unsettle him.

On the last leg of the long trip, Roosevelt rode by stagecoach. Two fellow travelers were boys about his age. They were bigger than Roosevelt, as most of his peers were. "I have no doubt they were good-hearted boys, but they were boys!" he recalled years later. The tedium of travel led to trouble. "They found that I was a foreordained and predestined victim, and industriously proceeded to make life miserable for me," said Roosevelt. Without mercy, they tormented the small kid who must have looked and felt out of place: "The worst feature was that when I finally decided to fight them I discovered that either one singly could not only handle me with easy contempt, but handle me so as not to hurt me much and yet to prevent my doing any damage whatever in return."[1]

Roosevelt was keenly aware of his own vulnerabilities, but this may have been his first experience with the social dimension of personal weakness. Unless he developed his scrawny physique, he risked further humiliation. Shortly before the encounter on the stagecoach, Roosevelt had read a poem that seemed to taunt him as much as the bullying boys. It was typical of Roosevelt to compare an event from his own life with something he had read in a book. In this case, he thought of several lines from "The Flight of the Duchess," by Robert Browning.

He had read them shortly before the trip to Maine. They made such an impression on Roosevelt that he remembered them for the rest of his days, as he confessed to one of his first biographers, Hermann Hagedorn. Browning's poem describes a young duke, born into privilege and the heir of a distinguished ancestry. Yet the duke lacked ambition and vigor. He was a feeble boy: "the pertest little ape / That ever affronted human shape . . . all legs and length / With blood for bone, all speed, no strength." In these words, Roosevelt perceived a sorry reflection of himself.[2]

On the way to Moosehead Lake, Browning's poem became a disturbing reality: "The experience taught me what probably no amount of good advice could have taught me. I made up my mind that I must try to learn so that I would not again be put in such a helpless position; and having become quickly and bitterly conscious that I did not have the natural prowess to hold my own, I

decided that I would try to supply its place by training."[3] He resolved to take up a competitive sport. He would become a boxer.

At this point, it is possible to see Theodore Roosevelt begin
to emerge from the shell of his invalid boyhood. Asthma would
remain a significant challenge, but other problems would begin to
correct themselves, partly through the dint of his own effort but
also through happy circumstance. Roosevelt started to observe the
connection between sports and fitness in his own life—experiences
that would make him an apostle for a certain kind of living later
on. The first flicker of the Progressive impulse that would animate
so much of his presidency also appeared. The boy would come to
believe that not every difficulty is irreversible and that determination can matter more than determinism. Self-improvement was
not only a possibility, but an imperative.

BEFORE THAT FATEFUL trip to Moosehead Lake, Roosevelt
received his first gun. It was a gift from his father: a 12-gauge,
double-barreled shotgun imported from France. For a boy of Roosevelt's size, the gun would have delivered quite a kick—enough
to knock him over if he failed to set his legs and feet properly. He
did have his share of mishaps: "I tattooed myself with partially un-
burned grains of powder more than once," he wrote.[4] Yet the gun's
greatest effect was not to blemish the boy or push him backward.
Instead, it propelled him forward into a life of sportsmanship. In
time he would become identified with hunting more than any
other sport. He had always appreciated the natural world, from
the moment he encountered it between the covers of the books in
his parents' library. When he had the chance and his health permitted, he would hike through field and forest. He simply loved
the outdoors. From this point on, he would enter it armed.

As an adult, Roosevelt would go on to stalk big game—
buffalo and grizzly bears on journeys across the American West,

and impala and elephants on a postpresidential safari in Africa. When he was not hunting, he was often writing about his hunting expeditions: He authored books with titles such as *Hunting Trips of a Ranchman* (1885), *Ranch Life and the Hunting-Trail* (1888), *The Wilderness Hunter* (1893), and *African Game Trails* (1910). During and after his time in the White House, Roosevelt was probably the most famous hunter in the world.

Oddly enough, his best-known hunting exploit did not involve the bagging of a beast at all. It was quite the reverse. On a presidential excursion to Mississippi in 1902, Roosevelt went for several days without killing anything larger than a pig. A guide, presumably embarrassed by this disappointing result, decided to take desperate measures. He located a small bear and whacked it over the head, stunning the animal. Then he called for Roosevelt and suggested that the president shoot the dazed creature. But Roosevelt refused, on the grounds that it was unsporting to kill an animal that had rendered insensible. Newspapers cheered his conduct. A cartoonist for the *Washington Post* began to draw bears alongside his renderings of the president. Within a few weeks, F.A.O. Schwarz and other toy merchants in New York City were marketing what has since become one of the most popular items of childhood. Long after Roosevelt's face crumbles off the side of Mount Rushmore, children will still go to bed clutching their teddy bears.[5]

If Roosevelt himself had grown up with security objects, he most likely had put them away before he loaded his new weapon for the first time. Yet he was fascinated by stuffed animals—not the cuddly ones of youth, but rather the mounted and preserved specimens of creatures that once had lived. He had become a voracious collector of critters and operated what he called the "Roosevelt Museum of Natural History." Its first item was the skull of a seal that he had obtained from a city market in Manhattan. Baby squirrels and snapping turtles also took up residence in the

Roosevelt home. The boy kept snakes in a guest room water pitcher. His family tolerated these enthusiasms, but his siblings and parents did have their limits. After a while, Elliott requested his own room when they stayed in hotels, on account of his brother's habit of leaving animal entrails in the washbasin. Mrs. Roosevelt once discovered that her son was storing dead mice in an icebox. When she deposited them in the trash, the boy lamented "the loss to Science! the loss to Science!" Another time, he hid a toad beneath his hat. When he met a distinguished lady on the street, etiquette called for the hat's removal. The amphibian hopped from his hair to its freedom, startling all who witnessed it.[6] Eventually Roosevelt took lessons in taxidermy from John G. Bell, who had worked with John James Audubon, the influential painter of birds. As always, Roosevelt was ready with a literary reference: Bell, he wrote, "had a musty little shop, somewhat on the order of Mr. Venus's shop in *Our Mutual Friend*," the novel by Charles Dickens.[7]

For Roosevelt, a new gun meant a new and improved ability to amass animal specimens. In creating this opportunity, however, it exposed a different problem that neither Roosevelt nor his family had come to appreciate. It came into focus when he went tramping with his brother and their friends in the wilds around Dobbs Ferry, a small town on the Hudson River just north of New York City. The Roosevelts often retreated to it when they wanted a short break from urban life. Almost a century earlier, during the American Revolution, it was a base of operations for George Washington and his patriot army. In 1781, when Washington left for Yorktown and final victory over the British, he departed from Dobbs Ferry.

Perhaps Theodore and his gang crashed through the brush while shouting "the Redcoats are coming!" More likely, they tried to remain as quiet as possible, at least when they searched for prey. For Roosevelt, noise was not the problem. Instead, he struggled with his vision. His friends would spot targets and shoot. He was baffled. He simply could not see what they did. At one point, a deer stood about forty feet away from Theodore—and still he did not see it, even as his brother, Elliott, had no trouble at all.[8]

Before long, the source of the problem became clear: "One day they read aloud an advertisement in huge letters on a distant billboard, and I then realized that something was the matter, for not only was I unable to read the sign but I could not even see the letters." Roosevelt talked to his father about his eyes. It turned out he was badly nearsighted. Anything beyond about thirty feet was rendered obscure. Like a fish that is unaware of the water in which it swims, Roosevelt had grown so accustomed to his handicap that he did not even know that it afflicted him. He obtained his first pair of glasses. Suddenly everything looked different, and better. "I had no idea how beautiful the world was until I got those spectacles," he wrote. "I had been a clumsy and awkward little boy, and while much of my clumsiness and awkwardness was doubtless due to general characteristics, a good deal of it was due to the fact that I could not see and yet was wholly ignorant that I was not seeing."[9]

He wore the glasses to Moosehead Lake, and the image of a boy who was not only small but also in spectacles probably encouraged those harassers on the stagecoach. Did they mock him as a "four eyes"? Whatever the case, their actions led to Roosevelt's embrace of an activity that would require him to remove his glasses. Just as they had improved his eyesight, the boxing ring would build his muscles.

UP TO THIS point, Roosevelt's sporting activities had not involved formal competition. His exercise was primarily a solitary pursuit. Hunting was much the same. It may have fed a competitive spirit, as boys tried to hit targets and bring down quarry, but these contests would have been more convivial in nature. Boxing was different. It would force Roosevelt to get in a ring and fight. There were rules and customs to follow. There would be winners and losers.

When Roosevelt first showed up for lessons with John Long, a onetime prizefighter, he probably did not look like a winner. He was still the puny boy who had suffered from abuse on his way to camp. Yet he returned from Maine with a desire to take boxing lessons. His father soon arranged for him to work with Long.

Roosevelt sparred in a room lined with color pictures of famous fights. One featured an image of bare-knuckle boxers Tom Hyer and Yankee Sullivan in their 1849 match near Baltimore. Another depicted an 1860 contest between English pugilist Thomas Sayers and American John Heenan. It was a bare-knuckle bout as well. More than a thousand spectators had turned out to see it in the English countryside, a short train ride from London. If Long ever shared the story of the fight with his students, Roosevelt may have taken some inspiration from Sayers, who weighed about thirty pounds less than his foe from the United States. It was not exactly David versus Goliath, but most casual observers would have viewed Heenan as the likely victor. Early in the fight, Heenan appeared to gain the upper hand. Yet he could not finish off Sayers. Round after round went by. The smaller man simply refused to surrender. The two men pounded each other for two hours, across three dozen rounds. In the thirty-seventh round, Heenan forced Sayers against the ropes. One of the onlookers then interfered, possibly in an attempt to save Sayers from serious injury. Chaos erupted. A referee declared a draw. Heenan and his supporters felt cheated. If Sayers and his backers felt relief, they did not express it: They thought the fight should have continued and said so. Both sides had to settle for a frustrating and controversial nonresult.[10] As an American nationalist by nature and conviction, Roosevelt almost certainly would have favored Heenan. Yet the scrappy Sayers probably would have earned his respect. At some level, Roosevelt may even have identified with him.

In his training with Long, Roosevelt first would have learned the fundamentals of boxing. Then he would have graduated to informal sparring. Finally he would have been ready for a public competition. It probably did not take more than a few weeks—and readiness is always a question of degree. Long scheduled a boxing tournament for his young charges. It sorted combatants by size and climaxed in a series of "championship" matches. Roosevelt was placed in the lightweight division. The winner of his category would take home a trophy: an inexpensive pewter mug. Roosevelt did not believe he would contend for it. Long was a skeptic as well. "Neither he nor I had any idea that I could do anything," recalled Roosevelt. "It happened that I was pitted in succession against a couple of reedy striplings who were even worse than I was." To the surprise of all, Roosevelt prevailed. "The pewter mug became one of my most prized possessions," he confessed.[11] This emblem of accomplishment provided a comforting reminder that he was not necessarily destined for a life of shameful defeats. From that point on, boxing would become one of Roosevelt's great enthusiasms.

YET HE WOULD not continue his training in John Long's ring. His father was appointed American commissioner to the Vienna Exposition of 1873 and his parents decided to use this as the occasion for another extended trip across the ocean. In October 1872, seven months before the exposition's May opening, the Roosevelts left New York City on what would become a roundabout journey to their final destination. They paid a visit to England and stopped elsewhere in Europe, but their initial goal was Egypt. They were to spend a couple of weeks in Cairo followed by a two-month excursion up and down the Nile River. The first purpose for Mr. and Mrs. Roosevelt was educational: Their children would come to learn about an important part of the world by seeing it firsthand. They also hoped that Theodore's and Corinne's bouts with asthma would vanish into the thin air of the desert, at least while they were breathing it.

They were successful on both counts. The children marveled at the sights: "How I gazed on it! It was Egypt, the land of my dreams; Egypt the most ancient of all countries!" gushed Roosevelt in his diary.[12] Moreover, his asthma seemed to disappear. So did his sister's. Elliott had misgivings about the trip, probably because of the previous experience in Europe, but he managed to buck up: "Perhaps it won't be so bad after all what with rowing, boxing, and Christmas and playing, in between lessons and the ruins."[13]

Roosevelt entered a phase that would become the longest period of uninterrupted good health in his young life. He began an adolescent growth spurt. Clothes that fit at the start of the journey upriver were too small by the time his family returned downriver. Most exciting of all were the birds. The Nile River is home to its own native fauna and also serves as a flyway for migrating species. Through his glasses, Roosevelt could see them clearly. They were everywhere. He immediately took to hunting and collecting, using his shotgun as well as a new breechloader that his father gave him for Christmas. Previously, birds had eluded the boy with poor vision. Now, with spectacles pinching his nose, he killed them with gusto. Most days he left the *Aboo Erdan*—a traditional, barge-like vessel known as a dahabeah—to probe the reeds and riverbanks of the Nile. The wildlife won no respite except on Sundays, when the guns fell silent for the sabbath. When Roosevelt was not creating a ruckus with his weapons, he was creating a stink in his open-air workshop. The deck of the Roosevelts' luxury riverboat became a scene of disemboweling, skinning, and stuffing.

"There has always been something to do," Roosevelt wrote in a letter to his aunt, "for we could always fall back upon shooting when everything else failed us." A sampling of the boy's diary entries, taken from early February (and collected by biographer Carleton Putnam), suggest that he did little else: On February 1, "We visited Karnac and I killed some specimens." On February

4, "Made beautiful time and reached here in the evening. Killed a ringed plover." On February 5, "Visited the beautiful and well preserved temple of Dendera. Shot a sand chat and an Egyptian plover and got a bat." On February 7, "Saw the temple of Abydis, which was quite interesting. Killed 17 pigeons." On February 8, "Rowed all day. Shot in the morning." On February 12, "Visited the Tombs of Beni Hassan. Interesting in subject but not in execution. Killed an owl and a kestrel."[14] Toward the end of his time in Egypt, Roosevelt summarized his activity and made a prediction: "I have procured between one and two hundred skins—I expect to procure some more in Syria."[15]

Roosevelt's passion for hunting and exploring was infectious. His father often joined him. "He is a most enthusiastic sportsman and has infused some of his spirit in to me," wrote Theodore Sr. "Yesterday I walked the bogs with him at the risk of sinking hopelessly and helplessly, for hours . . . but I felt I must keep up with Teedie."[16] During this period, there is no hint of the boy's suffering from asthma or any other illness. The link between sports, the outdoors, and good health grew in his mind.

The Roosevelts flew an American flag above their dahabeah's brown sail, providing an unusual sight for Egyptian onlookers. Yet they were not the only Americans on the Nile. Henry Adams was on the river that winter. Ralph Waldo Emerson was there as well. His home in Massachusetts had burned down the previous summer. During its reconstruction, he traveled abroad with his daughter Ellen. Emerson was approaching his seventieth birthday and beginning to lose his memory, but he hosted the Roosevelts aboard his boat and then paid his own visit to the *Aboo Erdan.* The man who once worried about the vigor of his country did not record his impressions of the Roosevelt brood, but Ellen did. "Enchanting children," she wrote, "healthy, natural well-brought-up, and with beautiful manners."[17]

On their slow journey from Cairo to the Nile's first cataract at Aswan and back—a trip of 583 miles each way—the Roosevelts had companions. Four Harvard men from the class of 1871 were making their own grand tours of Europe and the Middle East. They traveled on two dahabeahs. Future diplomat Augustus Jay, a great-grandson of John Jay, joined Harry Godey, who would become a doctor, aboard the *Gazelle*. The *Rachel* carried Francis Merriam and Nathaniel Thayer. Merriam would go on to manage estate and investment interests. Thayer would fail at politics, succeed in business, and marry a descendant of Paul Revere. All were bachelors.

Corinne called their group "a delightful circle." They socialized frequently and often included the children in their gatherings. Their presence may have influenced Roosevelt's enthusiasm for attending Harvard. Bamie, who celebrated her eighteenth birthday with a moonlight visit to an Egyptian temple, probably developed an interest in one or more of the Harvard men. Her attractions went unrequited, though Jay and Thayer stayed with the Roosevelts after their cruise on the Nile had come to an end. The camaraderie continued for another month as they visited Jerusalem and the Holy Land's other major sites. Outside Jaffa, Theodore challenged Jay to a horse race and won.[18] At the Dead Sea, Theodore and Jay experimented with diving below its buoyant waters. The boy abandoned the effort quickly; Jay managed to stay submerged long enough to accumulate crusted salt in his eyes and ears.[19]

It is sheer speculation to say that Roosevelt learned about football from these compatriots. Yet it is also plausible to think that they would have known about the game and may have shared some of their thoughts and observations with the dynamic boy who seemed so enthralled by sports and the outdoors. Football was still in the very earliest stages of establishing itself on campus, but it also had started to cause a stir at Harvard and elsewhere. In fact, it is hard to believe that Godey, Jay, Merriam, and Thayer would have known nothing of the game.

. . . .

AS FAR BACK as the 1820s, around the time William Webb Ellis supposedly picked up a ball and ran with it at Rugby, American students were playing versions of the game that would evolve into football. At Princeton, the undergraduates called it "balldown." They assembled on a big field and divided into two teams on the basis of last names. Apparently they could kick and punch the ball, but not carry it. Harvard students developed the tradition of "Bloody Monday," a game whose name suggests its level of roughness. Longtime Harvard librarian John Langdon Sibley commented on the game's "violence and brutality" and said the central mission of each team was to "kick the other and bark their shins as much as possible."[20] At Yale, freshmen and sophomores played something similar. A tongue-twisting song captures the spirit of the contest: "There were tearing of shirts, and ripping of stitches / and breaches of peaces, and pieces of britches." The violent nature of these games led to their prohibition. In 1858, the city of New Haven forbade Yale students from using the town green, effectively ending the play. Two years later, Harvard's faculty banned Bloody Monday.[21] In a letter to the fathers of the sophomore class, the professors complained that football had "degenerated into a match at boxing and fighting." The game was "coarse and violent in character."[22] The next year, students held a mock funeral service for their beloved game.

After the Civil War, however, the sport sprang back to life. In 1869, a group of students at Rutgers issued an invitation to students at nearby Princeton. On the afternoon of November 6, they played what is now often regarded as the first intercollegiate game of football. The rules were similar to modern soccer. They permitted kicking and heading. Players could catch the ball in flight, but they could not run with it. After a catch, they dropped the ball on the ground and took a free kick. Goals were scored when the ball traveled between a pair of posts set about twenty-five feet apart. There was no crossbar. Each team put twenty-five men on the field, which measured 360 feet long and 225 feet wide. The players did not wear uniforms, though several men on the Rutgers team put on scarlet head coverings similar to bandanas. They called them "turbans." There was no clock: The match would end after one team scored six times. About one hundred spectators gathered to watch.[23]

Early on, players learned the importance of brute force. Princeton earned the first point. But its captain, William S. Gummere (a future chief justice of New Jersey), became concerned about the Rutgers strategy. The men in red turbans tried to advance the ball by shielding it with bodies. Gummere ordered his biggest player, Jacob Michael, to break up this formation. "Time and time again, Michael, or 'Big Mike,' charged into Rutgers' primitive mass play and scattered the players like a burst bundle of sticks," recalled John W. Herbert, who played for Rutgers.[24] This tactic led to Princeton's second goal, giving it a lead of 2–0. Later in the game, when the ball stopped beside a fence, two players raced to grab it. One of them was Big Mike. "They reached the fence, on which the [spectators] were perched, and, unable to check their momentum, in a tremendous impact struck the fence, which gave way with a crash, and over went its load of yelling students to the ground."[25]

Despite its early lead and the aggressiveness of Big Mike, Princeton soon ran into trouble. Rutgers stopped putting the ball in the air, where Princeton's taller players appeared to have an advantage. The home team kept it on the ground, passing from foot to foot and finding ways to knock it through the posts. After three hours of play, Rutgers won by a score of six goals to four. Rutgers prevailed despite the fact that its team featured one of history's first wrong-way players, who became confused about which way to kick the ball and nearly scored on his own goal.[26]

Princeton had its revenge the next week, when the players met again in a cow pasture near the Princeton campus. It was within sight of a mansion that Grover Cleveland would occupy after finishing his second term as president.[27] The rematch was perhaps most notable for an ongoing equipment failure. "The ball . . . was too hard to blow up right," remembered Henry Green Duffield, who had watched the contest as a boy. "The game was stopped several times that day while the teams called for a little key from the sidelines. They used it to unlock the small nozzle which was tucked into the ball, and then took turns blowing it up. The last man generally got tired and they put it back in play somewhat lopsided."[28] Despite this frustration, Princeton seemed to have no trouble beating Rutgers: It won, eight goals to none.

The next year, Columbia and Cornell started to play football. At Yale, students tried to revive the sport as well. This time they showed more persistence. When they started to play on the city green in New Haven, police ordered them away. Instead of quitting, they moved to an empty lot and continued. These games still resembled soccer. They were rougher and more physical, but the rules barred players from carrying the ball in their hands.

Harvard, however, had a different idea. In the spring of 1871—when Theodore Roosevelt's companions on the Nile would have been finishing their studies—a group of students gained permission to play football according to the rules of what they called the "Boston Game." This was not a revival of the old Bloody Monday ritual, but a new game that would not scandalize the faculty. Or so they claimed. The precise origins of its rules are unclear. It seems to have developed among boys who attended elite secondary schools such as Boston Latin and Dixwell's. As these young men moved from high school to Harvard, they brought their game with them.[29] Under its rules, players could pick up the ball and run with it. Kicking remained a dominant feature, but the element of rushing with the ball separated Harvard's pastime from football on other campuses. This hybrid version was one part soccer and one part rugby.

. . . .

WHATEVER THE TRUTH about Roosevelt's exposure to football from his traveling companions, the boy had more pressing concerns. Upon leaving the Nile, the absence of asthma attacks came to a fitful end. Roosevelt hacked his way across the mountains of Lebanon. Other maladies beset him, too: He was seasick on the voyage to Greece and across the Black Sea. In Constantinople, he suffered abdominal pains. On his cruise up the Danube River, toward Vienna and its exhibition, asthma overtook him yet again. By the time he arrived, he was miserable.[30] If he had once imagined that his improvements in Egypt marked a turning point, by now he had learned otherwise. He had experienced a pleasant interlude rather than a permanent change in his condition.

Upon reaching Vienna, the Roosevelts split up. Theodore Sr. attended to his duties in the city. Bamie and her mother traveled through Germany, France, and England. The three younger children went to Dresden. At first the boys lived apart from Corinne, though soon they were reunited under the same roof. They lived with the Minckwitz family. The purpose of their five-month stay was to learn German and French. Lessons took up much of their time. On Sunday afternoons, however, they had their freedom. They usually gathered with a pair of cousins, John and Maud Elliott, the children of their mother's half brother, who happened to be in Dresden at the same time. Their favorite activity—at least for the boys—was boxing.

Before long, they were finding ways to fight just about every day, when their studies were done. Their father encouraged them from afar, sending them boxing gloves as gifts. One of Theodore's earliest surviving letters comes from this period. The gloves, he wrote, "are a source of great amusement to us."[31] The boys seemed to enjoy nothing more than beating each other up. "Boxing is one of Teedie's and my favorite amusements; it is such a novelty to be made to see stars when it is not night," joked Elliott. Like wrestlers who assume stage names, the Roosevelt boys invented nicknames for themselves. As the smaller member of the pair, Theodore went by "Skinny." Elliott was known as "Swelly." Both enjoyed chronicling their bouts. Here is how Swelly described one of them:

> 1st Round, Skinny-Swelly. Results: Skinny, lip swelled and bleeding. Swelly sound in every limb if nose and lip can be classed as such.
>
> 2nd Round. Results: Skinny, nose bleeding and cheeks of a carmine hue. Swelly, one cheek looking as if it had a mustard plaster on it.[32]

Theodore took a more narrative approach. Here is an account of a match with his cousin, whom he regarded as a better fighter:

> After some striking and warding, I got Johnie into a corner, when he sprung out. We each warded off a right hand blow and brought in a left hander. His took effect behind my ear, and for a minute I saw stars and reeled back to the centre of the room, while Johnie had had his nose and upper lip mashed together and been driven back against the door. I was so weak however that I was driven across the room, simply warding off blows, but then I almost disabled his left arm, and drove him back to the middle where some sharp boxing occurred. I got in one on his forehead which raised a bump, but my eye was made black and blue. At this minute "Up" was called and we had to separate. . . . If you offered rewards for bloody noses you would spend a fortune on me alone.[33]

It is easy to picture Mr. Roosevelt's delight at reading of these bouts: Here was his son, by turns sickly and vigorous, engaged in self-improvement through athletics rather than retreating into a suffocating world of books and beds. As always, the boy proceeded not with grim resolution but with a sense of high spirits. Theodore's mother seems to have been less charmed: "The children have just left after a boxing match in which bleeding noses and swelled lips were common," she wrote. "I think it a horrid amusement."[34] Yet these may be the words of a woman who secretly approved. One night, when she was visiting Dresden, Mrs. Roosevelt caught a glimpse of the man whom her boy would become. They were walking back from the Altstadt, the old section of the city. "When we passed some rather rowdy people, [Theodore] walked on the outside in a *protective* manner," she wrote.[35] The incident gave her a sense of comfort and, perhaps, motherly accomplishment.

Roosevelt's asthma was mild in Dresden. It remained in the background, not tormenting him but occasionally rising up to remind him that it was still there. Toward the end of his stay in Europe, he commented on "a small attack" in a letter to his father: "Except for the fact that I can not speak, without blowing like an abridged edition of a hippopotamus, it does not inconvenience me much."[36] His days were otherwise consumed by study and boxing.

The family returned to New York in the fall of 1873. Theodore's new project was to prepare himself for Harvard. This would require passing entrance exams and, more to the point, spending the time it would take to prepare for them. He had learned that he could build his body; now he would have to build his mind in order to meet his goal of admission. Because of his health, Roosevelt had never engaged in the routine of leaving home for school and learning his subjects bit by bit, day after day. He had certainly received an education, through a mix of tutors and travel. But the next phase of his life would involve a more methodical study of everything from Greek and Latin to math and history.

He continued to make time for sports and the outdoors. When he was not in New York City, his primary stomping ground was

Oyster Bay on Long Island, where his father leased a house and began to establish permanent roots. Roosevelt remained meticulous about physical activity and recorded his exploits in a diary. In the second half of 1875, he competed against his brother and several cousins in a series of athletic contests, such as running, jumping, wrestling, and boxing. There were fifteen events in total. Teedie went undefeated, prevailing in fourteen of these activities and taking a draw in the fifteenth.[37] Even the cold of January and February failed to keep him huddled inside, where he might enjoy the warmth and safety of a comfortable home. "Last winter we had so much skating, and I was hurt while on the ice, falling on my head and being senseless for several hours," he wrote to a friend.[38]

Roosevelt was on the verge of manhood. He stood five feet, eight inches tall. He weighed 124 pounds. He was wiry and muscular. According to his own calculations, his chest measured thirty-four inches and his waist twenty-six and a half inches.[39] He grew a muttonchop beard, which he would wear to Harvard as a freshman in the fall of 1876. Best of all, his asthma was under control. It did not leave him entirely, but it would never again haunt him the way it did when he was young. Whether he had defeated it through his own efforts or simply outgrew it cannot be known. Yet it is easy to think that Roosevelt believed an act of willpower, manifested in a devotion to fitness and sports, had allowed him to conquer his affliction.

Chapter Four

CAMP DAYS

For the fifteen hundred fans who watched Harvard and Yale play football in 1881, the most obvious feature of the day was the rain: The two rivals faced each other in a torrential downpour. The field turned to slop. Players had trouble with their footing. The ball seemed to resist possession as it squirted out of hands like a fish flopping madly for release. If the deluge from above and the mud from below were not challenges enough, burly defenders made it all but impossible to score goals.

The game took place on November 12, in New Haven's Hamilton Park. It marked the sixth time the two colleges had met to play their young sport. In the first contest, in 1875, Harvard had prevailed. In the four games since then, however, Harvard had failed to score even a single goal against Yale. The Elis had come to dominate the annual competition. Its players were routinely bigger and stronger. Football already bestowed great advantages on competitors with these traits. The bad weather in 1881 seemed to confer even more.

As time expired, the score stood at zero to zero. The result, however, was not a tie. Under a peculiar set of short-lived rules, safeties could make the difference when goals did not. If one team had four fewer safeties than its opponent, it would take the game. Harvard had four safeties. Yale had none. The streak continued for another year.

More than three hundred Harvard students had chartered a special train to travel from Cambridge and cheer for their team. By the end of the game, they were sopping wet. Yet their spirits were anything but dampened. They believed their team at least deserved credit for a moral victory. Yale, after all, had won by the slimmest of margins. Others, however, were frustrated by what they had seen. "It has been the custom since the beginning of football contests between Yale and Harvard for Harvard men to accuse Yale men of uncalled-for brutality, of a desire to win by maiming our men," complained a writer for the *Harvard Advocate*, a student magazine. "It is felt by nearly all Harvard men that Yale plays more violently than is necessary or in good taste." The *Advocate* did allow that Yale's team brimmed with ability. It paid particular attention to "the brilliant playing of Camp."[1]

This was a reference to Walter Camp, a twenty-two-year-old graduate student at Yale's medical school. He was in his sixth and final season as a member of the Yale squad. His collegiate career had started in the 1876 game against Harvard, the same game that Theodore Roosevelt had attended as a freshman. By botching a lateral pass that day, Camp had produced the odd bounce that gave his team its one good goal-scoring chance of the game—an unexpected opportunity that a teammate did not let go to waste. Roosevelt had grumbled about the result in 1876 much as the *Harvard Advocate* did after the rainy contest in 1881.

Camp was not one of Yale's "giants," as described by the *Harvard Advocate*. He was a man of average weight and slightly above-average height. Yet he enjoyed great success as a player. He was known for his speed as a runner, his skill as a kicker, and his talent as a tackler. If he had done nothing else for football but perform on its fields, he would still be remembered as one of the best players in the early days of the sport.

Yet this was his least contribution to football. More than a skillful player, Camp was a resourceful thinker. Starting in his student days, and continuing to the end of his life, he gave careful consideration to the game and how to improve it. He built upon traditions developed in England and carried across the ocean, inventing rules and strategies that gave birth to a distinctly American sport. He also defended football from its critics. Whenever controversy touched the game, Camp fought back. The history of football is full of essential men, but Camp stands first among them. More than anybody else, he deserves the title of football's founding father.

WALTER CHAUNCEY CAMP was born on April 7, 1859, in New Britain, Connecticut. He was the only child of his parents to survive infancy. In 1864, the family moved to New Haven, where Camp essentially would live for the rest of his days. His parents started out as teachers. His father, Leverett Camp, became the principal of Dwight School. His mother, Ellen Cornwell Camp, became a homemaker.

The Muscular Christianity movement shaped Leverett Camp's views on childhood education and physical fitness: He encouraged exercise among his students and helped form the Dwight School Cadets, a military group. Leverett earned a good salary from this primary job. Yet he also showed a flair for entrepreneurship and supplemented his income with real estate transactions. This extra money helped the Camps reside in an upper-middle-class section of the city that would have remained beyond the reach of a less ambitious breadwinner. The family was even able to employ a servant. They did not live in luxury, but they enjoyed many comforts of material advantage.[2]

As a boy, Walter Camp was brown-eyed and fair-complexioned, thin but not gaunt, and youthful in appearance. His cast of mind was serious and sober—he was said to have "sand," a word that indicated his willingness to work hard and absorb punishment on the way to success.[3] He almost certainly read *Tom Brown's Schooldays*. At the very least, he fell under the influence it was having on the culture of American boyhood, probably with his father's encouragement. Walter became a vigorous swimmer, camper, and fisherman. As he grew older, he played tennis and sailed. His parents owned a house on Martha's Vineyard, an island off the coast of Cape Cod. On one of his visits, Camp and a friend faced down a drunk who was harassing a group of vacationers. Another time, as a teenager, he took a job on a fishing boat but abandoned it after a single day. He considered the work filthy and swam to shore that night. It was said to be the only job Camp ever quit. He seems to have had due cause: His hair had become so infested with lice that it had to be shaved.[4]

Back in New Haven, Camp attended Hopkins Grammar School. He maintained a strong record of attendance and earned good grades. The principal was William L. Cushing, who coached crew at Yale. Athletics did not dominate school life, but the students played sports in their spare time. They took up baseball, which was gaining renown in the post–Civil War years, and Camp learned to throw a curve. One time, he and his classmates played against Yale freshmen, with Camp on the mound. The younger students prevailed, though the final score indicates that the game was anything but a pitchers' duel: 14–12. The boys of Hopkins Grammar also played a soccer-like version of football. It was an informal activity, less organized than baseball and other sports, and it involved kicking round balls. Camp and his peers had at least a passing familiarity with rugby's distinguishing elements. In 1873, when Camp was fourteen, he watched a game between Yale students and English sailors who had stopped in New Haven.

This contest may have involved picking up the ball and carrying it. Eleven men participated on each side, possibly for no better reason than this was the number of players the English team could field. That night, Camp spotted the sailors at the theater, where they had a box. "I am sure I looked at them a good deal more than I did the stage," he wrote.[5]

Two years later, in 1875, Camp moved from onlooker to participant. During his final year at Hopkins Grammar, he attended Yale's varsity football practices as the member of a scrub team whose purpose was to keep the varsity players sharp. Camp helped out in other ways as well. He put down the lines for the field at Hamilton Park, where Yale and Harvard would play their first-ever football game.

Yale preferred a form of football that resembled soccer. Harvard, on the other hand, had adopted rugby's practice of allowing players to grab the ball and run with it. The match, played on November 13, has become known as the "concessionary game" because Yale made concessions to Harvard: It agreed to try the rugby rules. Harvard dominated and came away with a 4–0 victory. If the loss dispirited Yale's players, it did not prevent them from making an objective judgment about the experience. They decided that they liked the game the way Harvard played it.

Camp loved what he saw, too. It is easy to picture him alongside the field he helped prepare, cheering for Yale and wondering whether his future would include putting on one of the school's football uniforms. Hopkins Grammar adjoined the campus of Yale—it stood on the site of what is now the law school—and sent many of its students there. Camp joined their ranks in the fall of 1876. At Hopkins Grammar, he had earned a reputation for athletic prowess. He was not a large person, weighing about 160 pounds. He would gain a little heft in college but never approach the bulging physique of so many football players. Yet he was deceptively strong, with muscles hardened during his constant outdoor activity and long runs around New Haven. Anybody who watched him on the field for a few minutes would have concluded that although he did not look like a football standout, Camp possessed a natural aptitude for the game.

AS A FRESHMAN at Yale, Camp would have participated in his first athletic event on the day before classes began. A school tradition at the time called for a class rush in which freshmen and sophomores battled each other in a pushing and wrestling contest on the grounds of Hopkins Grammar and then continuing along High Street. Students organized it on their own, away from the eyes of their professors, many of whom disapproved. In 1876, when Camp would have taken part, the annual ritual was said to have resulted in a draw.[6]

This unusual hazing event, whose purpose was to develop feelings of solidarity among classmates, marked the informal start to a long and distinguished career in college athletics. Camp went on to participate in baseball, crew, track, and tennis. If he had never shown an interest in football, he still would have gone down in the history of Yale athletics as one of his era's most accomplished sportsmen.

As a student, he was merely ordinary. His grade-point average was consistently unspectacular, ranging from a high of 2.77 in his freshman year to a low of 2.43 in his junior year. Yale's curriculum included Latin, Greek, English, physiology, astronomy, chemistry, logic, ethics, philosophy, and history. Not all of these courses were to Camp's liking. "Studied awhile on Ethics," he wrote in a journal that he updated sporadically. "I think this is the most useless study we ever had. Any man in his senses would know enough to do what this book tells him."[7] Camp was not above cutting class: Occasionally he skipped a lecture in order to play whist with friends in his room at Durfee Hall. He did admire one professor in particular:

William Graham Sumner. When Camp was a student, Sumner was well on his way to becoming one of America's leading intellectuals. Later, Camp and Sumner would become bound in more personal ways.

Yale students were required to pray at chapel every day and attend church on Sundays. In his leisure time, Camp read popular fiction, including novels by Wilkie Collins and Charles Dickens. He grew a mustache, became known as a snazzy dresser, and often took meals at Mory's, a private club near campus. It does not appear as though he had anything like a steady girlfriend. Instead, Camp went "snabbing," the slang term for flirting with young ladies. He wrote poetry and seems to have shown some talent for doggerel verse. He was no rabble rouser, but he did not always avoid mischief. As a sophomore, during a performance of *Richard III*, he and several friends abused one of the actors: "We pelted him from first to last with beans, onions, etc. . . . It is the best fun I have had since I have been here." (After the show, Camp noted in his diary "a row with the police" and observed five arrests.) Toward the end of his junior year, he was tapped to join Skull and Bones, the secret society of students and alumni. Upon graduation, he and two dozen classmates entered Yale Medical School. He planned to become a doctor.[8]

It was in football, of course, that Camp made his reputation. He became one of only two freshmen to make the varsity team. He also made the freshman squad, became its captain, and played for it simultaneously. There were no formal coaches in those days: The team captain was essentially a player-coach. Each morning during Camp's freshman year, Eugene V. Baker, the varsity captain, held a ninety-minute practice. Each night, players gathered again for a three-mile run on an indoor track. "We believed that we were making ourselves models of strength and endurance," said Camp. The language of Darwinism crept into his talk. Camp compared his team's training to the "survival of the fittest" principle.[9]

Camp had arrived at Yale in good physical condition, and it improved under Baker's direction. Even so, many thought Camp looked too small to join the varsity team. Before his first game against Harvard, according to one story, Harvard captain Nathaniel Curtis warned Baker not to "let that child play." Baker scoffed. "He is young but he is all spirit and whipcord," he replied. After the game, Curtis conceded the point. "You were right, Baker," he said. "The little fellow nearly put me out."[10] In another account—one that provides a sense of how the game was played when there were few rules—Camp really did put out a Harvard player that day:

> A fully mature Harvard player, breaded and brawny and strong, bore down on Walter Camp under the impression that Camp had the ball. As he was not in possession of it, the tackle should not have been made. But it was made. And Camp and the Harvard man engaged, then and there, in a private wrestling match on the field. They heaved and hauled, and at least, to everyone's astonishment, Camp threw his burly opponent and pinned his shoulders down.[11]

Rough play was of course a fundamental feature of football. Even so, an encounter later in the season rattled Camp. In a game against Columbia, on a bitterly cold day, one of the opposing players broke free from the pack. Only Camp stood between him and the goal line, so Camp made the tackle. "The ground was frozen hard and he struck on the back of his head, stunning him and making a slight scalp wound," wrote Camp. "To my freshman eyes his head had apparently cracked open and I ran to the Captain saying, 'I don't want to play any more. I've killed a man.' It took him only a minute or two to come to consciousness and go on with the game, to my great relief."[12] It would seem that Camp had inflicted a concussion.

Camp became a key contributor on an excellent team. In 1876, Yale played three games—against Harvard, Princeton, and

Columbia—and won them all. Yale's opponents failed to score a single goal. Camp went on to play for four years as an undergraduate. Then he played for two additional years as he attended Yale's medical school. Over the course of these six seasons, Yale earned twenty-five victories and suffered only a single defeat. (There were four ties.) For three of these seasons, Camp was Yale's captain. He assumed the role as a junior. He kept it as a senior. Then he stepped down, in the belief that graduate students should not serve in that capacity. In 1881, however, team captain Franklin M. Eaton broke his collarbone at a practice. With his friend injured, Camp agreed to set aside his reservations and lead the team once more.

He took the responsibility seriously. He carried around a notebook, in which he wrote down observations, devised formations, and developed plays. In 1878 he skipped a game against Amherst in order to scout Harvard.[13] It was the second time Yale was scheduled to play Amherst that season. In the first contest, Yale had won easily. Camp must have figured he would not be missed the second time around. Yet the game went poorly for his teammates. Although they held Amherst scoreless, they also failed to score a goal of their own. The result was a frustrating tie. A student newspaper criticized Camp's absence. It is impossible to know whether Camp's presence would have changed the outcome against Amherst, but it is possible to believe that Camp's decision prepared Yale for its big game. At Boston's South End Grounds, a pair of well-matched teams clashed. Two years earlier, a goal kick by Oliver Thompson had made the difference. History repeated itself: Once again, Thompson booted a ball through the uprights, giving Yale the only goal of the day—and a 1–0 victory over its archrival.[14]

As captain, Camp had to make difficult decisions away from the field. Before the Princeton game in 1878, John Moorhead, a Yale player, broke curfew. Camp wanted to drop him from the team. At a meeting in Durfee Hall, the other players objected: The loss of Moorhead would make them weaker, they said. "We had a very hot argument," Camp recalled. When an agreement seemed out of reach, Camp resigned his captaincy and left the room. "I wanted to play in the coming game, but I did not believe I could give my best efforts in behalf of a team with the members of which I was in such radical disagreement," he explained. That night, Camp had trouble sleeping. He did not care for argumentation—he was more of a soft-spoken persuader who led by example than a fist-pumping force of nature. The decision to walk out on his teammates would not have come to him easily, but it had the desired effect. The next day, Moorhead delivered a fulsome apology. He said he would quit if Camp would return as captain. This offer broke the impasse. Camp stayed on as captain and the regular team, including Moorhead, took the field against Princeton.[15] Unfortunately for Yale, Princeton carried the day. Yale suffered its only loss between 1876 and 1885.

Camp had planned to come back for a seventh season in 1882, but a hard blow to his knee stopped his return.[16] The injury effectively ended his career as a player. It would have happened soon enough anyway, as Camp's student days were drawing to a close. After two full years of medical school, Camp wanted out. He no longer aspired to become a doctor. Instead, he decided to pursue a career in business. The reason he gave for his change of heart was simple and memorable: "I can't bear the sight of blood."[17] This sounds like a quip, though the sentiment was hardly unprecedented. Years earlier, the messiness of surgery had nauseated Charles Darwin and caused him to abandon his initial career goal of becoming a doctor. For Camp, however, there may have been more significant reasons behind his choice. He had come down with a bad case of typhoid fever and struggled with his grades. About 60 percent of the students at Yale Medical School did not complete their studies during this period, so there was nothing unusual about Camp's decision to abandon his plans to become a doctor.[18] The sight of blood was common enough on the football field. If Camp was truly squeamish, he might not have devoted himself to the game.

FOOTBALL WAS IN fact gaining a reputation as a human blood sport. One of Camp's teammates boasted of visiting a slaughterhouse and dipping his uniform in blood. The purpose, he said, was to make it look "more businesslike."[19] The author of this grim aesthetic was Frederic Remington, the artist. In 1878, at the age of sixteen, he had enrolled in Yale's new art school. He was a big kid who would balloon to an adult weight of nearly three hundred pounds. It was said that when he dismounted, "the horse appeared glad to be rid of him."[20] Football fascinated Remington: His first published artwork appeared in the *Yale Courant*, a student publication. The full-page cartoon, titled "College Riff Raff," showed an injured football player. He sits in a chair by a desk with his head bandaged, his left arm in a sling, and his right foot in a cast and propped on a chair. He also appears to have a black eye or a bruised cheek. Bottled tonics lie on the desk, apparently for the relief of pain. A dapper-looking man has just walked into the room. Startled by the sight, he asks, "Good gracious, old fellow, what have you been doing with yourself?"[21] Remington played for only a single season, in 1879. When his father died, he dropped out of school and eventually found work as an illustrator. He went on to fame as an artist of the American West. Throughout the 1880s and into the 1890s, however, he occasionally returned to football as the subject of illustrations. His artwork appeared alongside articles and stories about football by Camp and others.

After suffering his injury in 1882, Camp stayed on at Yale as a coach. He went on to become one of the great coaches in the history of college football. Between 1876 and 1909, the years of

Camp's greatest activity as a player and coach, Yale's football teams dominated the sport. They won 319 games, lost 14, and tied 16.[22] In his two roles, Camp shaped the outcomes of games as they unfolded on the field. Yet his greatest influence may have been felt elsewhere, in his role as a football legislator. In this capacity he helped fashion the game itself. There was nothing inevitable about the direction football took. Its evolution as a sport was the result of personal willpower, conscious choices, and unintended consequences. Camp had a hand in almost all of it.

Others influenced football, too. In 1875, a pair of Princeton men, W. Earl Dodge and Jotham Potter, attended the Harvard-Yale game—the "concessionary game" played on the field prepared in part by Camp. They were more accustomed to a soccer-style sport, but came away impressed by the rugby elements that Harvard was introducing to the game. Upon returning to their own campus, they tried to convert their classmates.

One of their allies was a young man whom everyone called "Tommie" but whose full name was Thomas Woodrow Wilson. Born in Virginia and raised in Georgia, Wilson had learned about football from veterans of the Civil War. As an undergraduate at Princeton, he was both a prolific writer of editorials in the campus newspaper and a sports nut. He often combined these interests. Of the seventy-two editorials he penned for the *Daily Princetonian*, twenty-two dealt with athletics. His favorite sport was football. Wilson hailed victories, bemoaned defeats, and criticized anybody who did not share his passions. In an article that defended football against the charge that it was "most brutal and dangerous," he wrote that "all croakers in our midst must be silenced."[23] Wilson did not compete as a player, but he helped his classmates strategize. Wilson and Dodge would concoct plays and sketch them on a tablecloth. "He had," recalled a classmate, "clear-cut notions of how the game should be played and insisted on them." Wilson also took a strong and active interest in the organization of football, serving as an officer in Princeton's football program. One season, he was responsible for setting ticket prices—and suffered jeers when he boosted the cost to fifty cents per game. The proceeds, however, allowed the football team to pay off the baseball team's deficit, in what may be the first example of a football team's gate receipts subsidizing another college sport.[24]

When Dodge and Potter introduced their classmates to the new way of playing football, they encountered substantial resistance. Yet over time, with help from Wilson, they persuaded their fellow students to adopt the rugby-like format they had seen in New Haven. Then they called for a conference of the leading football teams and issued invitations for student representatives from Columbia, Harvard, and Yale to gather at the Massasoit House in Springfield, Massachusetts, on November 26, 1876.

THIS WAS THE birth of the Intercollegiate Football Association. The idea was to formalize the rules and eliminate the need for team captains to meet before games and make ad hoc agreements on how they would play. The attendees established a standard field size of 140 yards by 70 yards. They called for each game to have a neutral referee, so that captains would not have to settle disputes. They also set up a scoring system and declared that teams could field fifteen players. On these last two points, Yale's representatives objected. They believed that only kicks after touchdowns, rather than the touchdowns themselves, should count for points. They also wanted to limit the number of players to eleven. On both points they failed to sway the other schools. Despite these disagreements, Yale continued to send representatives to the association's annual meetings.[25]

These conferences would become the venue of Camp's great innovations and the source of his deepest influence on the sport. Camp attended his first meeting on October 9, 1878. As with his predecessors from Yale, he suggested reducing the number of players to eleven. It would create more space on the field, he reasoned, allow for livelier play, and make it easier for teams to travel to away games. He also proposed that safeties count in the scoring. Both of these ideas were rejected. He offered them again the following year and, once more, they went down to defeat.

The annual rules meetings took on added significance because football was growing in popularity. The conference's decisions affected more teams, players, and fans every season. The Princeton-Yale game in 1878 drew four thousand spectators—a figure previously unimaginable.[26] By the start of the next decade, the game had spread up and down the eastern seaboard, where it was played by Brown, City College of New York, Dartmouth, Pennsylvania, Stevens, Trinity, Tufts, Wesleyan, and Williams. To the west, schools such as Michigan and Racine joined in. Administrators saw football as a marketing tool. In 1878, the president of Princeton wrote to an alumnus in Kentucky, suggesting that if the newspapers in Louisville offered coverage of Princeton's football exploits, the school would attract more students from the region. At the same time, many onlookers noticed that the skills of players and the overall quality of the games were improving.[27]

DURING CAMP'S DAYS as a player in the late 1870s and early 1880s, football was still in its infancy. A fan from the 21st century would barely recognize it. Players had just started wearing uniforms. Instead of helmets, the men went bareheaded or put on stocking caps whose purpose was ornamental rather than protective. They did not use pads. Kicking was the game's dominant feature, especially in terms of scoring. Between plays, teams did not keep possession of the ball. Instead, players formed a rugby-style scrum, locking arms and waiting for an official to toss the ball between them. At this point players would try to kick the ball up the field or knock it back to their teammates. Blocking was illegal. So were tackles below the waist. Teams struggled to maneuver around the scrum by placing guards alongside ballcarriers, who tried to dash toward the goal line or put themselves in position to kick the ball through the goalposts. Players could toss the ball backward or laterally. Forward passes were forbidden. Ordinary roughness frequently turned to violence as players heaved each other to the ground, threw elbows, and piled on top of one another. A single referee simply was not able to see all the abuses. Many officials routinely chose to allow what they did see.

By 1880, Camp had become something of an elder statesman among his peers. He had completed four seasons on a top team. He was the veteran of a young game. Whereas the football association's other delegates were undergraduates, he was a graduate student. They naturally looked to him for leadership. Again, he proposed the eleven-man rule—and this time the other schools gave their consent.

This was a significant and lasting change, but Camp was far from done. He introduced another reform that would mark a permanent break from British-style rugby and allow football to become a distinctively American sport. Camp proposed a possession rule:

> A scrimmage takes place when the holder of the ball puts it on the ground before him and puts it in play while on-side either by kicking the ball or snapping it back with his foot. The man who first receives the ball from the snap-back shall be called the quarter back and shall not rush forward with the ball under penalty of foul.[28]

In other words, the ball would not go up for grabs between plays. Rugby's "scrummage" became American football's "scrimmage." A team in possession of the ball would keep it. Plays would start with a snap to the quarterback—essentially a new position, invented by Camp. Over time, football's quarterback would become the single most important position in any team sport.

Camp was a methodical planner who wanted football to gain a more strategic dimension. His new rule moved the sport away from a chaotic free-for-all and toward a system that emphasized planning and organization. Suddenly, the offensive team had the ability to call plays, based on tactics designed to push the ball forward. Players would still make quick decisions in response to the actions of others, but they would also give advance thought to what they would do on each play. There was less spontaneity. This heightened the importance of coaching and practices. The decision to reduce the number of players from fifteen to eleven increased the importance of each one, and therefore the technique of proper positioning as well.

The possession rule was designed to bring order to the game. At first, however, it simply sowed confusion. It led directly to a series of stalemates that threatened football's popularity. The problem was that the game still had no concept of downs. Camp and his fellow rule makers assumed that when a team discovered it could not move the ball forward, it would maintain the custom of punting it away. This was not what happened in actual games, however. Teams learned that they could just hang on to the ball. If defenses pushed them back and they ran out of space, they could retreat into their own end zone and take safeties, which did not count against them. A safety merely let them put the ball on their own 25-yard line and start over.

As the possession rule came into effect for the 1880 season, Princeton was regarded as the sport's defending champion. The claim derived from the results of the 1878 season, when Princeton had defeated Yale in the last game of the year, and the fact that the 1879 season had produced too many ties to determine an undisputed champion. In 1880, Princeton prepared to face an undefeated Yale in the last game of the season—a de facto championship game. Princeton reasoned that in the event of a tie, it would keep its title. Following a scoreless first half, Princeton took the ball in the second half and held on to it. Its players took eleven safeties. The result was a 0–0 tie in what must have been one of the most boring games of football ever played. Writers condemned it as a "block game." Princeton nevertheless considered itself triumphant. Yale and others disagreed.

At the next rules meeting, Camp wanted to eliminate the prospect of more block games. He suggested that safeties serve as tiebreakers. In the case of ties, "the side which makes four or more safeties less than their opponent shall win the game."[29] Under this arrangement, Yale would have beaten Princeton in 1880. Then again, maybe not: Princeton would not have taken so many safeties, and the game would have been played in an entirely different fashion.

Once again, however, Princeton found a loophole. Instead of taking safeties, it put the ball into an area called the "touch-in-goal," which was formed by the extension of the sideline and the goal line, diagonal to the playing field. This ploy functioned as a safety but without the scoring implication—it allowed teams to put the ball on the 25-yard line and keep possession. In the Princeton-Yale game of 1881, Princeton kept the ball for the entire first half. Then Yale kept it for the entire second half. The result was another scoreless tie. The block game lived. It was hard to believe, but the game was even duller than it had been a year earlier. The championship went to Yale on the grounds that its defeat of Harvard was more convincing than Princeton's. All were dissatisfied.

The real solution came the following year, at the 1882 rules meeting. Camp proposed the concept of downs. Teams would have three downs to move the ball. If they advanced it forward five yards or lost ten yards, they would keep possession. If they failed in three consecutive tries, they would surrender the ball to the other team. The origin of this idea is obscure. It almost certainly did not come from Camp. It may have come from Canada, where Camp possibly watched a couple of teams use the rule.[30] Whatever its ultimate source, its adoption proved Camp's abilities as a problem-fixing consensus builder. He identified a flaw with the game, found a way to repair it, and rallied others around a solution. The rules of possession would continue to undergo refinements, but once the concept of downs was in place, they were essentially complete.

Measurement became a vital feature of the game. Referees now had to determine when the ball had moved a sufficient distance to earn a first down. To help them, football fields acquired painted lines at five-yard intervals. This met with aesthetic objections. One critic said the lines would turn the field into a "gridiron." He meant the term as a pejorative, suggesting that it would render the field unsightly and hurt the game. He was wrong about that—but his word survives, without the negative connotation.

IN JUST A few years, Camp had reinvented football. It started as a sport that had resembled a rugby-soccer hybrid and became a new game. It still lacked a few key features, such as the forward pass, but it shared many fundamental elements with its modern version. Several formations became standard, as players took spots along an offensive line and in the backfield. Linesmen still stood upright—the crouch would come later—but they understood that their job was to provide interference for the ballcarrier. Their positions took on familiar names. The snap back became known as the center because he stood at the center of the line. To his immediate left and right came players whose primary duty was to protect the center. They were called guards. Then there were the tackles because, when they lined up on the defensive side of the ball, they were involved in more tackles than other players. Behind the line came the backs. The quarterback and the halfbacks stood midway between the center and the fullback. At one time, Harvard referred to its fullbacks and halfbacks as goaltends and halftends. These variations succumbed to the trend of standardization. As with so much of the sport, the positional names developed informally among players. They were not officially recognized in the rulebooks until 1909.[31]

Camp began to assemble his players in what came to be known as the T-formation. Once players were aligned, in the T-formation or some other arrangement, quarterbacks would call a play. They used coded signals, introducing the element of deception. At Princeton, for instance, the quarterback would shout "What's the matter?" This indicated that he would deliver the ball to the fullback because the first word of the sentence started with a *W*. Later on, teams switched to numerical signals.[32]

More schools adopted football. At Lehigh, Richard Harding Davis, who would make his name as a war correspondent, helped organize a team, began a long rivalry with Lafayette, and scored his school's first touchdown.[33] Bucknell, Cornell, Dickinson, Fordham, Haverford, Johns Hopkins, Massachusetts Institute of Technology, Navy, and Swarthmore also started to play. Most notably, football spread outside the Northeast. In the South, Virginia took it up. In the Midwest, Indiana, Minnesota, Notre Dame, and Purdue began to play. On the Pacific coast, California, Southern California, and Washington started programs.[34]

Scoring was a subject of dispute for several years. In 1883, the rules committee settled on a formula. A touchdown was worth two points, a goal following touchdown four points, a goal from the field five points, and a safety one point. At the end of the season there were further modifications. Touchdowns were increased to four points and the kick afterward to two points. The value of a safety was doubled, to two points. These numbers would remain in place for the next fourteen years.

During this period, Camp's student days came to an end. In

1883 he left medical school and took a sales job with the Manhattan Watch Company in New York City. He rented a room in the city but returned frequently to New Haven, where he would stay with his parents. He coached the Yale football team, though the position was more advisory than it would become in later years. He also refereed the sport and was considered so scrupulously fair that he even judged games involving Yale, with the consent of Yale's opponents. During a game in 1885, he disallowed a Yale touchdown and ruled in favor of a game-winning Princeton touchdown even though several fans believed that Princeton's man had stepped out of bounds on his run.[35]

After about a year with the Manhattan Watch Company, Camp took a sales job with the New Haven Clock Company. It was headquartered in his hometown, but he continued to work primarily in New York City for several years. He rose through its ranks, eventually becoming company president and chairman of the board. All the while, he segregated his business and athletic lives. It was said that if his clock company colleagues did not read about sports in the newspapers, they would not have known of Camp's involvement with Yale football. Likewise, many of Yale's football boosters were unfamiliar with Camp's business career.

Yet his business and football activities were not wholly separate. In their way, both involved salesmanship. Camp sold timepieces to consumers, and also tried to sell the sport of football to an American public that was in the market for athletic diversions. A questionnaire once asked Camp: "What was your ambition when you were a boy?" Camp replied with concision: "To write."[36] And this was the primary means by which he promoted football. He began to pen articles on the game for newspapers and magazines. As the man most associated with the sport and its development, Camp discovered a demand for his byline. He was a proficient writer rather than an artful one. His prose was perhaps most notable for clear expression, as it jumped from fact to fact.

Many of his articles simply explained the intricacies of the sport, often to an audience that had never before watched a game. It also positioned him to respond to an emerging concern about football: the disturbing fact that it was so violent.

THE SPORT'S ROUGH play was directly tied to its popular appeal. Spectators enjoyed the clash of teams, the hard tackles, and the grit that players had to display as they shook off blows and ignored bruises. Many early commentators called attention to everything from the limping men who played through their pain to the casualties who had to be helped off the field. Nothing like this happened in baseball or tennis. A school of criticism began to emerge, in the belief that something was wrong with a pastime that demanded so much of its participants. When Harvard lost to Yale in 1881, a student newspaper responded with an article that mixed sour grapes with genuine concern: "It has been the custom since the beginning of football contests between Yale and Harvard for Harvard men to accuse Yale men of uncalled for brutality. . . . Yale plays more violently than is necessary or in good taste."[37]

Claims such as these irritated Camp. In responding, he took the concerns of the Muscular Christianity movement that had influenced his own boyhood and refashioned them in secular terms. An article in 1885 echoed the view expressed in *Tom Brown's Schooldays*. Camp argued that there was more to education than books and lectures: "How many parents urge their sons on coming to college to study hard and stand high! How few exhort them to play hard and be athletic!" It is necessary to build the body and the mind together, wrote Camp. Moreover, the claims about the hazards of football were greatly exaggerated. "If the critics who call one of the college sports brutal and dangerous could be persuaded to spend the necessary time in learning the game, they would change their opinion," he wrote. "Players [do not] think of tumbling about so violently on the ground without a previous preparation which accustoms them to the falls and renders them safe by the very hardness of their muscles." Finally, Camp wondered whether the public would ever stop worrying about young people: "Cartooned and caricatured for years as a hollow-chested consumptive, all brains and no physique, the student opened his eyes one day to find himself portrayed as all muscle and no brains."[38]

BY THE MID-1880s, Camp was a minor celebrity. More than anyone else, he was associated with the rise of football and had become a figure of public interest. He welcomed the attention, in large part because it allowed him to promote the sport. Yet it also led to at least one strange incident, when Camp was accused of involvement in a bizarre love triangle and arrested for attempted murder.

On March 3, 1887, at around one o'clock in the morning, George Condit Smith suffered a bullet wound to his right shoulder. The incident apparently took place at Madison Square Park, in New York City. Suspicion immediately fell on Camp, who was said to be a rival for the hand of Sallie Barnes, an attractive young woman who resided in Paterson, New Jersey. A detective began to shadow Camp and police questioned him about the crime at the clock company's office in New York. Then, on March 5, as Camp was about to board a train for New Haven, they arrested him.

Newspapers covered the episode breathlessly. It had all the ingredients for a sensational story: celebrity, sex, and murder. The *New York Times* noted that Camp "was always popular with the ladies."[39] Another report said that he and Barnes had been engaged, but that their pending marriage had been broken off. Had Camp tried to kill a rival?

Camp proclaimed his innocence: He said he was not even in Manhattan when the shooting occurred. Instead, he was at a skating rink in New Haven until 11:15 P.M. Hundreds of people saw him there. Afterward he went home, caught a few hours of sleep, and boarded the seven o'clock train the next morning for New York. It appears as though Camp had courted Barnes a year or two earlier, but they were never engaged.

A police captain took Camp to the hospital and put him before Smith. "Is this the person who fired at you?" asked the officer. Smith said it was not. Camp was released. He went straight to the train station and returned to New Haven, embarrassed by the publicity. The press quickly turned against the police, mocking the arrest. "Every college man in the country knows of Walter's prowess as an athlete, but no one, except the astute limbs of the law, ever yet supposed him capable of being in New York and New Haven at the same time," said the *Boston Globe*.[40]

It later came out that Smith had shot himself in an attempt to win the sympathy of Barnes. His weird ploy appears to have worked: Seven months after the incident, Smith and Barnes were married.[41]

CAMP HIMSELF WAS headed toward marriage. The previous August, he had sent a note to his former professor, William Graham Sumner: "I write, with the consent of your sister, to ask your permission to marry her as soon as my position will warrant."[42] Before meeting Camp, Alice Sumner had shown virtually no interest in athletics. As Mrs. Camp, however, she would exhibit a strong interest in the game—to the point where some of Yale's players trained in front of her more often than they did in front of Camp himself.

The Camps had met at the house of Alice's brother. William Graham Sumner was one of America's leading intellectuals, a champion of free trade, market economics, and academic freedom. He helped give birth to sociology as an academic discipline. An admirer of Herbert Spencer, Sumner sought to apply the evolutionary principles of Charles Darwin to the study of human customs. As a result, he is commonly regarded as a Social Darwinist. He possessed a wide-ranging mind and is credited with coining terms such as "the forgotten man" and *ethnocentrism*. At Yale he was a popular teacher, known for making practical points about the news of the day, sometimes even passing out copies of newspapers to his students. Camp had experienced this firsthand. "This morning Billy Sumner gave us a very good talk on Sociology," he wrote in his diary in 1880. "He claims that everything Government does is wrong, and I guess he is nearly right."[43]

Sumner's working-class father was a two-time widower. He was born to his father's first wife and raised primarily by his second wife, a frugal woman whose relentless determination to save money probably made his college education possible. Their home was almost devoid of books and Sumner had to search elsewhere to find the serious tracts that interested him even as a youngster. He was an uncommonly sober boy who partook in almost no sports apart from skating, an activity that, as one of his biographers noted, "does not necessarily involve sacrifice of dignity or complete cessation of thought on more important matters."[44] Although his faith was strong enough to make him consider a career in the ministry, he was virtually untouched by the spirit of Muscular Christianity. One snowy day, he returned home to find his father and stepmother sledding down a hill. He criticized them for wasting their time, saying that grown people had better things to do.[45] As a student at Yale in the early 1860s, he kept to himself and seemed to prefer books to people. "He took very little exercise," commented a roommate. "He was not athletic."[46]

Alice was his much younger half sister, the daughter of their father's third wife. In 1881, their father died and Sumner, who had married a decade earlier, became the head of the family and took charge of Alice. By then he was a well-established professor at Yale, a big-boned man known for his deep voice. He was a heavy cigar smoker until just before his fortieth birthday. Then he quit, cold turkey—not because of any specific health reason, but because he decided that he was spending too much money on tobacco. He did not exercise until late in his life, when a doctor urged him to take up bicycling.

For Sumner, sports were not a source of amusement. "What do I know about football?" he blurted out at a faculty meeting in 1905. "The last game I attended was on Thanksgiving Day, 1876."[47] Yale's football greats occasionally would enroll in his courses, and their classmates were amazed to learn that their professor had no idea that they were well-known athletes. Sumner once called on a student to stand for a recitation. "While he was on his feet, I forgot his name. I often did that," he recalled. "So I asked, when I got through with him: 'Name?' and the whole class seemed to be a little shocked." The student was Amos Alonzo Stagg, one of the greatest players ever to put on a Yale jersey and a man who would go on to a storied career as a coach.[48]

Walter Camp hardly could have found a better partner than Alice, or "Allie," as friends called her. She possessed some of her brother's intellectual bent, but not his aloofness from sports: Allie found herself drawn to the thinking side of football. After the Camps married in 1888, she plunged into her husband's world. He often missed practices due to the demands of his job at the clock company. Yet Allie was always there, serving as his eyes and ears. She became such a familiar presence that the players began to call her "Mrs. Walter." During their first year of marriage, according to Stagg, Allie "was more the coach than he. She was out every afternoon for practice and made a detailed report from notes at night to her husband."[49] In the evenings, as Yale players gathered at the Camp home, they discovered that Allie had told Walter exactly what had happened during the day. She was such a part of their lives that when the 1888 team held a dinner years later for its twenty-fifth anniversary, the souvenir booklet listed "Mr. and

Mrs. Walter Camp—Head Coaches of the Yale Football Team of 1888."[50] In later years Allie became less involved in football as she committed herself to raising two children and participating in the social life of New Haven.

William Graham Sumner, for his part, never became a football fan. But he knew his brother-in-law well. They even lived together for a time, when a fire at the Camp home forced Walter and Allie to move in with Sumner.[51] A fellow professor once asked Sumner what Walter Camp thought of a football matter. "What do I know about what Camp thinks?" said Sumner. "Get him in here and he'll tell you. He can say plainly what he thinks, and he isn't afraid to."[52]

Chapter Five

THE CAPACITY TO INFLICT PAIN

As Walter Camp conquered the gridiron, Theodore Roosevelt jogged around the campus of Harvard in a crimson football jersey. The future president enjoyed the sport that Camp was reinventing, but he did not play it. One of his closest friends was Robert Bacon, a star on the varsity team—and a man who would serve in Roosevelt's presidential administration. Roosevelt probably knew better than to go out for the game himself. He lacked size. Owen Wister, a fellow student who would become a well-known author of Westerns, said Roosevelt was a man "of slight build."[1] He looked nothing like the barrel-chested figure of his White House years. Roosevelt's poor eyesight would have posed a problem as well. Nobody was foolish enough to wear spectacles onto a football field.

Yet he had the vigor of a determined athlete. Roosevelt earned a reputation among his fellow students for combativeness. In the classroom, he often jumped out of his seat and challenged his professors. ("See here, Roosevelt, let me talk. I'm running this course," said one of them in an anxious reply.) Among his peers, he was quick to start fights. At meals he would throw food in anger. Elsewhere he would put up his fists, forcing friends to restrain him. He once smashed a pumpkin on the head of a rival. Another time, he shot a dog that had snapped at his horse.[2]

Normally, Roosevelt found better outlets for his boundless energy. In addition to schoolwork, his daily routine included two or three hours of exercise. He filled his diary with short notations: "Threw Ellis wrestling" and "Gave red-haired Coolidge a tremendous thrashing in the gymnasium boxing."[3] He also attended the theater, enrolled in dancing classes, and taught Sunday school. In the winter, he sledded down snowy hills and skated on frozen ponds. During one foray onto the ice, Roosevelt's companion was Richard Welling, a student known for his strength. Welling had once regarded Roosevelt as "a youth in the kindergarten stage of physical development." As cold winds whipped them, Roosevelt seemed impervious to the elements. Welling reconsidered his earlier observation: "Never in college was my own grit so put to the test," he wrote. "I recall my numbed fingers grasping the key to my room and unable to make a turn in the lock. That afternoon of so-called sport made me realize Roosevelt's amazing vitality."[4]

Roosevelt never seemed to relax. Instead, he was a perpetual-motion machine. He went on expeditions into the wilderness of Maine, where he hunted deer, caribou, and lynx. He climbed Mount Katahdin, the tallest peak in the state. He also canoed on streams and took long hikes, often with a Bible in hand. In the summer, he continued to compete with his brother, Elliott, at everything. "As athletes we are about equal," Roosevelt said. "He rows best; I run best; he can beat me sailing or swimming; I can beat him wrestling or boxing; I am best with the rifle, he with the shotgun." One day he rowed across Long Island Sound from the family's summer home in Oyster Bay. The round trip was more than twenty-five miles.[5]

This surge of activity had many sources, from Roosevelt's own inclinations to the welcome fact that his health had improved. He would never fully escape from the clutches of asthma. As he entered adulthood, however, the scourge of his boyhood loosened its grip. In his letters and diary, he complained about it less and less. He was not by nature a complainer, and so this is not simply an artifact of his reserve. He really was feeling more vigorous.

He was also in love. Roosevelt wanted to marry Alice Lee, the neighbor of a Harvard classmate. Their courtship started in 1878. He called it love at first sight. She apparently did not share his infatuation: She resisted his first marriage proposal. Roosevelt, however, was relentless in pursuit of her hand. She eventually consented to give it. "If loving her with my whole heart and soul can make her happy, she shall be happy," he wrote in his diary. "I made a vow that win her I would if it were possible; and now I have done so, the aim of my whole life shall be to make her happy, and to shield her and guard her from every trial."[6]

Alice was present at what may be the most recounted event of Roosevelt's student days: his participation in a boxing tournament sponsored by the Harvard Athletic Association on March 22, 1879. In his journal, Roosevelt barely mentioned the episode, but it made a vivid impression on those who saw it. He entered the lightweight category, weighing 135 pounds. Roosevelt prevailed in his first bout, having "displayed more coolness and skill than his opponent," according to the *Harvard Advocate*. This victory allowed him to advance to the championship round against C. S. Hanks, another senior.

As Alice looked down from the balcony, Owen Wister watched from ringside. He described the fight in the opening pages of his biography of Roosevelt:

> We freshmen on the floor and those girls in the gallery witnessed more than a spirited contest; owing to an innocent mistake of Mr. Hanks, we saw that prophetic flash of The Roosevelt that was to come.

Time was called on a round, Roosevelt dropped his guard, and Hanks landed a heavy blow on his nose, which spurted blood. Loud hoots and hisses from the gallery and floor were set up, whereat Roosevelt's arm was instantly flung out to command silence, while his alert and slender figure stood quiet.

"It's all right," he assured us eagerly, his arm still in the air to hold the silence; then, pointing to the time-keeper, "he didn't hear him," he explained, in the same conversational but arresting tone. With bleeding nose he walked up to Hanks and shook hands with him.[7]

Another observer called the fight "distinctly gory." Hanks was the more skillful boxer. His punches had a longer reach. Yet Roosevelt proved a dogged foe. "You should have seen that little fellow staggering about, banging the air," said a student. "Hanks couldn't put him out and Roosevelt wouldn't give up. It wasn't a fight, but, oh, he showed himself a fighter!"[8] Although Hanks won the championship, Roosevelt made a lasting memory. Witnesses understood in retrospect that a public sporting event had allowed Roosevelt to reveal important aspects of his character.

A year later, Roosevelt was finishing his time at Harvard. At a physical examination, he completed a "measurement card." It asked, "Have you always had good health?" Roosevelt's answer: "No." He identified asthma as his affliction and noted that he had suffered from it "badly until I was twelve."[9]

The doctor who treated him was Dudley Sargent. Instead of merely helping his patient fill out a form, Sargent studied Roosevelt's health. Then he issued a warning: Roosevelt owned a weak heart. Sargent urged Roosevelt not to exert himself. He even cautioned against running up the stairs. A life of vigor was absolutely out of the question. Sargent advised Roosevelt to take an occupation that would permit a sedentary existence. The consequences of doing otherwise could be fatal.

"Doctor," replied Roosevelt, "I am going to do all the things you tell me not to do. I've got to live the sort of life you have described, I don't care how short it is."[10] Roosevelt did not discuss this exchange for decades. Even Alice seems not to have known about it. Roosevelt mentioned it late in life to one of his biographers.

SARGENT'S PRESENCE AT Harvard acknowledged America's growing interest in health and fitness. It was also something of an innovation—one of several that was propelling the school to preeminence. The doctor, a pioneer in physical education, had recently arrived on campus. Born in Maine in 1849, Sargent had joined a circus before pursuing an advanced education. He earned his undergraduate degree from Bowdoin College and then a medical degree from Yale. He had wanted to join his former professors on the faculty in New Haven, but failed to obtain a position. So he moved to New York City, where he opened the Hygienic Institute and School of Physical Culture. This was a private gymnasium much like the one that Roosevelt had attended as a boy. A year later, Harvard called. Sargent jumped at the opportunity to attach himself to a college.

The man behind his summons was Charles W. Eliot, Harvard's president. During Roosevelt's student days, Eliot was in the midst of becoming the most influential person in the development of higher education in the United States. In 1869, when Eliot assumed the presidency, Harvard enjoyed a very good reputation as a leading college. For much of his time in office, it was the largest university in the country. When Eliot retired forty years later—no other president in the school's history has come close to serving for so long—Harvard was a model of the elite 20th-century research university.

Eliot's tenure coincided with football's growth from a peculiar hobby played by a small number of amateur enthusiasts to a big-time college sport performed in front of thousands of cheering spectators. Although he was a prime mover behind many of the trends in college life, Eliot resisted the rise of football with fervor. Along with Sargent, he tried to ban the sport at Harvard. For a time, he actually succeeded. Yet his ambitions were larger than his own campus. He fought football's development everywhere. The country's leading voice in higher education wanted to wipe out the sport. Eliot was football's prohibitionist.

ELIOT WAS BORN in 1834 to a privileged family of Bostonians. Despite many material advantages, Eliot from his earliest days had to learn to live with a handicap: An enormous reddish-brown birthmark stained the right side of his face. It did not affect him mentally or physically, but the social impact was profound. Whenever people met him, the first thing they noticed was the big blotch. Eliot could not remove it, but sometimes he could conceal it. Photographs of him are almost always in profile, showing the left side of his face and hiding the right. Even in group shots, when others looked straight at the camera, Eliot would tilt his head just enough to obscure the birthmark. Seen individually, none of these images is remarkable. Examined together, they show a man who made a deliberate effort to disguise his mottled countenance. Over time, he must have built up a natural resistance to the stares of others. During his childhood, however, the birthmark was a curse. As a cousin observed, "You must realize that when he was a boy he was hooted off the Boston Common because of his face."[11]

He grew up shy, but not a recluse. His many playmates included four sisters and an assortment of relatives. They bounced balls, ran footraces, and, in winter, hopped on sleds.[12] The Eliots owned a summer home in Nahant, a town on a rocky peninsula near Boston. Surrounded by water, Eliot devoted himself to swimming, fishing, rowing, and sailing. In 1850, he wrote to his father about reading the novels of Sir Walter Scott, and also described what appears to have been his primary activity: "I am out of doors the greater part of the time, chopping wood, pumping water, and taking a good deal of general and some particular care of the horses."[13]

Team sports did not form a part of his boyhood. They had yet to take root in the culture. *Tom Brown's Schooldays*, which shaped Roosevelt and his generation, was not published until Eliot was grown. The schools he attended as a youth, such as Boston Latin, provided nothing in the way of physical education or organized athletics. For that, Eliot's family sent him to a private gymnasium, where he learned how to use ladders, parallel bars, and the vaulting horse.[14] It was another solitary activity for a boy who felt uncomfortable in the presence of strangers. Even if team sports had been an option, Eliot possibly would have avoided them.

The problem was not confined to the birthmark and its social effect. If Eliot had devoted himself to kicking goals or hitting fastballs, he almost certainly would have failed. Another handicap, this one unseen, also plagued him: He was badly nearsighted—much worse than Roosevelt. Years passed before he or his parents noticed. "This defective vision cut me off from some desirable sports and entertainments," admitted Eliot.[15] His eyesight was so poor that he could not recognize friends from more than a few feet away. He understood that his eyes were weak from birth and believed that squinting at books in dim lamplight had compounded the problem. Whatever the cause, the nearsightedness was so severe that even thick-lensed glasses did not supply full relief. For Eliot's whole life, a part of the world was a blur.

Eliot entered Harvard in 1849, at the age of fifteen. He was a good student—he would graduate second in a class of eighty-eight—but he did not have a passion for all of his subjects. At the time, Greek and Latin were a central part of the curriculum. After finishing his intensive coursework in these languages, Eliot probably never bothered to read a book in them again. He was far more interested in math and science, especially chemistry. His classmates included several figures who would go on to distinguished careers in a variety of areas, such as William Le Baron Jenney, the architect who designed the first skyscraper (Chicago's ten-story Home Insurance Company Building, completed in 1885). Yet Eliot did not make many friends. He seems to have kept mostly to himself. He may have been happy simply to get through his days without having too many people gawk at him.

Eliot was tall and thin: He stood six feet and weighed 138 pounds. Harvard lacked a gym and Eliot avoided anything resembling a ball game or a team sport, but he was an ardent exerciser. He went boating on occasion and also took boxing lessons. His main activity, however, was walking. He went on long excursions around Cambridge. After graduation, he embarked on a series of scientific field trips—walking tours to study geology, ranging from Canada to Pennsylvania. He once traveled 250 miles across New Brunswick in ten days.[16]

"None of us can have an effective life without a strong, healthy, cheerful servant in the body," wrote Eliot, who lived to the age of ninety-two.[17] Eliot attributed his longevity to his personal commitment to fitness, which he also encouraged in others. He came of age at the dawn of the Muscular Christianity movement and many of his own views were consistent with its admonitions. He once suggested "that the attention of a community once Puritan or Calvinistic should be withdrawn from those Bible passages which express a deep sense of vileness of the body, and should be turned toward those passages of opposite tenor which extol the holiness of our bodies."[18] At the same time, Eliot cautioned against placing too much emphasis on athletics: "It is a wholesome thing to enjoy for a time, or for a time each day all through life, sports and active bodily exercise. These are legitimate enjoyments, but if made the main object of life, they tire. They cease to be a source of durable satisfaction. Play must be incidental in a satisfactory life."[19]

His own concept of a satisfactory life led him to reject a career in business and gravitate toward the academy. After graduation from Harvard, he returned as a tutor—a kind of postgraduate teacher—and eventually became an assistant professor of math and chemistry. He continued to exercise and joined the crew team. His fellow boaters included four undergraduates and another young member of the faculty, Alexander Agassiz. In 1858, they took part in a three-mile race on the Charles River that would go down in school lore. Shortly before it began, all six tied red silk handkerchiefs around their heads. It contributed to their esprit de corps and also made the Harvard boat easy to spot from shore. This was the origin of crimson as Harvard's school color. "It was the purest accident in the world," recalled Eliot years later. "We might as well have bought blue."[20]

The morning of the race, Eliot began to write a letter to his fiancée: "I had rather win than not, but it is mighty little matter whether we beat or are beaten—rowing is not my profession, neither is it my love—it is only recreation, fun, and health."[21] He also promised not to row too hard. Although these words sounded like a preemptive rationalization for defeat, Eliot sincerely believed them. He enjoyed rowing, but more as a pleasant exertion than as an excuse to compete against others. As it happened, the debut of Harvard's crimson was a big success: Eliot and his teammates won by several lengths. A couple of weeks later, in a six-mile race, the Harvard rowers put on their red bandanas again and triumphed once more. The victory carried a prize of one hundred dollars. In later years, Eliot joked that accepting his part of this purse had turned him into a professional athlete.

· · · ·

WHEN THE CIVIL War erupted, Eliot felt the call of duty. He even received an offer to serve as a lieutenant colonel in a regiment of cavalry. Many men of his economic and social class bought their way out of service, as did Theodore Roosevelt, Sr. Eliot said that he wanted to accept a commission, but he feared that he could not perform effectively in the field: "I was very near-sighted; and to this day I have never been able to find spectacles that would give me anything like natural vision. This physical defect had cut me off from many sports."[22]

He had also tied himself to Harvard, or so he thought. In 1863 the college chose not to reciprocate his affection: It refused to give him the full professorship that he dearly desired. One of his major detractors was Louis Agassiz, a pioneering glacial researcher who became the first person to suggest that the earth had experienced an ice age. Before Charles Darwin published *On the Origin of Species* in 1859, Agassiz may have been the most renowned scientist of his day. He was also the father of Alexander Agassiz, who had been one of Eliot's fellow crew members at the famous race more than a decade earlier. This personal tie did not matter. Louis Agassiz believed another man was more suitable for the job. He was not Eliot's only critic. William James, then a student, questioned Eliot's capacity as a scholar: "I don't believe he is a very accomplished chemist," he wrote.[23]

Just as Eliot had once retreated from the company of other boys on the playground, now he retreated from Cambridge. He embarked on a tour of Europe. His ostensible purpose was to visit the continent's great universities and increase his knowledge of chemistry. His interest in organization soon supplanted his interest in science: He was drawn to the European system of higher education, with its emphasis on research and advanced studies. The German universities especially impressed him—and he believed that if higher education in the United States was to keep up, it would have to Germanize. Eliot would succeed at shifting colleges and universities in this direction, but along the way he would come into conflict with a different vision of schooling, one that had been on display in *Tom Brown's Schooldays*: the notion that the goal of education was not merely to turn out chemists but more fundamentally to make men.

UPON HIS RETURN to the United States, Eliot became a professor at the Massachusetts Institute of Technology. He also began to comment on the structure of higher education. In 1869 he authored a pair of articles for the *Atlantic Monthly*. On the pages of the same magazine that had helped to import the ideas of *Tom Brown's Schooldays*, Eliot laid out a plan for the American research university. Coincidentally, Harvard was looking for a new president. Eliot's articles made him a contender. He met with opposition, but other candidates encountered resistance as well. In the end, the college settled on Eliot. At the age of thirty-five, he became president of Harvard.

It was a moment of triumph and tragedy. Just as Eliot was selected for the job of his life, his wife died. She left him with two young sons. A little more than a decade earlier, after he became engaged to Ellen Derby Peabody, her family received a letter of congratulations that praised Eliot's character: "He is a regular cedar-post, firm, sound, and always in the same place."[24] These traits served him well as he tried to balance the demands of single fatherhood with the duties of his new academic post. This combination of personal and professional stress would have overwhelmed many men. Eliot once reflected on how he survived. "I was probably saved from physical breakdown by two practices," he wrote: daily horseback riding and summer camping.[25] These activities kept him fit, though it never will be said that Eliot's camping excursions were grueling experiences in an unforgiving wilderness. He and his boys frequently traveled with a cook and a maid.[26]

As a college professor, Eliot had been a competent teacher. As a college president, he demonstrated a genius for administration. In his forty years at Harvard's helm, he oversaw a long period of steady growth. The number of students and faculty members roughly quadrupled.[27] Yet his real legacy was not quantitative but qualitative. He improved Harvard's standards and implemented a series of reforms that changed the face of higher education. He introduced the elective system that now dominates American colleges and universities, pushing Harvard away from a core curriculum that permitted students to make few choices in their course selections and toward a more open system that accommodated a range of interests. He encouraged scholarship and research among professors and created opportunities for graduate studies. He promoted the study of science. He ended the rule of compulsory worship. He also stopped the practice of compulsory attendance. Faculty and alumni met each initiative with doubts. One student's father lit into Eliot when he learned that his son was registered at Harvard but vacationing in Havana.[28] Yet Eliot usually prevailed. Sometimes he simply outlasted his critics. Over the course of his forty-year presidency, he won many battles of attrition.

In retrospect, he may be judged a champion of student freedom: He abolished requirements and introduced an element of choice into the academic and religious life of the college. Yet Harvard's students tended to dislike him. They saw him as solitary, detached, and frugal. Eliot was not personable. He did not chat with students or even wave to them across Harvard Yard. He once said that the university president must be like the captain of a ship—a man who takes his meals alone and avoids the temptation of friendship because it threatens sound judgment.[29] He was once asked to name the most important quality for a person in his position to have. His reply: "The capacity to inflict pain."[30] Even though he developed a bold vision for Harvard, in other areas he lacked imagination and seemed utilitarian to a fault. On his tour of Europe in 1864, he condemned some of the Old World's greatest architecture (in a comment that also displays anti-Catholic prejudice): "Cathedrals are bad things—they are infinitely costly, they inspire feelings of superstitious awe in ignorant minds, they are magnificent theatres for the ceremonies of Catholicism, and when a people abandon this idolatry, these huge temples are of no use for rational worship."[31]

There were also stories of Eliot's kindness. In 1873 he moved out of his house so that a student who was stricken with smallpox could occupy it and avoid the perils of a public hospital. And despite his reluctance to establish friendships, he seemed to know when circumstances demanded a personal touch. One time, Harvard received a telegram that said a student's father had died. Eliot waited in the young man's dormitory room so that he could deliver the awful news in person.[32]

ELIOT ONCE COMMENTED that a university president must possess a variety of characteristics, such as administrative ability and patience. He also noted the need for "physical toughness."[33] His regimen of horseback riding and summer camping kept him in good shape—and he encouraged Harvard's students to adopt their own habits of daily exercise. His notes from a talk to freshmen on how to achieve success after college show how he connected exercise with lifelong fitness: "An available body. Not necessarily the muscles of an athlete. Good circulation, digestion, power to sleep, and alert steady nerves."[34]

Under Eliot's leadership, Harvard built the Hemenway Gymnasium and developed a program of physical education. Dudley Sargent, the doctor who warned Roosevelt not to exert himself, collaborated with another member of the Harvard faculty, George

W. Fitz, to create a bachelor of science degree in physical training.[35] In time, Sargent would push for students to receive academic
credit for physical education courses. Although Eliot resisted this
effort, he and Sargent were usually allies in their commitment
to student exercise. Eliot believed Harvard's attention to fitness
paid off: "The average physique of the mass of students has been
sensibly improved," he wrote. "The ideal student [has] been transformed from a stooping, weak, and sickly youth into one well-
formed, robust, and healthy."[36]

Eliot's primary concern was for personal health—and he remained skeptical of activities that required more than a single participant. "Any outdoor sport which does not require a team, so to
speak, is valuable through life," he wrote. "Those which require a
combination of many players, of course, cannot be kept up through
life."[37] He approved of the notion of a seventy-two-year-old man
going on a brisk walk through the woods but found absurd the
concept of a team of seventy-two-year-olds tossing a ball around a
field. Eliot did not object entirely to team sports. He thought they
could teach students about cooperative behavior. But he thought
the same thing about symphony orchestras and theatrical produc-
tions. They delivered precisely the same benefit.

What bothered Eliot most, it seems, was competition—and
how it motivated players to conduct themselves in ways he considered unworthy of gentlemen. If baseball and football were honorable pastimes, then why did they require umpires and referees? "A
game that needs to be watched is not fit for genuine sportsmen,"
he said.[38] Moreover, a pitcher who threw a curveball engaged in
an act of deception, reasoned Eliot. One time, Eliot suspended a
baseball player from Harvard's team due to poor grades. He observed that this was no great loss because baseball was just a game
of trickery. The players objected to this comment and a couple of
sympathetic professors intervened. When they challenged Eliot,
the college president replied in exasperation: "Why! They boasted

of his making a feint to throw a ball in one direction and then throwing it in *another*!"[39] The very idea outraged him.

Football distressed him even more. Eliot believed it was improper for a running back to attack the weakest part of an opposing team's line—he thought the honorable thing required him to attack the strongest. He liked almost nothing about the sport. He thought it caused student athletes to neglect their studies. He worried that its rising popularity placed too much emphasis on elite performers and not enough on a widespread commitment to student fitness. Even the behavior of spectators appalled him. Before the start of a game against Yale in Cambridge, he heard a group of his students chant, "Three cheers for Harvard and down with Yale!" He regarded this as bad mannered: "Of course it's right to be enthusiastic for your own side, but why sing a song that's rude to our guests?" So he proposed an alternative: "Why wouldn't it be better to sing 'Three cheers for Harvard and one for Yale'?"[40] His suggestion did not catch on.

By frowning on the sports that were becoming immensely popular among students, alumni, and the public, Eliot burnished his reputation as a killjoy. The problem was not merely his negative attitude toward football, but the concrete actions he took against it: In 1885, Harvard banned the sport.

It was hardly the first time football faced prohibition. In 1314, King Edward II outlawed the ancestral version of the game that Eliot despised: "Forasmuch as there is great noise in the city, caused by hustling over large footballs from which many evils arise, which God forbid, we command and forbid on behalf of the king on pain of imprisonment such game to be played in the future."[41] The ban must have failed because several of Edward's successors felt the need to repeat it. Scottish royalty also denounced the game. In 1457, James II demanded that "football and golf be cried down utterly."[42] Bans of football also had a pedigree in the United States. In 1860, Harvard's faculty barred the Bloody Monday football game.

By the early 1880s, as football and other intercollegiate sports grew in popularity and attracted thousands of fans to the biggest games, Eliot wanted to obtain more control over them. He was instrumental in the creation of an athletic committee appointed by the faculty to oversee and regulate sports at the college. Formed in 1882, it immediately began implementing rules on conduct and eligibility and issuing reports. Charles Eliot Norton, an art historian as well as a cousin of Harvard's president, served as chairman. John W. White, a professor of Greek, was a member of the panel, too. The third and final member was Sargent. As director of the gymnasium, he received an automatic appointment to the committee. Sargent shared Eliot's animus toward competition. He called it the "crying evil of the age" and "the arch-enemy of all true culture."[43]

Here was the incipient voice of the Progressivism that would come to dominate American politics within a generation. Competition was increasingly seen not as the source of opportunity but as a threat that had to be managed or, in some cases, actually suppressed. The immediate concerns of Harvard's athletic committee were more mundane, and safety topped the list. One of the committee's first decrees stated that members of the crew team must know how to swim.[44] Before long, Sargent and his colleagues turned their attention to football. In 1883, the committee heard allegations about the game's violence and resolved to study the controversy. Its members informed the football team that they would monitor games during the 1884 season.

Others shared their concerns. Newspapers often focused on violence in their coverage of football, as in this account of the 1884 game between Princeton and Yale, held on the Polo Grounds in New York City:

The spectators could see the elevens hurl themselves together and build themselves in kicking, writhing heaps. They had a general vision of threatening attitudes, fists shake before noses, dartings hither and thither, throttling, wresting, and the pitching of individuals headlong to earth; and all this was an exceedingly animated picture which drew from the volley after volley of applause. . . .

Judges, reporter, and so on saw something more. They saw real fighting, savage blows that drew blood, and falls that seemed as if they must crack all the bones and drive the life from those who sustained them.

Came a crush about midway of the field. All the maddened giants of both teams were in it, and they lay there heaped, choking, kicking . . . gouging and howling. One smaller man lay under them. He held the ball hugged to his breast. . . . His chin rested upon it and his white face looked out from the ruck as the face of a man might look who was on the rack.[45]

The Harvard committee observed four games in 1884, not all of them involving Harvard. At a Princeton-Wesleyan contest, the committee watched one player throw another out of bounds, push him down as he tried to get up, and seize the football from him, all while the referees looked on without objection.[46]

Sargent and his colleagues issued a strong condemnation. "In every one of these games there was brutal fighting with the fists, where the men had to be separated by other players, or by the judges and the referee, or by the bystanders and the police," said their report. "Unfair play, often premeditated and sometimes concerted, was a prominent feature in all of the games, and, although not always successful, was rarely punished. Intentional off-side play and unlawful interference with opponents who were not running with the ball were the rule rather than the exception. The game is demoralizing to the spectators mainly through its brutality; unfair play they usually fail to recognize."[47]

The committee recommended a ban on intercollegiate contests. The faculty approved the proposal and Harvard sat on the sidelines during the 1885 season.

HARVARD'S MOVE WAS unpopular among both students and alumni, who watched as teams from Yale, Princeton, and other colleges continued to compete. New schools joined them. Rather than setting an example for its peers, as Harvard had done in so many areas, it looked petty and irrelevant. A year later, after the 1885 season, the athletic committee reversed course. "The game of football has been much improved during the past season," claimed its report.[48] The ban on intercollegiate football was lifted.

Alumni influence had a lot to do with this. Graduates of colleges and universities were starting to exert more control over their alma maters as they joined governing boards and sought a greater voice in campus life. Their power would only grow in the years ahead. Toward the end of the 19th century and into the 20th, they became especially important to athletics because their financial support underwrote everything from team travel to the construction of new football stadiums. Camp encouraged this trend away from faculty oversight because he saw professors as meddlers and alumni as boosters. "College athletic organizations if left to themselves would soon work out their own salvation," he said, meaning that students and alumni could manage and reform sports programs without the interference of historians and mathematicians.[49] At Harvard, alumni gained seats on Harvard's athletic committee—a development that would make it more difficult for the opinions of Eliot and his faculty allies to trump football's popular appeal. Although Eliot remained a foe of football, presidents at other schools understood that they owed their positions to trustees who were far more likely to be fans of the game than critics of it.

During Harvard's self-imposed exile, football did not become more peaceful. If anything, its violence grew. The Harvard-Yale game of 1886 made a vivid impression upon Yale's Amos Alonzo Stagg. Although his team defeated Harvard by a wide margin—the final score was 29 to 4—he felt Harvard's men had roughed up Yale's players: "George Woodruff brought home a broken nose from Cambridge; George Carter, guard, came out of the game with a cut over the eye needing eight stitches; and [Eddie] Burke, who had beaten me out for right tackle, was a campus curiosity for several days. Both his eyes were closed and his lips were mangled and hideously swelled."[50]

Yale's players presumably recovered from their injuries. At Harvard, however, time did not heal all wounds. When Sargent came up for a full professorship in 1889, Eliot reported favorably on his candidacy to a board of overseers that had the final say. The board was controlled by alumni, many of them football fans. Not only did they refuse to approve the promotion, but they actually stripped Sargent of his faculty status. This rendered him ineligible for further service on the athletic committee. He remained director of the gymnasium but no longer had any influence over varsity sports.[51]

On June 30, 1880, Charles W. Eliot handed Theodore Roosevelt his Harvard diploma. Roosevelt graduated magna cum laude, ranking twenty-first out of a class of 177 students. Eliot barely knew Roosevelt as an undergraduate—but then he knew few students well. He once recalled Roosevelt as a "feeble" boy who read a lot but never got "to the bottom of things." When asked if he could detect Harvard's influence on Roosevelt, Eliot responded simply: "No."[52]

Chapter Six

THE VIRILE VIRTUES

After his graduation from Harvard, Theodore Roosevelt immediately devoted himself to doing the types of things that Dr. Sargent had specifically warned against. He went to Oyster Bay, where he went swimming and riding. He also played tennis, adopting a distinctive method: "He gripped the racket way up the handle with his index finger pointed along the back," commented his son years later. "When he served he didn't throw the ball into the air but held it in his left hand and hit it in between his fingers."[1]

On a trip to Maine, Roosevelt hiked and climbed. Although he came down with a stomach illness, ailments had receded into occasional inconveniences. They were no longer the constant nemesis he had endured in his boyhood. Alice nursed him back to health—an experience that Roosevelt found so pleasant he almost wanted to stay sick. When she was not tending to her future husband, she proved her own athletic prowess, winning the Mount Desert Ladies' Tennis Tournament.[2] On October 27, 1880, in Brookline, Massachusetts, she officially became Mrs. Theodore Roosevelt. It was her husband's twenty-second birthday. She was nineteen.

On the night of their wedding, the couple traveled to Spring-field, Massachusetts, and stayed at the Massasoit House, which, coincidentally, was the site of the Intercollegiate Football Association's annual meetings. They went on to Oyster Bay for a brief sojourn and finally arrived in Manhattan on November 13. Roosevelt's father had died two years earlier, which meant that young Roosevelt not only established a formal residence with his new wife but also assumed the role of family patriarch. Within days of his arrival, he started law school at Columbia. Yet studies did not occupy all his time. On November 20, just a week after he and Alice had returned from Oyster Bay, Roosevelt took a train to Boston for the Harvard-Yale football game. Although he was now a married man and burdened by new responsibilities, he thrilled at the contest, just as he had during his student days. Roosevelt, according to his sister, "nearly went wild & wished he was with the fellows."[3] He certainly did not enjoy the result: Yale won, by a score of one goal to none. A decade would pass before Harvard's alumni would celebrate a victory over their rivals.

As usual, Roosevelt was a flurry of activity. He attended his law school classes, went to dinners with Alice, and even found time to work on the manuscript he had started at Harvard. It would become *The Naval War of 1812*, a book that would shape his future in ways he could not foresee. A revisionist triumph, it claimed that Americans had prepared well for war and outfought their foes. Roosevelt also became interested in politics, forming a Free Trade Club and showing up at Republican Party meetings. During the summer of 1881, he and Alice took the extended honeymoon that they had skipped right after their wedding. On vacation in Europe, they visited a number of popular attractions. At one museum, the Roosevelts studied the art of Peter Paul Rubens. Probably influenced by the form of his slender, tennis-playing wife, Theodore disapproved of what he saw: "I don't like a chubby Minerva, a corpulent Venus, and a Diana who is so fat that I know she could never overtake a cow, let alone a deer."[4] Their tour of the Old World was anything but leisurely, with stops in Ireland, England, France, Italy, Austria, Switzerland, Germany, the Netherlands, and Belgium. Roosevelt did not search for opportunities to relax his mind or his body. Instead, he packed his bags with book-writing materials and planned long hikes.

Sargent had urged him not to climb so much as a staircase, but Roosevelt set his sights on the Matterhorn. The most famous mountain in the Alps, it remained unconquered until 1865, within Roosevelt's own lifetime. Its pointed peak, standing at 14,692 feet, represented an irresistible challenge for an American who wanted adventure. "It was like going up and down enormous stairs on your hands and knees for nine hours," he wrote in a letter to his sister. "I was anxious to go up it because it is reputed very difficult and a man who has been up it can fairly claim to have taken his degree as, at any rate, a subordinate kind of mountaineer. . . . There is enough peril to make it exciting."[5]

Here was Muscular Christianity in action. When Roosevelt scaled the Matterhorn, he did not decorate himself with crosses or describe his expedition as a religious pilgrimage. Yet he participated in precisely the sort of bodybuilding pursuit that a generation of intellectuals had advocated. As the boys who had grown up reading *Tom Brown's Schooldays* reached adulthood, they sought to apply the lessons of their youth to the way they lived as men. Physical achievements were important to them, whether they took the form of single events such as the ascent of a tall mountain or longer episodes such as striking out for the territories—something Roosevelt would do soon.

ROOSEVELT CAME TO embody the spirit of the age, but the last decades of the 19th century were about more than personal feats of physical accomplishment. The cultivation of certain individual habits had a broader impact on the American way of life. It created the conditions for a variety of behaviors and beliefs. Some were amusing and healthy, such as a bicycle craze that saw millions of Americans suddenly take up a new form of exercise. Others would influence national life, such as the conviction that the United States should develop and utilize its martial power. These trends also fed the growth of sports, turning them into mass events that had widespread commercial appeal, but whose fundamental attraction depended on the belief that they improved the physical and moral well-being of all who partook of them.

When the Roosevelts returned to the United States from their honeymoon in Europe, New York was entering a new political season. A day after his first anniversary and twenty-third birthday, Theodore was nominated as the Republican candidate for a seat in the state legislature. There was almost no way he could lose. The district was a safe one for the GOP. Moreover, the Democratic candidate had just been fired as director of Blackwell's Island Lunatic Asylum.[6] Roosevelt cruised to an easy election. Two months later, at the start of 1882, he arrived in Albany and began his career as a public official.

Initially, Roosevelt's colleagues regarded the young newcomer as a rich dandy from the big city. Roosevelt soon set them straight. One day, after a walk with a pair of friends, Roosevelt settled into a saloon for a drink. A figure from the Tammany political machine insulted Roosevelt's pea jacket: "Won't mamma's boy catch cold?" Roosevelt bristled at the taunt. "Teddy knocked him down," recalled a witness, "and he got up and [Roosevelt] hit him again, and when he got up he hit him again, and he said, 'Now you go over there and wash yourself. When you are in the presence of gentlemen, conduct yourself like a gentleman.'"[7] In Roosevelt's view, a proper gentleman did not turn the other cheek—he knew how to fight and was not afraid to prove it.

New York held annual elections for its state legislature and Roosevelt would win two more races, in 1882 and 1883. "I rose like a rocket," he once said of this period.[8] Indeed, the Republicans put him forward as a candidate for Speaker of the House, possibly the most powerful political office in the state, after the governorship. Roosevelt was the youngest member of the assembly. He did not win, but his political life definitely had taken flight.

All the while, he nurtured his interest in competition, even when it involved animals rather than people. One time, at the invitation of two political compatriots, he attended a cockfight near Albany. Roosevelt was famously incorruptible—he did not take bribes or visit prostitutes, at a time when getting away with either would have been simple—but in this instance he broke the law. The cockfight was illegal. The police raided the event, and Roosevelt slipped away before he could be arrested.[9]

He also resumed the boxing lessons that he had abandoned for several years. Roosevelt hired a trainer—"a second-rate prizefighter"—to come by his rooms in Albany each morning.[10] They sparred for half an hour. "I felt much better for it," he wrote to Alice, "but am awfully out of training. I feel much more at ease in my mind and better able to enjoy things since we have gotten under way; I feel now as though I had the reins in my hand."[11] Soon, however, everything would seem to skid out of control. A few weeks after sending this letter, his life changed forever.

In his diary, Roosevelt would mark February 14, 1884—Valentine's Day—with a big, black X and write below it: "The light has gone out of my life."[12] Within hours of each other and in the same house, his mother and his wife died. Roosevelt had rushed down from Albany to be with them, helpless to do anything but witness their final breaths. Martha Bulloch Roosevelt succumbed to typhoid fever. Alice died of Bright's disease, a kidney ailment, following the birth of her only child. Theodore would name the infant for his wife. Yet he would speak of the original Alice Lee Roosevelt almost never again. Her name does not appear in his autobiography. The memories apparently remained too painful even years later, following a happy and fruitful second marriage. In Roosevelt's voluminous writings, this subject is the great silence. The only other topic of comparable importance that he refused to discuss was his father's behavior during the Civil War.

THE WEST SAVED Roosevelt. "The romance of my life began here," he once said of the Dakotas.[13] He had made his first extended trip there in 1883, while Alice was still alive. It led to an investment in a ranch operation near Medora, in what is now North Dakota. For the next several years, he traveled back and forth between there and New York.

In the 1880s, the cowboy had not yet developed as a mythic figure in the American imagination. That would come later, as the images of Frederic Remington, the novels of Owen Wister, and the work of their successors planted themselves in the national culture. Roosevelt would play a part in this development, both as a participant who lived and worked in the West and as a chronicler who described what he saw for an eastern audience that would never gaze upon the fruited plains or towering mountains of the American interior. Roosevelt described his own experiences and celebrated the lives of others in a series of books, including one that Remington illustrated when it appeared as a magazine serial. This work culminated in his multivolume history, *The Winning of the West*.

When a biographer suggested that his time in the West was "a kind of idyll," Roosevelt responded with enthusiasm: "That's it! That's exactly what it was."[14] These years may have been an idyll, but they certainly were not idle. Roosevelt always had found comfort in action—and out West there was plenty of it.

Early on, the West acted as a kind of salve that healed him during a time of emotional need. When he said that the Badlands of the Dakotas looked the way Poe sounded, he was probably not referring to the writer's macabre stories but rather his elegiac verse. Specifically, he may have had in mind one of Poe's most popular poems, "Annabel Lee," whose titular character—a woman who dies young—almost shares a name with his dead wife.[15] This is exactly the type of observation that he would have made—and, because it touched on the memory of Alice, would have left unrecorded.

Over time, the West shaped his idea of how physical vigor contributed to the good life. When he first arrived in the Dakotas, the professional cowboys immediately saw him as an interloper. They would mock his glasses, at least when he was out of earshot. They also marveled at his odd way of talking. He sounded like a character out of Shakespeare the time he ordered one of his men to "hasten forward quickly there!"[16] Beneath the alien exterior, however, the cowboys discovered Roosevelt to be a man of determination and toughness. A couple of times, horses threw him. He cracked a rib and broke a bone in his shoulder. He refused to complain. On another occasion, he set out with companions to locate stray animals. At camp a torrential downpour soaked their blankets. The men shivered in the wet and cold. One of them heard Roosevelt speaking, apparently to himself, "By Godfrey, but this is fun!"[17] He also proved his mettle as a hunter. On one of his expeditions, he shot and killed a grizzly bear from eight paces away. The beast weighed twelve hundred pounds and stood nine feet tall when it reared up on its hind legs. "The bullet hole in his skull was as exactly between his eyes as if I had measured the distance with a carpenter's rule," wrote Roosevelt.[18]

By his own admission, Roosevelt never became adept at roping and he was at best an average horseman. Yet he possessed one of the most important qualities of the Western man, at least as he has developed in the American mind: the ability to fight. One time, Roosevelt went searching for lost horses near the border of what is now Montana and North Dakota. At a dingy little bar in a remote town, he encountered "a bully who for the moment was having things all his way." When a bespectacled Roosevelt entered the room, the bully spoke: "Four eyes is going to treat." Roosevelt tried to laugh it off, but the bully shadowed him, holding guns and spewing taunts and cusses. He repeated his order for Roosevelt to buy drinks. "Well, if I've got to, I've got to," said Roosevelt, getting up from his chair. In his autobiography, he described what happened next:

> As I rose, I struck quick and hard with my right just to one side of the point of his jaw, hitting with my left as I straightened out, and then again with my right. He fired the guns, but I do not know whether this was merely a convulsive action of his hands or whether he was trying to shoot at me. When he went down he struck the corner of the bar with his head. It was not a case in which one could afford to take chances, and if he had moved I was about to drop on his ribs with my knees; but he was senseless. I took away his guns, and the other people in the room, who were now loud in their denunciation of him, hustled him out and put him in a shed. . . . When my assailant came to, he went down to the [train] station and left on a freight.[19]

Half a lifetime earlier, Roosevelt had failed to fend off a couple of bullies on a stagecoach in Maine. So he learned how to fight. It led to recreational success at Harvard. The skills he developed came in handy later on, in Albany when he wanted to prove a point to a thuggish politician and then in the Dakotas when they may have saved his life from a boorish gunman who was probably drunk. These experiences—combined with the simple fact that he was roughing it out west—allowed him to project an image of manliness to easterners who could only marvel at his exploits. "It would electrify some of my friends who have accused me of representing the kid-glove element in politics if they could see me galloping over the plains day in and day out, clad in a buckskin shirt and leather chaparajos, with a big sombrero on my head," he told a newspaper reporter in 1884. "For good healthy exercise I would strongly recommend some of our gilded youth to go West and try a short course of riding bucking ponies, and assist at the branding of a lot of Texas steers."[20]

Roosevelt certainly reveled in this image, which he nurtured and promoted, but his time in the West was not just about mere appearances. He found himself becoming the man he always wanted to be, from the days when he was a tike who lugged around a big book by David Livingstone, the African explorer and missionary. As one of his friends noted in 1885, Roosevelt had become "physically a very powerful man . . . with broad shoulders and stalwart chest, instead of the city-bred, slight young friend I had known earlier."[21] As his body grew, so did his thinking about the way physical activity shaped character—both in individuals and, more broadly, in the nation. When he heard about skirmishes along the border with Mexico, he began to fire off letters to public officials, promising to raise "an entire regiment of cowboys." The clashes never amounted to a war, to Roosevelt's disappointment. "If war had come off," he wrote, "I would surely have had behind me as utterly reckless a set of desperadoes as ever sat in the saddle."[22] On a personal level, Roosevelt was always ready for a fight. He believed that the United States should be ready for a fight as well.

A devastating winter in 1886–87 ended Roosevelt's direct involvement in ranching. Later on, he liquidated his investments for a substantial loss. Even in the absence of harsh weather, his ranching years probably were coming to an end. Political and personal ambitions tugged at him. In 1886 he ran for mayor of New York, coming in third place. A month later he married Edith Carow, his childhood sweetheart. Roosevelt must have known that his future lay in the East, not in the West.

Yet the aura of rugged accomplishment in a hard land always surrounded him. Shortly after quitting the Dakotas, he founded the Boone and Crockett Club, which dedicated itself to the hunting and conservation of North America's big-game mammals. By now he was a prolific writer of books and magazine articles, too. His writings frequently focused on Western themes, though he often tackled other subjects as well. He might have gone on to a career as something of a public intellectual, or at least a popular writer who took on big subjects. Yet he always wanted to be more than a mere observer of the passing scene. Roosevelt wanted to participate in the great events of the day, and to direct them.

IN 1889, ROOSEVELT returned to public service for the first time since leaving Albany: President Benjamin Harrison appointed him to the three-member Civil Service Commission, in Washington, D.C. From this perch, he became a crusader for honest government. Questions of virtue were never far from his mind—his parents had seen to that—but now they became a fundamental part of his job. His responsibility was to identify and eliminate corruption in federal employment. He spearheaded investigations that took him to Baltimore, Indianapolis, and Milwaukee.

For a man of his intellectual curiosity, Roosevelt did not require much prompting to turn his thoughts from professional ethics to the cultivation of virtue in the young. Perhaps if children benefited from the right kind of upbringing, there would be less of a need to monitor vice in adults. In 1893, he suggested a solution: athletic training: "In a perfectly peaceful and commercial civilization such as ours there is always a danger of laying too little stress upon the more virile virtues—upon the virtues which go to make up a race of statesmen and soldiers, of pioneers and explorers by land and sea, of bridge builders and road-makers, of commonwealth builders— in short, upon those virtues for the lack of which, whether in an individual or in a nation, no amount of refinement and learning, of gentleness and culture, can possibly atone."[23]

Roosevelt echoed the concerns of the original generation of Muscular Christians, warning against "the evil consequences of a merely sedentary occupation." But he updated their recommendations, taking note of the way sports had spread through American culture. He approved of all exercise, but applauded certain kinds of it: "sports which call for the greatest exercise of fine moral qualities, such as resolution, courage, endurance, and capacity to hold one's own and stand up under punishment." Boys who engaged in these activities would make better men. "The true sports for a manly race are sports like running, rowing, playing football and baseball, boxing, and wrestling, shooting, riding, and mountain climbing," he wrote. Then he singled out one of them in particular: "Of all these sports there is no better sport than football."[24]

IN THE 1880s, as Roosevelt toiled in the Dakotas, football grew into a popular spectator sport. In 1882, many college games attracted hundreds of onlookers, though major rivalries drew larger crowds. The Harvard-Princeton game had 1,000 fans in attendance and the Harvard-Yale rivalry boasted 3,000. Two years later, Princeton and Yale played before 15,000 people on Thanksgiving in New York City. Three years after that, the Harvard-Yale championship took place in front of 23,000. Football was not merely for sports fans. It was becoming a social event. "You would go to see the English Derby whether you cared for horse racing or not, wouldn't you?" asked the *Evening Sun* in 1890. "Well, then, you've got to go to the American Derby, to the greatest sporting event in the country, where there will be more to see and hear for your money than you can find anywhere else on Thanksgiving Day, or any other day in the year."[25]

The game was catching on at colleges and universities everywhere, from Michigan and Minnesota in the Midwest to Georgia and Texas in the South. On the other side of the continent,

California and Stanford tried to duplicate the Harvard-Yale rivalry with their own contest. Their first meeting, held in the spring of 1892, had all the marks of success: waving flags, tooting horns, and thousands of spirited fans. Unfortunately, they forgot to bring a football. Nobody noticed the oversight until kickoff. The start of the game was delayed for an hour.[26] One legend has it that a Stanford freshman named Herbert Hoover was responsible for the ball. This seems not to have been the case, though Hoover did help organize later games.[27]

Missionaries from established programs spread the gospel of football far and wide. By 1890, forty-five former players from Yale had gone on to coach elsewhere. Princeton supplied another thirty-five. Harvard produced twenty-four, including Vernon L. Parrington, a nonvarsity quarterback who became a coach at Oklahoma and, later, an influential historian of the Progressive Era.[28] Even Walter Camp joined the movement, agreeing to coach Stanford in the fall of 1892, following the completion of Yale's football season. California hired Thomas Lee McClung, also of Yale. They worked with their teams for about two weeks. Their practices drew thousands of spectators. The game itself attracted fifteen thousand fans and ended in a tie.[29] The fame of Camp grew. "There is only one man in New Haven of more importance than Walter Camp, and I have forgotten his name. I think he is the president of the university," wrote Richard Harding Davis in 1893.[30] He was only half joking.

Before the advent of radios and television, football relied on the print media for publicity. Newspapers and magazines were happy to provide it to an eager readership. In 1883, Joseph Pulitzer introduced journalism's first separate sports department, to take advantage of the growing interest in football and other athletics. A decade later, the *Evening Sun* assigned Davis plus seventeen other reporters, artists, and photographers to cover a single game between Princeton and Yale. In 1895, William Randolph Hearst paid

Davis five hundred dollars for an article on the Princeton-Yale game. This was an astonishing figure for the time. Davis claimed that it was "the highest amount of money ever paid for a single piece of reporting." The investment seems to have made sense: The edition of Hearst's *New York Journal* that carried the article by Davis sold out. Soon Hearst's newspaper would boast not only a sports department, but also journalism's first sports section.[31]

CAMP FED THE ravenous appetite for football through his own writings. Nobody was more closely tied to the game and editors jumped at the chance for him to write season previews and summaries. He was more of a booster than a journalist: He wanted to promote the game rather than analyze its strengths and weaknesses. In 1889, Camp and Caspar Whitney, a leading sportswriter, came up with the concept of the All-America Team—a team of college all-stars chosen by Camp himself. The idea seems to have been a quickly considered gimmick that arose in the face of deadline pressure. However unplanned, it became a great success—and gave birth to an enduring tradition in college football. Camp's annual list became a major topic of discussion in the press. Writers and readers loved to argue about who should make the team and who should not. These debates provided yet another boost to the sport.

Much of football's popularity stemmed from views similar to Roosevelt's: the belief that the game built men. One of the men on Camp's first All-America team was Edgar Allan Poe—not the famous writer, who died in 1849, but his grandnephew. Poe quarterbacked Princeton's team, which went undefeated in 1889. One time, after a game against Harvard, a spectator asked if Princeton's quarterback was related to "the great Edgar Allan Poe." A Princeton fan replied, "he *is* the great Edgar Allan Poe."[32] Poe graduated from Princeton with honors and later would be elected as attorney general of Maryland. Yet he is perhaps best remembered for his athletic achievements.

In 1890, Poe wrote about his sport for *Harper's Young People*, calling upon "every boy who is not physically deformed" to play. The game offered countless benefits, both to individuals and their communities: "It makes a boy a true boy, and prepares him to be a man in the best sense of the term. It implants and develops in him courage; it strengthens him in his every joint and muscle, and lays the foundation of an iron constitution that will be of inestimable service to him after he has become a man. It also makes him self-reliant, sturdy, and quick-witted, for the head now plays as important a part on the football field as the body. There is no more gratifying scene to me than a crowd of youngsters playing football. I always feel that the community in which they live will be the stronger and more useful as a direct consequence of it."[33] A year later, Poe tried to take advantage of his fame as a sports star and published *Poe's Football*, a sixty-four-page rulebook.[34]

The game that Roosevelt and Poe admired in the first part of the 1890s was different from the one that had existed just a few years earlier. It was becoming more violent. They may have loved football for the benefits it delivered to participants, but they also knew that the sport needed defenders who could refute the charges of its most aggressive critics. As Poe wrote, "The only objectionable feature still existing in the game is occasional unnecessary roughness; but this evil is being rapidly wiped out by stringent rules and regulations."[35]

This was not true. The game was definitely becoming more brutal, thanks in large measure to the ways its rules and customs had evolved. In the early 1880s, players were not allowed to block with their arms, but they started to "interfere"—they would use their bodies to protect the ballcarrier and thwart tacklers. The difference between blocking and interfering was often in the eye of the beholder. Referees maintained different standards. Over time, interference became more and more acceptable. Then, in 1884, Princeton's team introduced the V-trick, a wedge play that would begin to change the fundamentals of football.

FOOTBALL ALWAYS HAS been a game of strategy and advance planning, but the V-trick was not invented on the drawing boards of a locker room or during practice. It was born in the heat of an actual game. In a contest against Penn, Princeton became frustrated with its inability to move the ball forward. Then inspiration came to R. M. Hodge: "It suddenly struck me that if the rush-line would jump into the shape of a V with the apex forward and with [the ballcarrier] inside, the formation ought to gain ground."[36] The first time Hodge and his teammates tried their stunt, they drove the ball from midfield to Penn's five-yard line. The next time they deployed the V-trick, against Yale, they made another big gain. Princeton must have believed that the success of the V-trick owed much to its ability to surprise, because it used the play sparingly. Yet it made an instant impression. "There came a crush on one of the edges of the field about midway between the goals," wrote a reporter for the *New York Sun*. "All of the maddened giants of both the teams were in it and they lay heaped, kicking, choking, hitting, gouging, and howling."[37]

Within a few years, however, the V-trick and versions of it would become a dominant play in football, with players locking arms around each other and trying to knock over opponents in their efforts to protect the ballcarrier. Two rule changes in 1888 prompted this development. Walter Camp advocated both. In all likelihood, he did not foresee the far-reaching effect these alterations would have on the fundamentals of the game. Whatever the motivation, the result was soon clear: A rowdy sport became even more hazardous to play.

The first change involved blocking and interference. Technically, it said that players could not block opponents with their arms outstretched. More significant was what it left unsaid: It did not say that blocking itself was impermissible. Suddenly there was tacit recognition of the fact that blocking with the body had gained acceptance on the football field. This style of play had developed organically. The rules of the sport were catching up to its realities. Even so, the revision granted the technique an imprimatur it previously had lacked—and football would embrace blocking with fresh enthusiasm.

The other rule change affected tackling. Previously, defenders were not allowed to tackle below the waist. Now anything above the knees was fair game. Safety served as the primary motivation—specifically, the concern that too much tackling around the neck posed a threat to ballcarriers. The acceptance of low tackles, however, encouraged defenders to put their bare heads near the knees of charging runners. Whatever the new rules did to protect against neck injuries was more than compromised by how it exposed defenders to concussions.

It also made open-field tackling much easier. Combined with the new rules about blocking, this encouraged teams to compress their formations. It marked the end of what was later remembered as the "open game." Rather than spreading out across the width of the field, players now started to converge on single points. They stood shoulder to shoulder at the line of scrimmage, bumping and grappling as ballcarriers tried to plunge through small gaps. For most plays, the best outcome was a short gain. Games became shoving matches, as piles of men tried to push and pull themselves forward and backward. Football began to place an even higher premium on big players.

The result became known as mass play. It led inexorably toward early football's most spectacular and controversial tactic: the flying wedge. Its precise evolution, starting from Princeton's invention of the V-trick, is a matter of some dispute. There is no general agreement about which players and coaches deserve credit for each step in its development. Suffice it to say that the late 1880s and early 1890s were a period of creativity and experimentation as teams adapted to the new rules.

The appearance of players began to change, too. Some put straps on their canvas uniforms so ballcarriers could grab hold as they plowed forward. A few even removed the handles from suitcases and stitched them to the sides of their jerseys. Long hair became a fashion statement and supposedly provided an extra layer of cushioning. Nose guards made their peculiar appearance. These shoehorn-shaped devices, introduced about a decade before helmets, tried to protect one of the most vulnerable spots on the faces of players. They were regarded as concessions to safety, but they may have had the unintended consequence of encouraging aggression. With their noses properly guarded, big men perhaps became even more fearless as they grappled with opponents and tackled ballcarriers. The subsequent advent of helmets and padding may have fueled the very types of behavior whose effects they were supposed to blunt.

Athletes also became conscious of their diets and habits. In the summer of 1899, before he arrived on campus as a student, Bill Reid received a note from the captain of the Harvard football team: "From now on you are expected to train for the foot-ball team, giving up all smoking, drinking, etc."[38] By contrast, Camp's approach was unusual. He urged his men to drink beer but not tea, to have a glass of cold water each morning, and to smoke only after a breakfast that included stale bread.[39] These were strange instructions—akin to Roosevelt's parents trying to treat their son's asthma with cigars—but also an honest attempt to create fit men who would gain advantages on the gridiron. In time, the link between nutrition and performance would become a virtual science. These were its first rumblings, a period of trial and error based on hunches and limited knowledge.

· · · ·

DEFENSES SOON FIGURED out how to frustrate the V-trick. It took wedge busters: players who would dive into the point of the V, trying to knock over members of the opposing team like pins in a bowling alley. Yale's William "Pudge" Heffelfinger, a giant of a man, took to leaping over the V and landing on the ballcarrier. Offenses responded by putting players in motion before the ball was snapped to the quarterback so they could achieve momentum before they collided with defenders. Each new method of play gave way to a countermethod. Yet football was more or less stalemated. When played between two well-matched teams, the sport became a glorified pushing contest without much scoring or excitement.

Then Harvard's Lorin B. Deland delivered a jolt of innovation. Growing up, he had not played football. He was a small man and probably would not have been very good at the sport. Moreover, he possessed an intellectual turn of mind that attracted him to chess and military history. He did not even see his first football game until 1890. Yet the sport immediately captured his imagination. The man who spent much of his spare time thinking about how to move pieces across checkered boards and armies around battlefields turned his attention to the gridiron. "One of the chief points brought out by the great French general [Napoleon]," he said, "was that if he could mass a large proportion of his troops and throw them against a weak point of the enemy, he could easily defeat that portion, and gaining their rear, create havoc with the rest."[40] This was the concept of the V-trick, of course. Deland borrowed the principle and came up with the flying wedge. Then he persuaded the captain of Harvard's team, Bernie Trafford, to try it in a real game.

It happened in 1892, before more than twenty-one thousand fans in Springfield, Massachusetts, during the annual contest between Harvard and Yale. Defense dominated the first part of the game. Halftime arrived without a score. At the start of the second half, Harvard's players set up in an unusual formation, with two lines of men slanting away from the ball at 45-degree angles. They arranged themselves well behind the line of scrimmage and went into motion, gaining full speed as they converged on a single Yale opponent, Alex Wallis. Meanwhile, Trafford snapped the ball to Art Brewer, a quick halfback. Brewer got behind the wedge, which rolled over Wallis on the way to a twenty-yard gain. Football fans had seen mass plays before, but not mass plays that also included such a buildup of momentum and a coordination of attack. It took timing and discipline to execute the flying wedge, which worked only for teams that had devoted themselves to practicing it. When it came off properly, as it did during the game in which Harvard unveiled it, the effect was stunning. Amos Alonzo Stagg called it "probably the most spectacular single formation ever."[41]

The *New York Times* described the effect: "About half a dozen big healthy youths in the prime of life form a V about twenty yards from the opposing line and, at a given signal, start on a dead run with the intention of mowing down one man—the one picked out to make the play against—so that the youth with the ball can find a convenient hole in the line to force his way through. Think of it—half a ton of bone and muscle coming into collision with a man weighing 160 or 170 pounds. What is the result? The victim is generally sent sprawling with his nose broken or his chest crushed."[42]

The flying wedge did not win the game for Harvard. Yale managed to eke out a victory, but Harvard had changed the sport. Soon every team was using mass-momentum plays, as they came to be called. Deland outlined sixty variations of it for Harvard's 1893 playbook. At the end of the season, the *Times* described the result: "Every day one hears of broken heads, fractured skulls, broken necks, wrenched legs, dislocated shoulders, broken noses, and many other accidents." This was no exaggeration, by the newspaper's own accounting:

On Saturday, Nov. 18, a team of the Farmington [Connecticut] Athletic Club played against a Yale eleven [not the varsity team]. Early in the game John White, a Farmington player, fell on the ball, and two Yale men fell on White. When the Yale giants got up, White was writhing in agony on the ground. He was taken at once to the hospital and, on examination, it was found that his neck had been terribly twisted and his spine badly injured. The doctors regarded his case as hopeless and confined all their skill to making him comfortable. White became completely paralyzed. He lingered for eleven days, and died on Nov. 29.

Hugh Saussy of 24 University Place was killed in a game played at Elizabeth [New Jersey] on Nov. 11. Saussy played left guard on the team of the College of the City of New York. Their opponents were the Elizabeth Athletic Club. During the game Saussy fell. He lay on the field like a corpse. When his friends went to him he was unconscious. They removed him to St. Mary's Hospital, and he died there at 8 o'clock that evening. Saussy's neck was broken by the fall.

Gelhert, the famous half back of the team of the University of Pennsylvania, had his ankle wrenched so badly in the game played at Philadelphia against the Princeton team on November 4 that he was unable to play in another game. For weeks his ankle was very weak, and he still limps.

In the game between Yale and the University of Pennsylvania, played on Manhattan Field on Nov. 11, Vail, the quarterback of the Pennsylvania team was badly hurt, and had to receive medical attendance. It was feared that he was internally injured. An abscess formed in the head, and Vail has been watching the games since then with his head swathed in bandages.

Frank Ranken, a son of ex-County Clerk Ranken of Brooklyn, played full back for the Montauks against the

Columbians, at the Eastern Park, Brooklyn, on Nov. 25. When running with the ball he was thrown violently to the ground and both bones in his right leg, about midway between the knee and ankle, were broken. Ranken had to be taken to St. Mary's Hospital.

In this same game J. McNally, who played right end for the Montauks, was thrown and fallen on. Several of his lower teeth were knocked out, and the shock incapacitated him for work for several days.

Several men were badly injured in the game played at Springfield between Yale and Harvard on Nov. 25. Two men were seriously injured. Capt. B.G. Waters of the Harvard team had his head injured by a fall and his leg badly wrenched. Two days after the game the doctors feared he was suffering from concussion of the brain and a battered knee cap.

Thorne, Yale's half back, was thrown down, fallen on, and had his nose broken. His nose bled so badly that the spectacle was a most disgusting one.

In the Yale-Princeton game on Thanksgiving Day Capt. Hinkey had his ear badly torn and Balliet, the centre of the Princeton team, received a severe scalp wound. Surgeons had to dress both these wounds before the men could go on playing. Hinkey had to retire for several minutes to be put in proper shape to proceed with the game. After the contest Hinkey went to the Fifth Avenue Hotel and was put to bed. In a short time he grew delirious and a physician was called in.

Phil King, the famous quarter back of the Princeton team, was injured early in the season internally. He had a steel plate made to protect his side in the region of the heart, and was unable to take part in many of the games. The Pennsylvania men heard of this plate and refused to allow King to wear it in the game played against their college.

Early in the season Butterworth, Yale's full back, had his leg badly hurt and was unable to play for several weeks. He used to attend the games, but could only move about with the aid of crutches.

Addis Herrald, the athletic director of the Richmond (Ind.) Young Men's Christian Association team, while engaged in a game a few weeks ago with his eleven against the team of Franklin College, had his breast bruised and received some severe scalp wounds. He was carried from the field, and for a time his life was despaired of.[43]

Football had experienced controversies before, but the rise of mass-momentum plays led to the sport's first crisis. The sport always had a reputation for violence. Now, however, the public began to see violence as more than just the random by-product of a physical game. It was an integral part of football. Many disapproved. The president of Northwestern, Henry Rogers, began to suggest the game's prohibition to his colleagues at other schools.[44] President Grover Cleveland actually took the step, after reading a report on the Naval Academy's football team. Injuries had taken a severe toll on midshipmen: Twenty-four had been admitted to the hospital and they had suffered eighty-two sick days.[45] He put an end to the annual Army-Navy football game. It did not resume until 1899.

AT THE END of the 1893 season, Theodore Roosevelt weighed in on the growing controversy. Writing in *Harper's Weekly*, he defended football against "the noisy crusade" of the prohibitionists. "Sports are good things for the men taking part in them, and for our people generally," he wrote. "It would be a real misfortune to lose the game of football." Roosevelt did not merely accept the perils in the game. He embraced them: "The sports especially dear to a vigorous and manly nation are always those in which there is a certain slight element of risk," he wrote. "It is mere unmanly folly to try to do away with the sport because the risk exists." Yet even Roosevelt, for all of his cheerleading, acknowledged football's problems. "The brutality must be done away with and the danger minimized," he wrote. "The rules for football ought probably to be altered so as to do away with the present mass play, and, I think, also the present system of interference, while the umpires must be made to prevent slugging or any kind of foul play."[46]

Walter Camp recognized that he would have to try to reduce football's violence. At the off-season meeting of the rules committee, he suggested several reforms that involved blocking and kicking. He also called for increasing the distance necessary for a first down from five yards to ten. None of these ideas won the approval of his colleagues, though Camp would not abandon the ten-yard proposal. In the years ahead, he would continue to advocate it, sometimes to the exclusion of almost everything else. Despite these failures, the rules committee did want to solve the problem of brutality. It concluded that mass-momentum plays such as the flying wedge would have to go, and banned the practice of more than three men beginning to move before the start of a play.

This change in the rules brought an end to the playmaking detour introduced by Deland and his innovations. It possibly made the game safer. Yet it did not make the game safe, at least not according to its critics. Football's violent streak would live on.

BACK AGAIN TO HARD STUDY

This 1902 cartoon satirized football as a collegiate obsession. Tens of thousands of fans attended the biggest games and the sport became a moneymaker.

Chapter Seven

LET THEM BE MEN FIRST

W hen the football teams of Harvard and Yale clashed on November 24, 1894, Harvard had won only two of the sixteen games they had played, going back to 1875. Four years had passed since Harvard had so much as put a point on the board against Yale. Harvard was supposed to lose again in 1894. A lot of the betting did not involve the final result, but whether Harvard would even manage to score. Yet the annual ritual generated a tremendous amount of enthusiasm, as it always did. Students and fans in Cambridge and New Haven crowded onto trains bound for Springfield, where the two teams would square off. The day was brisk, clear, and windless. By the afternoon, twenty-five thousand spectators had gathered at Hampden Field. They were about to see what football historian John Sayle Watterson has called "the bloodiest and most appalling display of out-and-out violence yet witnessed in a big game."[1]

For Harvard, the game began poorly. It won the coin toss and elected to receive. Yale captain Frank Hinkey booted the ball deep into Harvard's territory, almost to the goal line. Harvard pushed the ball out to its own twenty-yard line, but then was forced to punt. On the attempt, Jim McCrea of Yale burst through the line and blocked the kick. The ball bounced across the goal line, with McCrea in hot pursuit. He landed on the ball, scoring a touchdown. The kick after succeeded as well. Under the rules then in effect, a touchdown was worth four points and the kick afterward was worth two. Only a minute of time had ticked off the game clock and Yale already had posted a lead, 6–0.

The ball traded hands several times, with Harvard missing a couple of field goal attempts. One kick hit the crossbar. Another was blocked. Then Harvard's Charlie Brewer, the brother of the player who had carried the ball on the first-ever flying wedge, went down with an ankle injury. He rolled on the field in pain and had to leave the game. His replacement, a player named Hayes, struggled to gain ground against Yale's tough defense. At last he broke through and crossed the goal line, with the help of teammates who pushed. For the first time since 1890, the Crimson had scored against Yale. Yet they failed to make the most of their opportunity: On the kick after, Harvard fumbled the ball and lost the chance to gain two additional points. The score was now 6–4.

Then the game took a bad turn. Harvard's Bert Waters jammed a finger into the eye of Yale's Frank Butterworth. Blood gushed forth, but Butterworth stayed on the field, "staggering around the ball, weak and useless."[2] A little while later, Yale punted the ball to Harvard's Edgar Wrightington, who caught it and fell to the ground. Yet Hinkey of Yale jumped onto him, driving his knee into Wrightington's neck and shoulder. Wrightington's collarbone snapped. He left the field in agony, his season over. Hinkey felt no remorse. He was just following his own advice. The night before the game, he had urged his teammates to ignore Harvard players who called for a fair catch. "Tackle them anyway," he said, "and take the penalty."[3] Hinkey took the penalty for his illegal hit on Wrightington. To the consternation of Harvard's partisans, he remained in the game. They thought the referee should have thrown him out.

A series of other injuries followed. Yale's Fred Murphy took a hard blow to the head. It left him so disoriented that his teammates had to point him repeatedly in the direction of his own goal. He exacted his revenge by poking the eye of Harvard's Mott Hallowell.[4]

By halftime, Yale had scored another touchdown, giving it 12 points to Harvard's 4. The Crimson players were frustrated by their performance. If they had not botched a few key plays and scoring opportunities, they would have held the lead rather than Yale. Each team harbored grievances about the other's rough play. Harvard decided to change its approach. "They soon were confronted by so much viciousness," said an advisor to the team, "that if they wished to be in the game they must give as well as to take."[5]

The violence carried into the second half. "It was a game in which an unusual amount of bad blood and foul playing was shown," commented the *New York Times*. "Prize fighting seems a tame and perfectly harmless game in comparison with the sort of thing that people saw on the field here to-day."[6] In an attempt to gain control of the event, the referee ejected Armstrong of Harvard and Hayes of Yale, for slugging. Yet the melee went on. Hallowell broke his nose and several other players suffered their own scrapes. Yale's Murphy had perked up during the break, but a new blow in the second half leveled him. He left the field on a stretcher. As he lay on the sidelines, a reporter was astonished by his "mud splashed and corpselike face turned to the skies and his battleworn hands lying at his side."[7]

Neither team scored in the second half, giving Yale another win over its bitter rival. That evening, Murphy slipped into a coma and went to a local hospital. Rumors of his death spread through Springfield. Although untrue, they provided an unnerving reminder of what football players could do to each other.

The city of Springfield had imported a force of about a hundred police officers from Boston to help with crowd control. In a grim aside to its account of the game, the *New York Times* suggested "that New York City be called on to furnish an ambulance corps and a body of surgeons to supplement the Boston police when next year's football game is played." Yet there would be no game the next season, or the season after that. In the wake of the violence, relations between Harvard and Yale broke down. Their football teams did not meet again until 1897.

THE SPECTACLE AT Hampden Field revealed that, even after the elimination of mass-momentum plays, football still had a serious problem. For some, the trouble was that Harvard kept losing. That was Roosevelt's view. "I can't believe that we haven't got in Harvard as much athletic talent as they have at Yale," he wrote. "Unquestionably the evil development of Harvard is the snob, exactly as the evil development of Yale is the cad; and upon my word of the two I think the cad the least unhealthy." He blamed Harvard's leadership for this sorry state of affairs. "I think President Eliot's attitude in some respects a very unfortunate one for the College," he wrote. "His opposition to athletics and his efforts to Germanize the methods of our teaching work real harm. The main product we want to turn out is men. Incidentally let them be professors, chemists, writers, anything you please, but let them be men first, and they can't be turned out if we don't have the instructors themselves men, and not bloodless students merely."[8]

Opposition to football, previously scattered, began to form into a movement. The controversy played into the hands of Eliot, who had continued his crusade against football. Ten months before the fateful game at Springfield, Harvard's president had issued his most energetic attack on football up to that point. He delivered it within his annual report to Harvard's board of overseers, a document he presented each January. These reports provided an overview of the school's activities and frequently they would discuss certain matters in considerable detail. Athletics always made up one section and Eliot typically praised Harvard's physical education. By the early 1890s, he believed that students were in better condition than they had been a generation earlier, when he was new to the presidency.

Yet the growth of intercollegiate athletics, especially football, bothered him. Sports distracted students from intellectual pursuits. Big games generated substantial gate receipts, making money rather than education a driving force behind their continuation. They also produced "an unwholesome desire for victory," which Eliot likened to the "supreme savagery" of war. Football posed special problems. It induced "severe nervous strain" in its participants. They entered "an overwrought and even morbid state, from which return to normal life is difficult." From a physical standpoint, the game was becoming "more and more dangerous." He listed its risks: "sprains, wrenches, congestions of the brain, the breaking of bones, the loss of teeth, and the enlargement or stiffening of joints." He praised sailing, riding, mountain climbing, and hunting as "manly sports" that developed "courage, presence of mind, and promptness of decision." Football did none of this. Instead, it was "the least useful of the games as a promoter of open-air physical exercise." Worst of all, it actually encouraged players to hurt each other. "No other athletic sport used in colleges requires of the players this habitual disregard of the safety of opponents," he wrote. "Football cultivates strength and skill kept in play by all the combative instincts, whereas the strength most serviceable to civilized society is the strength which is associated with gentleness and courtesy." Eliot concluded by recommending ways to reduce "the evils of athletic sports." He suggested that "no football should be played until the rules are so amended as to diminish the number and the violence of the collisions between the players, and to provide for the enforcement of the rules." If football and other intercollegiate sports failed to change, they should be "abolished altogether."[9]

Eliot lacked the authority to do this on his own. If he meant to spark a public debate about the merits of football, however, he succeeded. The next month, at the Art Club of Philadelphia, a pair of professors met to argue a question: "Ought Football to be Encouraged?" Speaking for the affirmative was Princeton's Woodrow Wilson.

After graduating from Princeton, Wilson had remained enthusiastic about the game. He went on to teach at Wesleyan and helped coach its football squad. Wilson held team meetings in his recitation room and drew plays in chalk on his blackboard. During this period, coaches did not roam the sidelines and issue commands as they would come to do later. Instead, they helped teams prepare for games. Team captains made tactical decisions during games. Yet coaches still could make their presence felt. In a game against Lehigh in 1889, Wesleyan fell behind by two touchdowns. "Then suddenly from the bleachers, a man wearing a black raincoat, heavy rubber boots and carrying a rolled umbrella came out to face the glum Cardinal fans from the sidelines," according to one account. It was Wilson. "He chided them for not cheering, urging, 'Now is just the time to yell.' Whereupon he began to lead them in the Cardinal cheer . . . all the while beating out the rhythm with his umbrella. The stands came alive." Wesleyan fought back and earned a tie.[10]

In 1890, Wilson returned to Princeton as a professor. Although he did not take up coaching again, he remained an avid fan who attended practices and served on advisory committees. At least one of Princeton's players believed that Wilson could have made a career as a coach. The sport mesmerized him. One time, on a train ride from New York, he became so involved in a discussion about football that he missed his stop at Princeton Junction and had to get off at Trenton. In 1892, when "despised Penn" upset Princeton, Wilson blamed it on "incredibly stupid coaching." After the defeat, Wilson's wife commented on her husband's anxiety. "Really I think that Woodrow would have some kind of collapse," she wrote, "if we had lost in politics too." As it happened, Wilson's fellow Democrat, Grover Cleveland, had just been elected president.[11]

Shortly before the debate in Philadelphia, Wilson had discussed football with Princeton alumni in Baltimore. "In the criticisms of foot-ball lots has been said that is true and more that is untrue," he said. "Athletics are a safety-valve for animal spirits, and if these don't have a safety-valve, they mix kindly with other spirits. If the men don't play foot-ball they will play less legitimate games."[12]

At the debate in Philadelphia, Wilson made a positive case for the sport. "I believe it develops more moral qualities than any other game of athletics," he said. "Ordinary athletics produce valuable qualities—precision, decision, presence of mind, and endurance. No man can be a successful athlete without these four qualities." He added that football also taught cooperation and self-subordination. "These are things to be encouraged, and they unquestionably come from the game of football," he said. "In football I have been close enough to it to understand all its developments." Wilson also wondered about the motives of its critics. "Why is it that Harvard don't win in football?" he asked. He thought it might have something to do with the elective system, introduced by Eliot to give students more freedom in choosing their courses. "The elective man is never subject to discipline," he said. Wilson also speculated that opposition to football had its roots in failure at the game—a dig at Harvard and Eliot that probably was not accurate, but may have made his audience snicker.[13]

Wilson's rival was Cornell's Burt G. Wilder, a professor of zoology who had studied under Louis Agassiz at Harvard. Wilder had a flair for public performance—he once pulled 150 yards of silk from a spider, astonishing his audience. Yet he was fifteen years older than Wilson, and so had grown up before the rise of organized sports. During the debate, Wilder claimed to have played a version of football in his youth, though it was clear to many in his audience that he was out of touch with the contemporary version of the sport. If football instills moral values, he asked, then why does it require a referee? Surely well-bred young men should be able to police themselves.[14] He regarded this as a decisive point.

Unlike Harvard, Princeton, and Yale, Cornell had not established itself as a football powerhouse—and this may have shaped Wilder's views as well. Indeed, the sport had other critics in Ithaca. One of the school's co-founders, Andrew D. White, assailed the game: "the sight of a confused mass of educated young men making batter-rams of their bodies, plunging their heads into each other's stomachs, piling upon each other's ribs, or maiming each other for life—sometimes indeed . . . killing each other—in the presence of a great mass of screaming, betting bystanders, many among them utterly disreputable, is to me a brutal monstrosity."[15]

Just a few days after the Wilson-Wilder debate—which Wilson seems to have won, at least from the perspective of his audience—a bizarre incident at Cornell inflamed football passions further. The freshmen had planned a dinner to celebrate a series of interclass athletic victories over the sophomores. Before it started, however, members of the two classes began to brawl. Police had to break up the fight and the banquet went on as scheduled. Then, a little before midnight, a group of freshmen staggered out of the building in which they had feasted, gasping for air. An elderly black woman who had helped prepare their food also emerged, coughing badly. The newspapers identified her as "Mrs. Jackson." Within a few minutes, she died. It turned out that someone had planted a jug of chlorine gas in a room beneath the kitchen, bored holes into the ceiling, and inserted rubber tubes that carried the poison to the chambers above. All assumed the culprit was a sophomore and Cornell's administration issued threats of mass expulsions, but nothing was ever proved.[16]

THE SCANDAL AT Cornell made headlines around the country—and one influential writer decided to blame the whole thing on football. "It is more than a chance coincidence," wrote E. L. Godkin, "that this recent revival of brutality accompanies the over development of college athletics and the football craze." Godkin cited Eliot's report to Harvard's board of overseers as evidence.[17]

To some readers, this seemed like a stretch. Yet Godkin represented an important segment of American opinion. Born in 1831, in Ireland but of English ancestry, he eventually became perhaps the most important newspaper and magazine editor in the United States in the final decades of the 19th century. Early in his career, he was one of the first civilian journalists to serve as a war correspondent, when he covered the Crimean War for the *London Daily News* in the 1850s. (Before then, British editors took their war news from the foreign press or letters from junior officers.) Later, he married a relation of abolitionist author Harriet Beecher Stowe and settled in New York City, where he became a contributor to the *North American Review*, edited by Charles Eliot Norton—the cousin of Harvard's president and the man who would become one of the driving forces behind the college's short-lived ban on football in 1885.

Norton appreciated Godkin as a special talent and tapped him to run the *Nation*, a weekly magazine that he and others had founded in 1865. It became a voice of liberal Republicanism with a strong streak of idiosyncrasy. Godkin favored free trade and free markets and opposed U.S. territorial expansion and government graft. In 1873, Mark Twain announced the arrival of the Gilded

Age, a pejorative term that has come to imply a period of gaudy wealth and widespread corruption. Godkin had his own moniker for the era: He called it "Chromo-Civilization" and he railed against what he perceived to be its worst aspects. The *Nation* eventually merged with the *New York Evening Post*, becoming more or less a weekly edition of the daily newspaper. From 1883 until his retirement in 1900, Godkin oversaw both publications.[18]

The *Nation* did not enjoy a large audience, but its elite readership was uncommonly influential. For fans of football, Godkin's decision to crusade against the sport marked an unwelcome development. He let loose a barrage of editorial abuse. He called football "not only brutal but brutalizing." The controversial game between Harvard and Yale in 1894 had involved so many injuries that it was as deadly as the Union assault at Cold Harbor during the Civil War, "the bloodiest battle of modern times." Godkin attacked the concept, advanced by Roosevelt and Wilson, that football improved character: Football "cannot fail to blunt the sensibilities of young men, stimulate their bad passions, and drown their sense of fairness," he wrote. "How, in the name of common sense, does it differ in moral influence from the Roman arena?" The time has come "to end this great scandal," wrote Godkin. "It may be laid down as a sound rule among civilized people, that games which may be won by disabling your adversary, or wearing out his strength, or killing him, ought to be prohibited, at all events among its youth."[19]

GODKIN'S TALENT FOR arousing strong feelings delivered a loyal readership—and also detractors. One of them was Roosevelt. He regarded Godkin as a "peevish fool."[20] In 1884, they had disagreed over which candidate to support in the presidential election. The *Evening Post* declared that "no ranch or other hiding place in the world" could shield Roosevelt from its fury. In response, Roosevelt accused Godkin of suffering from "a species of moral myopia, complicated with intellectual strabismus."[21] He was capable of much worse. Elsewhere, Roosevelt labeled Godkin a "malignant and dishonest liar" and a "traitor to the country."[22] In his autobiography, published years after Godkin's death, the editor still provoked him. Godkin, he wrote, "was not a patriotic man."[23] When it came to football, Roosevelt had no patience for Godkin or his publication: "Much of the feeling against this game, and against athletics too, has been stirred up by the persistent and very foolish attacks upon them made by various publications, the *Evening Post* being the chief, and, on the whole, the least rational offender," wrote Roosevelt in 1893. "Such attacks as those in the *Post* are in part due to ignorance, and in part to the fact that some persons, who are by nature timid, shrink from the exercise of manly and robust qualities if there is any chance of its being accompanied by physical pain."[24]

Roosevelt's voice was strong, but football needed a more comprehensive defense. The supporters of the game knew that they had to respond to the wave of assault generated by Godkin and other critics. Roosevelt's old friend from college, Robert Bacon, had joined Harvard's board of overseers in 1889—and this former football player bristled at the way Eliot denigrated the sport. So did many other members of the board. Following the conclusion of the 1893 football season, Bacon visited Walter Camp in New Haven. On behalf of Harvard's board, he proposed that Camp chair a committee to investigate the controversies surrounding football. Camp agreed and convened a meeting in New York between himself, Bacon, and several educators, including the Reverend Endicott Peabody of the Groton School. The committee endorsed a plan to survey prep school headmasters, college professors, and former football team captains about the sport. The results were published in a book written by Camp, *Football Facts and Figures.*[25]

Inviting Camp to coordinate this project suggested that the intent of Bacon and Harvard's board was something other than an open-minded examination of violence in football. Indeed, *Football Facts and Figures* mounted a vigorous defense of the sport. It did include facts and figures. Readers who wanted to know how many of Harvard's varsity and class-team players suffered various injuries between 1890 and 1893 learned that there were fifty-two sprained ankles, twenty-four broken noses, and twelve "scalp wounds."[26] Yet the book was mainly a collection of anecdotes and opinions. These were not uniformly positive about football—there was some complaining about mass plays—but the response was overwhelmingly favorable.[27]

School leaders reported on how football improved the character of boys. Ex-players suggested that their injuries were tolerable. Former Princeton quarterback Edgar Allan Poe's reply to the committee is perhaps typical: He described a broken nose as his "most serious injury," said that it caused a permanent scar, and described his current physical and mental health as "good."[28] Other players said that the sport amounted to a form of extracurricular education.

Frederic Remington, in his contribution, expressed dismay at the entire controversy. "Who the devil is making you all this trouble?" he asked the committee. "They are not going to pass any State laws against [football], I hope. . . . I do not believe in all this namby-pamby talk, and hope the game will not be emasculated and robbed of its heroic qualities, which is its charm and its distinctive quality. People who don't like football as now played might like whist—advise them to try that."[29] When he wrote these words, Remington almost certainly had the likes of Eliot and Godkin in mind. Their views were largely absent from the book, except for the purpose of denunciation. On several polemical pages, Caspar Whitney, Camp's collaborator on the All-America teams, took specific aim at Godkin: "The futile crusade against football into which the editor of the *New York Evening Post* has recently flung himself with well-developed hysteria and a Roget's thesaurus would hardly excite comment were it not that undoubtedly many worthy readers of the *Post* are as ignorant—if less irascible—on the subject as is the editor."[30]

Football Facts and Figures may have shored up the sport's defenses, but it did nothing to stop the Harvard-Yale game in 1894 from turning into a bitter and contentious mess. Eliot's next report to Harvard's board of overseers, presented on January 9, 1895, contained yet another attack on the game.

> The evils of the intercollegiate sports . . . continue without real redress or diminution. In particular, the game of football grows worse and worse as regards foul and violent play, and the number and gravity of the injuries which the players suffer. It has become perfectly clear that the game as now played is unfit for college use. The rules of the game are at present such as to cause inevitably a large number of broken bones, sprains, and wrenches, even during trial or practice games played legitimately, and they also permit those who play with reckless violence or with shrewd violations of the rules to gain thereby great advantages. What is called the development of the game has steadily increased its risks, until they have become unjustifiable.[31]

The public's approval of football, wrote Eliot, was "partly ignorant and partly barbarous." The game was no different from "the prize-fight, the cock-fight, or bull-fight, or . . . the sports of the Roman arena." He cited football's "fatal accidents" and warned that "in every strenuous game now played . . . there is the ever present liability to death on the field." Football, in short, "is not fit for genuine sportsmen."[32]

The next month, Harvard's professors voted to ban football. They did not have the authority to do this, but they could recommend action. Specifically, the faculty urged the athletic committee "to put a stop to all intercollegiate football contests."[33] The athletic committee, which had voted to abolish football a decade earlier, was certainly concerned about the sport. But enemies of the game no longer controlled it. The committee's chairman, law professor James Barr Ames, had contributed to *Football Facts and Figures*. He praised the way football instilled character, but he also noted that "the game hitherto has been unnecessarily dangerous."[34] He hoped that rule changes would reduce risks. In the wake of the game against Yale at Springfield, the committee had asked the coaches of the football teams to find ways to cut down on injuries. Yet it was not ready to accept an end to football. In a letter to the faculty, Ames summarized the views of his colleagues: "They have no illusions as to evils of intercollegiate football in its present condition, but they are reluctant to believe that Yale and Harvard teams cannot compete with each other in the spirit of gentlemen." Even so, he conceded that without improvements to the sport, "all further attempts to save the game at Harvard shall be abandoned."[35]

Roosevelt was flabbergasted by Harvard's president and its professors. "What fools they are at Harvard to try to abolish football," he wrote to his friend Owen Wister.[36] Sports were frequently on his mind—and his interest in them had taken an unwelcome personal turn. His brother, Elliott, had started to dissipate in a fog of alcoholism, which may have contributed to a series of sporting accidents that worsened his condition.[37] It was quite a reversal. Theodore had lived a life of personal improvement, rising from sickly boy to hearty man. Elliott had traveled in the opposite direction. By the summer of 1894, he was dead, leaving behind three children, including a daughter, Eleanor, who would marry a distant cousin and become a first lady.

. . . .

DURING HIS TIME on the Civil Service Commission, Roosevelt kept up his sharp interest in athletics, especially at Harvard. Before the year was over, he would join his friend Bacon on the college's board of overseers. ("I felt like a bull-dog who had strayed into a symposium of perfectly clean—white—Persian—cats," he once commented to Wister.)[38] He would also switch jobs, accepting an appointment to the New York City Police Commission, a four-member body that would make him its president. Before leaving Washington, however, he wrote a long letter to Camp, thanking him for sending a copy of *Football Facts and Figures*. Roosevelt described reading a portion of the book to John Procter, the head of the Civil Service Commission. "One of Mr. Procter's sons is a midshipman. He was on the Annapolis [football] team, and put out his knee just before the game with West Point," wrote Roosevelt. "Neither the boy nor his father cared a rap about the injury, except because it prevented the boy from playing the great game. His other son is a freshman at Harvard. Last year he was trying for the team there and broke a bone in his arm; and of course all that either father or son cared about the accident was the fact that it barred the boy from the team."[39]

The rest of the letter, dated March 11, 1895, is one of Roosevelt's most passionate statements on the importance of athletics and the value of football:

> I am very glad to have a chance of expressing to you the obligation which I feel all Americans are under to you for your championship of athletics. The man on the farm and in the workshop here, as in other countries, is apt to get enough physical work; but we were tending steadily in America to produce in our leisure and sedentary classes a type of man not much above the Bengal baboo, and from

this the athletic spirit has saved us. Of all games I personally like foot ball the best, and I would rather see my boys play it than see them play any other. I have no patience with the people who declaim against it because it necessitates rough play and occasional injuries. The rough play, if confined within manly and honorable limits, is an advantage. It is a good thing to have the personal contact about which the New York Evening Post snarls so much, and no fellow is worth his salt if he minds an occasional bruise or cut. Being near-sighted I was not able to play foot ball in college, and I never cared for rowing or base ball, so that I did all my work in boxing and wrestling. They are both good exercises, but they are not up to foot ball. Since I left college I have worked hard in a good many different ways, and sport has always been a mere accessory to my other business; yet I managed to ride across country a good deal, to play polo, and to shoot, and the like. I was knocked senseless at polo once, and it was a couple of hours before I came to. I broke an arm riding to hounds, and I broke my nose another time; and out on the roundup in the West, I once broke a rib, and at another time the point of my shoulder. I got these injuries when I was father of a family, and while of course they caused me more or less inconvenience, and my left arm is not as strong as it might be now, nothing would persuade me to surrender the fun and the health which I could not have had save at the risk; and it seems to me that when I can afford to run these slight risks college boys can afford to take the chances on the foot ball field. . . .

I am utterly disgusted with the attitude of President Eliot and the Harvard faculty about foot ball, though I must also say I feel very strongly in favor of altering the rules, so far as practicable, to do away with needless roughness in playing, and, above all, in favor of severe umpiring, and the expulsion from the field of any player who is needlessly rough, even if he doesn't come quite within the mark of any specific rule. I do not know anything about umpiring foot ball games, but I have a good deal of experience in umpiring polo games. However, personally though I would like to see the rules change and to see the needless brutality abolished, I would a hundred fold rather keep the game as it is now, with the brutality, than give it up. . . .

I do not give a snap for a good man who can't fight and hold his own in the world. A citizen has got to be decent of course. That is the first requisite; but the second, and just as important, is that he shall be efficient, and he can't be efficient unless he is manly. Nothing has impressed me more in meeting college graduates during the fifteen years I have been out of college than the fact that on the average the men who have counted most have been those who had sound bodies. Among the Harvard men whom I have known for the last six years here in Washington, [Henry Cabot] Lodge, the Senator, was a great swimmer in college, winning a championship, and is a great horseman now. [Bellamy] Storer, a Congressman for Cincinnati, played first base in our nine. [Charles Sumner] Hamlin, the Assistant Secretary of the Treasury, also played on the nine. Sherman Hoar, another Congressman, was on our class crew, and so on and so on, and I am inclined to think that even more good than comes to the top-men from athletics comes to men like myself, who were never more than second-rate in the sports, but who were strengthened in every way by them. The Latin I learned in college has helped me a little in after life in various ways, but boxing has helped me more.

Now, my dear sir, you see what you brought on yourself by sending me the book. I had no idea of inflicting this tirade on you when I began to write.

This was vintage Roosevelt: a mix of courtesy (it starts out as a thank-you note), blunt talk, and forceful opinion. It shows an interest in character development, an appreciation for manly virtues, and an acceptance of risk as a necessary part of life. It also includes a racially charged line ("Bengal baboo") that reveals Roosevelt's anxiety, shared by many of his contemporaries, for America's national health. He did not want the United States to be merely one country among many, but the best in every possible way.

Within a few months, Roosevelt and Camp began to collaborate on bringing Harvard and Yale together. Ever the promoter, Camp wrote to everybody who he thought might be helpful. Charles Francis Adams, a prominent Harvard man and a descendant of two presidents, received a copy of *Football Facts and Figures*. Camp clearly wanted to recruit him as a supporter of football, but Adams preferred to occupy a middle ground. In a reply, Adams thanked Camp for the book and said he enjoyed it. Yet he did not want to speak out in favor of the sport. "I do not quite take the view you take in regard to critics of foot-ball, especially the *New York Evening Post*," wrote Adams. "I am myself a friend of the game, yet it seems to me the critics are performing a most useful service. . . . The more severe the attack, the more the game will be brought under proper regulations."[40]

Later in the year, on September 17, 1895, Roosevelt wrote a "confidential" letter to Camp, proposing that they try to thaw relations between their two schools. "I am sure you understand my earnest desire to bring about a good feeling between the two Universities, who, by rights, ought to be, and at bottom are, natural friends and natural rivals; as neither can be with any other University."[41] A year and a half passed. Camp co-authored *Football*, a book with Deland, the Harvard man.[42] Finally, in March 1897, Harvard and Yale agreed to resume games. In the fall, when their teams met for the first time after skipping two seasons, they tied. The game was noted for its clean play.[43]

Elsewhere, football caught a brief glimpse of its future—a future that Roosevelt would help create. In 1895, Auburn coach John Heisman wanted to scout his opponents. He visited Atlanta to watch a game between North Carolina and Georgia, which was coached by Glenn "Pop" Warner. Near the end of the game, the teams were locked in a scoreless tie. North Carolina was stuck deep in its own zone and decided to punt, a job that fell to the fullback because the punter had not yet become a specialized position. When he received the ball, however, he did not kick it. Instead, he took a few steps to his right and tossed the ball forward. It traveled only a few yards, into the hands of a teammate, who raced the length of the field for a touchdown. The play was illegal, but the referee did not call it back. Apparently he had not seen it. Heisman speculated that many of the fans also had missed it, possibly thinking that the ball had been knocked loose rather than thrown. Warner protested loudly, but to no avail. "I had seen the first forward pass in football," recalled Heisman, many years later. "A touchdown had been made and a touchdown it remained."[44]

Football injuries were common from the start, as this 1891 illustration makes clear. In 1905, eighteen people died playing the sport.

Chapter Eight

ROUGH RIDING

Georgia's Richard Von Gammon hurtled himself into Virginia's oncoming rush and vanished beneath a pile of players. The score stood in Virginia's favor, 11–4. If Georgia had any hope of beating its opponent on October 30, 1897, Gammon and his teammates would have to prevent another goal. As the players got up, however, Gammon stayed down. "He raised his eyes in mute appeal, his lips quivered, but he could not speak," according to one account. Gammon was removed from the field, put in a horse-drawn carriage, and taken to the hospital. He died overnight. The doctors diagnosed a fractured skull and a concussion to the brain. His only headgear had been a thick mop of hair.[1]

A native of Rome, Georgia—a town whose name would resonate with critics who compared football games to gladiatorial combat—Gammon was a month shy of his eighteenth birthday. He was the perfect image of a sports-obsessed, latter-day Tom Brown. As a boy, Von and his brothers played football, baseball, and tennis. Athletic gear cluttered their backyard, everything from pole-vaulting equipment to a sixteen-pound metal ball for shot-putting. In a barn, the Gammons kept a trapeze. When Von arrived at the University of Georgia in 1896, he immediately went out for the football team. The coach, Glenn "Pop" Warner, put him at quarterback. The next year, with Warner gone and a smaller boy taking the quarterback spot, Gammon switched to fullback.

His death made headlines around the country and caused Georgians to question the value of football. The university canceled the rest of its season and announced plans to convert its football field into a bicycle track. The legislature passed a bill banning football in the state. Newspapers hailed the move. "We do not favor a game where brutality steps in and usurps the place of athletic development," wrote the *Athens Banner*. "It was a display of savagery which tarnishes the fair names of both of the great universities represented in this contest."[2]

Yet Rosalind Gammon, the dead player's mother, would have none of it. She was made of stern stuff: One time, when a telephone lineman arrived to cut the branches of an elm tree that she prized, she sat beneath its boughs with a double-barreled shotgun until he left. Shortly after her son died, she wrote to the governor, William Atkinson, in defense of football. Her letter spoke the language of clean-living Muscular Christianity. Football, in her view, was no social blight: "The conditions necessary to its highest development are total abstinence from intoxicating and stimulate drinks—alcoholic or otherwise—as well as from cigarettes and tobacco in any form; strict regard for proper and healthiest diet and for all the laws of health; persistent regularity in the hours of going to bed and absolute purity in life." Mrs. Gammon also contacted several state legislators, urging them not to outlaw football. "His love for his college and his interest in all manly sports, without which he deemed the highest type of manhood impossible, is well known," she wrote. "Grant me the right to request that my boy's death should not be used to defeat the most cherished object of his life."[3]

Her appeal worked. Atkinson vetoed the legislature's bill. He said that football caused fewer deaths than hunting, boating, fishing, and other activities. Banning it, he said, would violate the rights of parents and "suppress in our schools and colleges a game of so great value in the physical, moral, and intellectual development of boys and young men."[4]

Football would survive in Georgia. The national controversy over the sport also carried on, fueled by Gammon's death. Concerns about violence remained prevalent. Not everybody accepted the proposition that football was just another pastime, no riskier than fishing. Legislators in Indiana, Nebraska, Pennsylvania, and Virginia considered bans.[5] "The deaths caused directly by playing football," commented *The Youth's Companion* shortly after Gammon's burial, "are as numerous in proportion to the numbers engaged as in a skirmish in a real war."[6] As fate would have it, a real war was coming: The Spanish-American War was just weeks away from erupting, in a conflict that arguably would test the mettle of the United States and its young men. If football and other rough sports built manliness, which in turn contributed to the strength of the nation and its ability to project military power, then football was about to receive its ultimate test. At the very least, the experience of war would shape Theodore Roosevelt's thinking on the subject.

THROUGHOUT THE 1890s, thoughts of war gripped Roosevelt. Early in the decade, when a mob killed a couple of American sailors in Chile, he seemed ready to wage war all by himself. "Do you remember," asked his wife, "how we used to call Theodore the Chilean Volunteer and tease him about his dream of leading a cavalry charge?"[7] After serving as a police commissioner in New York, he joined the new administration of President William McKinley in 1897 as assistant secretary of the navy. The appointment was born of both politics and policy. It certainly did not come from a mutual love of football. McKinley once attended a game between Princeton and Yale. He was puzzled by what he saw and demanded explanations. "They didn't have no game," he concluded. "They got into a scrap and kept fightin' all the time when they ought to have been playing ball."[8]

Roosevelt had campaigned for McKinley and was seen as a Republican with a bright future—his rocket was still rising. Yet he was also a true believer in a strong navy, going back to the days when he was writing his first book, on the naval aspects of the War of 1812. When he arrived in Washington, he clamored for a fight. In every theater of American influence, Roosevelt demanded action. He called for the annexation of Hawaii, the construction of a canal through Central America, and intervention in Cuba. "This country needs a war," he declared in a letter to Henry Cabot Lodge, a Massachusetts senator who was also a confidant. Roosevelt disdained those who did not see things as he did, and so he blasted the advocates of "peace at any price."[9]

These words stung Harvard's Eliot. In the 1850s, "peace at any price" was a slogan of the Know-Nothings, a short-lived political faction that sought to preserve the Union and avoid civil war at all costs, including the acceptance of slavery—a stance that Eliot, as a young man, had found repulsive. Back then, "peace at any price" was a concise statement of principle. By the time Roosevelt and others got hold of the phrase, however, they had drenched it in sarcasm: Eliot and his allies were not respectable pacifists, but in fact fearful appeasers whose intellectual roots stretched back to a discredited political movement.[10] In 1898, Eliot became a founding member of the Anti-Imperialist League, which dedicated itself to opposing the type of expansionist foreign policy that Roosevelt thought essential. Many leading figures shared Eliot's views. Other members of the league included journalists such as E. L.

Godkin and Carl Schurz, Harvard professors William James and Charles Eliot Norton, business leaders such as Andrew Carnegie, and Mark Twain.[11]

As Roosevelt awaited his shooting war, he traded barbs with Eliot in a war of words. Harvard's president never hesitated to make his political views known—he routinely announced his preferences in presidential elections, for instance. His broadsides against Roosevelt were blunt and vigorous, perhaps because he felt a special responsibility for the opinions of a Harvard man. Eliot excoriated Roosevelt's "doctrine of Jingoism, this chip-on-the-shoulder attitude of a ruffian and a bully." Roosevelt and Lodge, he added, were the "degenerated sons of Harvard."[12] For his part, Roosevelt regarded Eliot as a purveyor of American weakness. "I see that President Eliot attacked you and myself as 'degenerated sons of Harvard,'" wrote Roosevelt to Lodge, in a letter that begins in amusement but soon boils with outrage. "If we ever come to nothing as a nation it will be because the teaching of Carl Schurz, President Eliot, the *Evening Post*, and the futile sentimentalists of the international arbitration type, bears its legitimate fruit in producing a flabby, timid type of character, which eats away the great fighting features of our race."[13]

Meanwhile, Eliot continued his assaults on football. Harvard's intercollegiate athletics remain "unintelligent," he told the board of overseers in the annual report he presented in 1897. He lamented "the evils of overtraining and excessive exertion," especially as they applied to football. "It must be perceived and admitted that training which goes beyond pleasurable strenuous exercise is worse than useless, and that so-called sports which require a dull and dreaded routine of hardship and suffering in preparation for a few exciting crises are not worth what they cost," he wrote. "They pervert even courage and self-sacrifice, because these high qualities are exercised for no adequate end."[14]

The foes of football had yet to enjoy a major success. Football was still king, turning out thousands of fans on autumn weekends, selling untold numbers of newspapers, and generating enormous revenues. Even a high-profile death such as Gammon's at Georgia failed to result in meaningful reforms or political action. Yet their efforts did not go unheeded. The notion that football was too violent began to seep into popular culture. Arguments against the sport were not always accepted, but at least they were understood. In their apologias for the sport, Roosevelt, Camp, and other prominent supporters of football always felt it necessary to condemn the most flagrant examples of brutality.

The critique against football also began to broaden. As games became more lucrative, concerns about professionalism and profiteering arose. Desperate for football victories and the popular acclaim that they delivered, colleges often looked the other way as teams and their alumni supporters recruited ringers, often with money. Yale captain James J. Hogan became a spokesman for the American Tobacco Company. Students "buy our cigarettes, knowing that Hogan gets a commission on every box sold in New Haven," said a company representative.[15]

Eligibility became an issue. In 1893, in the first game ever played between the University of Georgia and the Georgia Technological School, a burly man named Leonard Wood scored three touchdowns for Tech, on the way to a 28–6 win. According to a newspaper account, Wood handled an opposing lineman "almost as if he were a child." Yet Georgia Tech's star player was no student: Wood was a thirty-three-year-old army doctor who had fought Apaches in the American Southwest and helped capture Geronimo. Later, Wood claimed that he had enrolled in a shop course in order to gain student status, but there is no record of his ever having attended a class at Georgia Tech. Posted to Fort McPherson, near Atlanta, he joined the college team simply because he loved to play football.[16]

The game, which took place in Athens, Georgia, was a spectacle of violence. At one point a Georgia player drew a knife on a Tech rival. Later a fan threw a rock that hit Wood in the head. Wood may have frustrated Georgia's fans, but he impressed its players: They invited him to play for their own team the next week against Vanderbilt. Wood declined, suited up a few more times for Tech, and finally retired from college athletics.[17]

These types of stories fueled the outrage of football critics such as Godkin. He argued that football and its winning-is-everything mentality were the products of a cultural sickness rooted in Gilded Age capitalism. "Lack of moral scruple which pervades the struggles of the business world meets with temptations equally irresistible in the miniature contests of the football field," he wrote.[18]

New voices built upon this point. One belonged to Thorstein Veblen, an aloof and eccentric intellectual who attacked commercial life in the United States. A native of Wisconsin, Veblen attended Carleton College in Minnesota and eventually earned a doctorate from Yale in 1884. In the 1890s, he began to publish a series of essays that culminated in *The Theory of the Leisure Class*, an influential book that tried to describe how wealth shapes behavior. It coined the popular term "conspicuous consumption" to describe the connection between consumer spending and perceptions of social status. A related term, not as well-known but nevertheless important to Veblen, was "conspicuous leisure." Sports, claimed Veblen, also represented a gratuitous display of social status. He scoffed at the Rooseveltian notion that athletics improved health and cultivated manly vigor. "The relation of football to physical culture is much the same as that of the bull-fight to agriculture," he quipped. To Veblen, football was nothing more than "a one-sided return to barbarism" that promoted "exotic ferocity and cunning."[19] It had no redeeming value.

Veblen's verdict flew in the face of mass opinion. Football attracted huge crowds and spread to more colleges, in all parts of the country. Games certainly created opportunities for conspicuous consumption, with high ticket prices at major events. Many prominent players, especially at Harvard and Yale, came from well-heeled families. At the same time, football's growth had a democratizing effect. Fans hailed from all walks of life. Football had mass appeal. Even the playing field was a leveler of privilege. The game did not discriminate in the way of campus fraternities and social clubs. It rewarded talent and hard work. A player could not step onto the gridiron and expect the financial bequests of earlier generations to help him. One of the first men to make Walter Camp's All-America team was William Henry Lewis, a black player at Harvard.[20] Although college football was far from color-blind, it did create an environment in which a man like Lewis could rise. Top universities were still dominated by an economic aristocracy, but a new kind of student suddenly was able to penetrate its ranks on the basis of athletic talent. The 19th-century school certainly was not blind to merit—admissions were based heavily on academic preparation—but now it was willing to define merit in different and broader ways.

The operations of the game were anything but democratic. The rules committee was a self-perpetuating body dominated by eastern schools. They met each year in New York. Many saw Camp as its reigning king. It was true that Camp, who continued to represent Yale, enjoyed enormous influence. Critics charged him with resisting the reforms that would have made football less brutal—and Camp surely saw no reason to overhaul a sport in which Yale excelled. Resentful of their exclusion, a group of midwestern schools started their own organization. They became known as the Big Nine, a forerunner to the modern era's Big Ten. The threat of a splinter group that would create a competing set of rules compelled Camp to act. He invited Amos Alonzo Stagg, who had become the University of Chicago's football coach, onto his committee. Stagg refused at first, but later joined. He provided

Camp's committee with the patina of regional diversity, though the grumbling about Camp and his allegedly iron-fisted control of football would persist.

FOOTBALL SOON GAVE birth to a literary subgenre: stories of derring-do on the gridiron, published in pulp magazines and dime novels. Richard Harding Davis, the journalist, wrote one of the first.[21] The most successful author in this field was Gilbert Patten, who wrote under the pen name of Burt L. Standish. In 1896, he invented Frank Merriwell, a modern-day Tom Brown. Merriwell was a sports-mad student who performed feats of athletic heroism on football fields and baseball diamonds. As a boy he attended the fictional Fardale Academy. Later he matriculated to Yale. Frank always played hard and he always played fair. He honored friendship, loyalty, patriotism, physical fitness, and clean living. (He was a teetotaler whose preferred drink was ginger ale.) Although Patten grew up in a home of pacifists and did not play sports himself, his character was the embodiment of Muscular Christianity, brought to life on the printed page for a modern audience of American readers.

Merriwell did not quiver at the prospect of rough play. Instead, he gloried in it. In one story, Frank competed in a scoreless football game against Harvard. Knocked around by the men clad in crimson, he was hobbled by injuries. With time almost out, Harvard fumbled the ball and Frank grabbed it. "Frank felt a fearful pain running through him." He ignored it and sprinted to the goal line. Hollender, a player for Harvard, caught up and took hold of him:

> Frank felt himself clutched, but he refused to be dragged down. He felt hands clinging to him, and, with all the fierceness he could summon, he strove to break away and go on.

His lips were covered with a bloody foam, and there was a frightful glare in his eyes. He strained and strove to get a little farther, and he actually dragged Hollender along the ground till he broke the fellow's hold. Then he reeled across Harvard's line and fell. It was a touch-down in the last seconds of the game.[22]

Frank's teammates carried him off the field, put him to bed, and called for a doctor to treat his wounds. There was no hand-wringing about brutality or overtraining, just pride in a job well done.

The stories of Frank Merriwell were an instant commercial success. Shortly after their debut, issues of *Tip Top Weekly*, which published Patten's athletic yarns, sold hundreds of thousands of issues. For seventeen years, Patten cranked out a weekly episode of twenty thousand words—a pace so tremendous that the author apparently had to hire a secretary because his fingers were constantly sore from his perpetual pecking at typewriter keys. The cast of characters in Merriwell's universe grew to include a long-lost brother, a son, and others. Several stories bound together made a book, and Patten sold perhaps 130 million copies of them.[23] Dozens of imitators tried to mimic his style and duplicate his success. Owen Johnson, the author of *Stover at Yale*, was probably the second-best-known writer of football fiction. Even Camp tried his hand at the form. Yet nobody outdid Patten. For years, sportswriters and broadcasters who grasped for ways to describe an amazing athletic triumph would refer to "a Frank Merriwell ending." They turned the phrase into a cliché.

If a certain segment of American literature was now concerned with heroism in sports, another branch concentrated on the much more serious problem of heroism in war. In 1895, Stephen Crane published *The Red Badge of Courage*, a novel about a young man who faces his first battle during the Civil War. Henry Fleming wants to demonstrate his bravery, but when he encounters actual fighting for the first time, he flees in panic. At one point, as bullets zip overhead, Fleming is said to duck "like a football player."[24] This mild anachronism speaks to how thoroughly football had seeped into the popular imagination. Yet the larger importance of *The Red Badge of Courage* involved a subject of great interest to Roosevelt and other supporters of football: How can society nurture men who will fight well in war?

Several observers already had drawn a connection between football and combat. Caspar Whitney, Camp's journalistic collaborator in producing the All-America football teams, covered the sport at the military academies in West Point and Annapolis. "If there is any game fitted to the training of a soldier, it is this one," he wrote in 1892. "The game is a mimic battle-field, on which the player must reconnoiter, skirmish, advance, attack, and retreat in good order; he must exercise strategy; be prepared to meet emergencies with coolness and judgment under trying circumstances," and so on.[25]

Some readers may have found this a glib comparison. What did Caspar Whitney, born on the day General William Tecumseh Sherman entered Atlanta in 1864, know of real war? They would not ask the same question of Oliver Wendell Holmes, Jr., the thrice-wounded veteran of Antietam and other battles. In 1895, the mustachioed Holmes, who had gone on to achieve fame as a legal scholar, delivered an address to the graduating class at Harvard. His words defied the pacifism of Eliot. "War is out of fashion," he said. Yet enduring peace is an illusion: "In this snug, over-safe corner of the world," he continued, "we may realize that our comfortable routine is no eternal necessity of things, but merely a little space of calm in the midst of the tempestuous untamed streaming of the world." Americans, therefore, must be "ready for danger." One route to preparedness involved athletics. "I rejoice at every dangerous sport which I see pursued," said Holmes. "The students at Heidelberg, with their sword-slashed faces, inspire me with sincere respect." He did not mention football specifically, but he made a point that was immediately familiar to all who had followed the debate over football's merits. "I gaze with delight upon our polo players. If once in a while in our rough riding a neck is broken, I regard it not as a waste, but as a price well paid for the breeding of a race fit for headship and command."[26]

Roosevelt loved the address. "By Jove, that speech of Holmes was fine," he wrote to his friend Henry Cabot Lodge.[27] The reference to students at Heidelberg would have made him think back to his own days in Dresden, boxing with his brother and cousin, bloodying his nose and theirs. The remarks on the importance of cultivating martial virtue spoke to one of the foremost subjects on Roosevelt's mind. Years later, as president, Roosevelt appointed Holmes to the Supreme Court—and his favorable reaction to this speech played an important part in the decision. Not all the responses to Holmes were so glowing, however. Wendell Phillips Garrison, the son of abolitionist publisher William Lloyd Garrison and a longtime colleague of Godkin's at the *Nation*, condemned the speech as "sentimental Jingoism."[28] To Roosevelt, this would have served as further credit to Holmes: He was making the right enemies.

A year later, Lodge echoed Holmes's sentiments in a speech to fellow alumni of Harvard. Lodge recalled the rowing and baseball victories of his undergraduate years in the late 1860s and early 1870s. Then he issued a direct rebuke of Eliot's hostility to football. "I happen to be one of those, Mr. President, who believe profoundly in athletic contests," he said. "The time given to athletic contests and the injuries incurred on the playing-field are part of the price which the English-speaking race has paid for being world-conquerors." Sports, said Lodge, helped to develop "the spirit of victory." Harvard was in jeopardy of losing it, to the detriment of both itself and the nation. "I want Harvard to play the part which belongs to her in the great drama of American life," he said. "Therefore I want her to be filled with the spirit of victory."[29]

. . . .

As THE TURN of the century approached, the United States was a rising force in the world—a development that was apparent not only to strategic thinkers who thought about long-term demographic and economic trends, but even to the lowliest European peasant. Millions of commoners steamed across the Atlantic Ocean and marched through Ellis Island. In the Darwinian struggle of nations, it was difficult to see the United States as anything but supremely fit. Meanwhile, Spain, a traditional power, was in severe decline, especially in the Western Hemisphere. A clash seemed inevitable.

On February 15, 1898, the U.S.S. *Maine* blew up in the harbor of Havana, killing 266 Americans and wounding many others. In a single, convulsive moment, the war for which Roosevelt had yearned finally presented itself. Roosevelt labeled the explosion "an act of dirty treachery" on the part of Spain.[30] His views were in line with those of the so-called yellow journalists, led by newspaper publisher William Randolph Hearst. Several months before the sinking of the *Maine*, Hearst had sent Roosevelt's friend Frederic Remington to Cuba, in anticipation of what was to come. Remington grew bored and cabled back: "Everything is quiet. There is no trouble. There will be no war. I wish to return." According to legend, Hearst replied: "Please remain. You furnish the pictures and I'll furnish the war."[31]

After the *Maine* went down, Roosevelt tried to furnish the war as well. He did everything he could in his capacity as assistant secretary of the navy to encourage it. The previous November, Eliot had invited Roosevelt to appear at Harvard in April and speak on police work. A week before the appearance, Roosevelt canceled. "I am exceedingly sorry, and I am sure you will understand that nothing but the impossibility of leaving a public office at this time would make me break my engagement," he wrote, in a note that misspelled Eliot's name.[32] From his post in Washington, Roosevelt tried to push McKinley and his administration toward a military confrontation with Spain. One day, McKinley asked a question of his doctor: "Have you and Theodore declared war yet?" The doctor replied, "No, Mr. President, but we think you should."[33]

The doctor was Leonard Wood, the former Apache hunter and Georgia Tech football player. After his posting at Fort McPherson, Wood had transferred to the War Department in Washington, D.C., where he became the physician to the president and several cabinet members. He also entered Roosevelt's social circle. "We soon found that we had kindred tastes and kindred principles," wrote Roosevelt.[34] The two men bonded over their experiences in the West and their fondness for football. They took long walks in the countryside around Washington. "In winter we sometimes varied these walks by kicking a foot-ball in an empty lot," reminisced Roosevelt.[35] During these excursions, Wood almost certainly shared stories from his athletic days at Georgia Tech. At the very least, Roosevelt probably heard the tales then in circulation about his friend. During one game, Wood had received a gash above his eye. He finished playing, returned to his office, and studied the cut in a mirror. Then he washed it out and sewed four stitches into his own eyelid. The incident "shows exceedingly well a certain Spartan side to Wood's nature," wrote an early biographer.[36]

Neither Roosevelt nor Wood wanted to spend the war with Spain behind a desk. When Congress authorized the creation of three cavalry regiments in the West, they saw their opportunity. By the end of April, Wood was colonel and Roosevelt was lieutenant colonel of the 1st U.S. Volunteer Cavalry. As they departed for a muster camp in San Antonio, Texas, the press dubbed them Roosevelt's Rough Riders—a nickname that Roosevelt first resisted and later embraced. Although he was second in command, the public perceived him as the regiment's true leader. If Wood had been as hungry for publicity as his friend, it might have strained their relationship.

In Texas, their biggest challenge was not in persuading men to join them, but in going through a flood of applications from all parts of the country. Because they did not have to accept all comers, they were selective, taking a mix of true westerners, Ivy Leaguers in search of adventure, and others "in whose veins the blood stirred with the same impulse which once sent the Vikings over the sea." Roosevelt placed particular value on men who had participated in college athletics, especially football. He brought in Dudley Dean, "perhaps the best quarterback who ever played on a Harvard Eleven," Bob Wrenn, "a quarterback whose feats rivaled those of Dean's," and "Princeton men like Devereux and Channing, the foot-ball players." A Cherokee recruit came to his attention because he had played football in school. Roosevelt also mentioned tennis players, high jumpers, steeplechase riders, and polo players. "They all sought entry into the ranks of the Rough Riders as eagerly as if it meant something widely different from hard work, rough fare, and the possibility of death," he wrote.[37]

In June, the Rough Riders sailed for Cuba. Wood received a promotion to brigade commander, which allowed Roosevelt to assume full command of his cavalry regiment. On July 1, outside the city of Santiago, Roosevelt led his dismounted men in the Battle of San Juan Hill. His famous charge up Kettle Hill drove Spanish soldiers from the summit. Roosevelt called it his "crowded hour."[38] It secured his place as a national hero. Although Roosevelt might have remained safely to the rear of his charging soldiers, he faced open fire and led them to the top of the hill. "It will never be forgotten as long as America has a military history," wrote Stephen Crane, who was in Cuba to report on the conflict.[39]

Remington made his own contribution to the legend of Roosevelt. Before the war, he had captured the romance of the West in his illustrations, but he had not witnessed actual combat. When he finally did observe it with his own eyes, his mind turned to his days as a football player at Yale and the game-day drawings he had supplied to eager publishers over the years. His full-color portrait *The Charge of the Rough Riders*, according to the historian David Mc-Cullough, "makes the war look more like a football game."[40] Roosevelt is in the foreground, dashing forward with a group of men. Had he been holding a ball instead of a pistol, he might have doubled for a rusher who streaks toward the goal line in a mass play.

Roosevelt and the Rough Riders were in Cuba for less than two months. On their journey home, the men talked of their adventures during and before the war, including "experiences on football teams which are famous in the annals of college sport."[41] It was a natural topic. In Roosevelt's view, the regiment's experience in Cuba confirmed the theory he had held for years: Athletics in general and football in particular had prepared his men for their great accomplishment. Whatever the sources of their success, the fact of it thrust Roosevelt to new political heights. In November, four months after his victory in Cuba, he was elected governor of New York. Two years after that, in 1900, he would find himself running for vice president on the Republican ticket of William McKinley.

In a letter to Roosevelt, John Hay, who had served as Abraham Lincoln's secretary and had known Roosevelt's parents, called the short conflict "a splendid little war." Many Americans agreed. They saw the Spanish-American War as a kind of coming-out party in which the United States emerged as a global force. It took control of Puerto Rico in the Caribbean and Guam and the Philippines in the Pacific. Cuba fell under U.S. military jurisdiction. After the island's independence in 1902, the Americans kept possession of a base at Guantánamo Bay. The balance of power in the world suddenly had shifted, sharply and swiftly, away from Europe and toward the New World.

George Hibbard, who would become mayor of Boston, applied his own adjective to the Spanish-American War: "It may now be admitted this was a 'sporting' war," he wrote. "There is a great deal of the spirit of sport in the spirit of Jingoism."[42] To some, the connection to football seemed more obvious than ever before. "Football is very much like a small war," wrote J. Hamblen Sears, "and the training of a team is not so different from the training of an army. . . . A brave man who cannot or does not obey orders in a regiment is well known to be not only useless himself, but a serious cause for the loss of discipline and efficiency on the part of all the other men in the regiment. It is precisely the same with football."[43] In their 1896 book *Football*, Camp and Deland observed "a very remarkable and interesting likeness" between "battles and the miniature contests on the gridiron."[44]

The anti-imperialists chafed at this type of talk. "My patriotism is of the kind which is outraged by the notion that the United States never was a great nation until in a petty three months' campaign it knocked to pieces a poor, decrepit, bankrupt old state like Spain," wrote William Graham Sumner.[45] Eliot responded as well. He prepared a set of statistics on Harvard students and alumni who served in the war, counting 384. There was some discrepancy as to how many had been athletes at Harvard, but Eliot suggested that 42 was a reasonable estimate—about 11 percent. From this, Eliot deduced that participation in sports did not incline students to enlist in the military. Then he took aim at football in particular: "It has been supposed that football was especially adapted to training soldiers; but the fact seems to be that nothing can be more unlike actual fighting than the bodily collisions which take place between football players," he wrote. "In modern warfare no one seems to see his adversary, and the constant thought of the men in line of battle is to conceal or cover themselves and their weapons while advancing or waiting."[46] Roosevelt, who exposed himself to fire as soldiers under his command were shot down, would have bristled at this description. He also might have seen that Eliot had snubbed him in his report. Whereas Eliot had mentioned Leonard Wood by name and half-correctly identified him as the commander of the 1st U.S. Volunteer Cavalry, he had skipped over Roosevelt's name entirely. It did not appear in the document.

In all likelihood, Roosevelt was too busy to notice. He had just become governor. He was writing *The Rough Riders*, his own account of what had happened the year before. He was also taking advantage of his burgeoning prominence to speak publicly and hold forth on subjects of special interest. On April 10, 1899, he addressed the Hamilton Club in Chicago and delivered one of his best-known speeches. "I wish to preach, not the doctrine of ignoble ease, but the doctrine of the strenuous life," he said. The bulk of his remarks concentrated on the challenge of empire and how America should govern the new territories that Roosevelt had helped to win. Yet the finest and most memorable passages involved the cultivation of "the great, fighting masterful virtues" upon which all great nations rely. "Who among you would teach your boys that ease, that peace, is to be the first consideration in their eyes—to be the ultimate goal after which they strive?" asked Roosevelt. "We do not admire the man of timid peace. We admire the man who embodies victorious effort . . . who has those virile qualities necessary to win in the stern strife of actual life." The self-satisfaction of individuals had nothing to do with it. Instead, Roosevelt was speaking of every citizen's duty to country: "It is only through strife, through hard and dangerous endeavor, that we shall ultimately win the goal of true national greatness." Roosevelt was a regular churchgoer, but he had taken many of the beliefs behind Muscular Christianity and secularized them into a doctrine that might be called Muscular Patriotism.

The speech was well received. Roosevelt himself thought highly of it—so much so, in fact, that when he published a volume of essays during his vice presidential candidacy in 1900, he chose

The Strenuous Life as its title. Years later, in his autobiography, he would say that he should have given his address a different name. An Italian edition had rendered it as *Vigor di Vita*. "I thought this translation a great improvement on the original, and have always wished that I had myself used 'The Vigor of Life' as a heading to indicate what I was trying to preach," he wrote.[47] Yet he continued to believe the central message of his remarks. He eventually felt compelled to say something he did not acknowledge in 1899: His own personal history provided a case study in the importance of embracing the vigor of life. "Having been a rather sickly and awkward boy, I was as a young man at first both nervous and distrustful of my own prowess," he wrote. "I had to train myself painfully and laboriously not merely as regards my own body but as regards my soul in spirit."[48]

One of the essays collected in the *The Strenuous Life* was called "The American Boy." Roosevelt wrote it some months after giving the speech in Chicago. It originally appeared in a children's magazine called *St. Nicholas*. In its essentials, "The American Boy" was a version of "The Strenuous Life," but modified for an audience of young readers. It brimmed with advice on how a boy can "grow into the kind of American man of whom America can be really proud." For Roosevelt, this meant playing sports. "The great growth in the love of athletic sports," he wrote, has "had an excellent effect in increased manliness." He singled out "the rough sports" for their development of pluck, endurance, and physical fitness. And he concluded with a direct reference to what many regarded as the roughest sport of all: "In short, in life, as in a football game, the principle to follow is: Hit the line hard; don't foul and don't shirk, but hit the line hard!"[49]

NEXT!
A president who "does" things.

Cartoonists made light of Roosevelt's frenetic activity. In this image, the president tries to manage a series of crises, including "Brutality in Football." (*Courtesy The Library of Congress*)

Chapter Nine

FOOTBALL IS A FIGHT

The game between Dartmouth and Princeton was barely under way on October 24, 1903, when Matthew W. Bullock, a star player for Dartmouth, collapsed in pain. His collarbone had snapped. The break would end his career as a college athlete. Broken bones were of course common in football. Yet many of Dartmouth's fans harbored darker thoughts. They suspected that Princeton's team had gone after Bullock intentionally. They sensed that his injury was not an unfortunate accident, but the result of a deliberate strategy to cripple an opponent. After Bullock left the field, Princeton cruised to a 17–0 victory over Dartmouth.[1]

Bullock was a top performer. If Princeton was going to attack a player, he was a likely target. He was also black. Other African Americans had played college football, such as Harvard's William Henry Lewis, the All-American. Yet they were a rare sight. Moreover, Princeton was known for its large number of southern students and their illiberal sympathies. The night before the game, the Princeton Inn had refused to rent rooms to Dartmouth, on account of Bullock. Had racism also played a part in Bullock's injury? Nobody knew for sure—or at least those who could verify it did not say.

A year and a half later, *McClure's Magazine* published a long exposé on corruption in college football. The writer, Henry Beach Needham, investigated Bullock's treatment. He reported on a conversation between an unnamed Harvard player who had gone to Andover with one of Princeton's men. The Harvard player accused his former teammate of prejudice: "You put [Bullock] out because he is a black man." The allegation upset the Princetonian. "We didn't put him out because he is a black man," he replied. "We're coached to pick out the most dangerous man on the opposing side and put him out in the first five minutes of the game."[2]

In denying the charge of racism, the player confirmed the reality of premeditated violence in football. Teams were committed to maiming opponents regardless of skin color. Needham's article presented neither the first nor the last credible claim of its type, but this one made an impression on an important reader: Theodore Roosevelt. It helped persuade him that football would benefit from reform.

Roosevelt held most muckraking journalists in low regard. He actually coined the term *muckraker*, in an allusion to a character in *The Pilgrim's Progress*, the 17th-century book by John Bunyan. Writers such as Upton Sinclair, Lincoln Steffens, and Ida Tarbell, according to Roosevelt, were "lurid sensationlists" who were "building up a revolutionary feeling."[3] Yet Needham was different. Roosevelt regarded him as an investigative reporter, not an agenda-driven, truth-distorting polemicist. He also considered Needham a friend—and invited him to the White House to discuss football's challenges. Importantly, Needham did not despise the sport, as did so many of its critics. His articles stopped well short of calling for the prohibition of football, in the manner of Charles W. Eliot and the *Nation*. Instead, Needham documented abuses of professionalism and fair play. His account of the attack on Bullock, as well as of athletes who jumped from college to college in a single season, spoke directly to Roosevelt's hatred of corruption.

Needham's articles were hot off the press when Roosevelt spoke at a dinner of Harvard alumni on June 28, 1905. The occasion was the twenty-fifth anniversary of his graduating class. Roosevelt used the forum to discuss football. "I believe in outdoor games, and I do not mind in the least that they are rough games, or that those who take part in them are occasionally injured," he said. "I have a hearty contempt for [a young man] if he counts a broken arm or collar bone as of serious consequence, when balanced against the charge of showing that he possesses hardihood, physical address, and courage." Yet Roosevelt also spoke strongly against the behavior that Needham had highlighted: "When the injuries are inflicted by others, either wantonly or of set design, we are confronted by the question not of damage to one man's body, but of damage to the other man's character," he said. "Brutality in playing a game should awaken the heartiest and most plainly shown contempt for the player guilty of it. . . . I hope to see both graduate and undergraduate opinion come to scorn such a man as one guilty of base and dishonorable action, who has no place in the regard of gallant and upright men."[4]

It was not the first time Roosevelt had condemned brutality in sports, but it was his clearest and most forthright denunciation. He certainly had not changed his mind about the value of football and remained a strong advocate. Yet he was increasingly sensitive to problems in the sport. Men whose opinions he trusted were telling him that something had to be done. He was also starting to think of football not merely as a fan, but also as a father—he had four boys, and the older ones were already playing the game. "I am delighted to have you play football," he wrote to the oldest, Ted, when he was a student at Groton in 1903. "But the very things that make it a good game make it a rough game, and there is always the chance of your being laid up."[5] Roosevelt never would support the elimination of football, but he began to recognize that the sport had to confront its worst abuses.

WHEN ROOSEVELT SPOKE to his former classmates in Cambridge, he was not just another voice in a debate that stretched back to his own student days. Instead, he was the president of the United States. William McKinley had tapped Roosevelt to run as his vice presidential candidate on the Republican ticket in 1900, figuring that a newly minted war hero and a proven vote-getter in New York would provide an electoral boost. Roosevelt worked hard for the ticket, almost losing his voice during the campaign and confessing that he felt like "a football man who has gone stale."[6] Yet with the younger man's help, McKinley secured a second term. He did not live to see much of it, however. On September 6, 1901, the anarchist Leon Czolgosz shot him in Buffalo, New York. McKinley lingered for a little more than a week and finally succumbed on September 14.

The day before McKinley passed away, Roosevelt hiked up Mount Marcy, whose peak is the highest point in the state of New York. Roosevelt did not merely preach about the benefits of the strenuous life to others—he was trying to live it himself. On his descent from the top, a messenger from Buffalo found him. Roosevelt rushed to McKinley's deathbed, on a journey that concluded with his taking the oath of office. Like John Tyler, Millard Fillmore, Andrew Johnson, and Chester Arthur before him, he had become an accidental president—a man who had ascended to the highest office in the land without having been elected to it directly.

Shortly after his swearing-in, Roosevelt worried that Americans would frown on his recreational enthusiasms. "I am going to curb my desire for hunting," he said. "I do not want the people to get the idea that they have a sporting President."[7] Roosevelt took promises seriously, but he violated this one often. From time to time, he certainly tried to downplay his love of sports. He had a wall built around a tennis court at the White House to prevent gawkers—or worse, newspaper photographers—from seeing him play. "I am fond of tennis, but I am not a great tennis player at all and would not care to be taken in tennis costume," he once wrote.[8] Yet this was an effort to control public perception, rather than an attempt to reduce his participation. Roosevelt had several dozen tennis partners, nicknamed the "tennis cabinet." Americans may have lacked photos of Roosevelt in tennis shorts, but they understood that they had a sporting president. Contrary to Roosevelt's fears, they seemed to like it rather than resent it.

As president, Roosevelt camped in Yellowstone and Yosemite. He hunted wolves in Oklahoma and bears in Colorado. Inside the White House, he received lessons in jujitsu from Japanese instructors. He also continued to box. During a bout with Lieutenant Dan Tyler Moore, a naval aide, Roosevelt took "a hot one" to his head. The blow ruptured a blood vessel in his left eye. His vision immediately blurred. Over time, it vanished. For the remainder of his term in office, he kept the injury a secret, even from Moore.[9] Roosevelt endured it without complaint, precisely the way he thought college football players should deal with their own scrapes. It was a wound manfully given and manfully received. Roosevelt's "extraordinary constitution" allowed him to become "the most intensely active man in America," wrote one admiring journalist—who happened to be none other than Needham, in a lengthy profile for *McClure's*.[10]

Most of the time, the actual business of the presidency occupied Roosevelt. His administration launched antitrust actions against railroads. Congress approved one of his favorite projects, the construction of a canal across Panama. He appointed Oliver Wendell Holmes, Jr., to the Supreme Court. He settled a coal strike. "You have made a very good start in life," joked Henry Cabot Lodge on Roosevelt's forty-sixth birthday, in 1904. "Your friends have great hopes for you when you grow up."[11] A week later, Roosevelt won the presidential election, capturing about 56 percent of the popular vote. He became the first accidental president to win an election on his own.

THE PRESIDENCY MADE Roosevelt proficient in the art of negotiation and compromise. During the summer of 1905, he mediated a peace accord between Japan and Russia. The two nations had gone to war in East Asia, with Japan emerging as the clear victor. Treaty talks took place in Portsmouth, New Hampshire. Japan went into the discussions with aggressive demands for financial and territorial concessions. Roosevelt's main achievement was to moderate Japan's ambitions, making it possible for Russia to accept terms. The next year, Roosevelt won the Nobel Peace Prize for his efforts. He was the sixth recipient of the award as well as the first American to win it.

Roosevelt brought his diplomatic skills to bear on other disputes, including football. He would need them, because the public seemed less willing to accept the game's casualty rate. Following the Spanish-American War, the sport remained as popular as ever. Yet standards of public health had improved. With this shift came the notion that just as diseases were preventable, so were physical injuries, whether received on assembly lines or athletic fields. The prevention of avoidable injuries became a priority. Albert G. Spalding, co-founder of the sporting goods company, began to sell protective gear for the nose and shins. In the early 1900s, the so-called head harness, a forerunner to the football helmet, went on the market.[12] Many players refused to wear this equipment, but these holdouts soon found themselves in the minority. This altered the aesthetics of football in a way that highlighted the game's

violence. For a generation, critics had compared football to gladiatorial combat. When players put on their armor, they looked the
part. Like Christians who protested the slaughter in Roman coli-
seums, politicians waded into the football debate: In 1905, South
Dakota legislators passed a bill to disqualify players who deliberately inflicted injuries.[13]

This obviously did not go far enough for prohibitionists
such as Charles Eliot. Yet Eliot must have sensed that perceptions about football were changing and that the sport was newly
vulnerable. He chose the occasion of his report on the 1903–04
school year, released at the start of 1905, to launch his most sustained attack on football. Although his words first appeared in
a document prepared for Harvard's overseers, they were widely
republished under a provocative headline: THE EVILS OF FOOT-
BALL. Eliot made the strongest case he could muster: "The risks
of football are exaggerated and unreasonable," he wrote, because
the sport so often resulted in players who suffered injuries that
led to "permanent weakness." As physical training, football was
not useful: "The mental qualities of the big, brawny athlete are
almost certain to be inferior to those of slighter, quicker-witted
men whose moral ideals are at least as high as his." These were
important and provocative claims, but Eliot was just warming up.
He soon arrived at his "main objection" to football: its "moral
quality," by which he meant its immorality. He despised "coaching from the side-lines," apparently because it was unfair. He also
believed the game's rules were unenforceable and therefore sus-
pect. And then there was the roughness: "disabling opponents by
kneeing and kicking, and by heavy blows on the head and par-
ticularly about the eyes, nose, and jaw." Worst of all, to Eliot the
pacifist, was how football resembled war: "The common justifica-
tion offered for these hateful conditions is that football is a fight;
and that its strategy and ethics are those of war." He despised its

promotion of "ruse, stratagem, and deceit" as well as the way in which "new tricks are always desirable, as surprises." Moreover, the strong preyed on the weak. No sport can be honorable if it embraces "the barbarous ethics of warfare."[14]

Eliot's words energized football's foes, but also inspired its defenders to speak out. A former Harvard player said that Eliot was severe simply because Yale kept winning the annual game. Michigan coach Fielding Yost pointed to Camp's *Football Facts and Figures*, published a decade earlier, as the only defense the sport needed.[15] The view from New Haven was a predictable blend of amusement and irritation. "Among the graduates [of Yale] there were many views expressed privately, but few for publication," noted the *Boston Globe*. Walter Camp refused to engage in a debate: "Yes, I have read Pres. Eliot's report. I would not care to discuss it."[16]

Roosevelt had no patience for Eliot's critique. "I think Harvard will be doing the baby act if she takes any such foolish course as President Eliot advises!" he scoffed in a letter.[17] He would say nothing so harsh about Harvard's president in public, though he did try to provide a balance to Eliot's rhetoric. Roosevelt's decision to bring up football at the alumni dinner was calculated: He had passed up opportunities to raise the subject in speeches at Clark University, College of the Holy Cross, and Williams College.[18] He knew his remarks would carry special weight if he spoke them at his alma mater.

Eliot had invited Roosevelt to stay with him in Cambridge. Protocol demanded nothing less. Yet he did not care for his guest. After the shooting of McKinley, Eliot expressed the hope that the wounded president would cling to life—if only to prevent Roosevelt from succeeding him. "Roosevelt as President would be dangerous," he wrote.[19] Several years earlier, he had written to E. L. Godkin about Roosevelt: "My belief is that he is a thoroughly honest man who wants to be serviceable in his day and generation, although he also wants to get on himself—that is, to hold place and have power. . . . Roosevelt seems to me hot, impulsive, and disinterested."[20]

When Roosevelt stayed with Eliot in 1905, the younger man's behavior violated the older man's sense of decorum. Harvard's chief seethed:

> He appeared very early in the morning, a very warm day in June. He said he was dirty. I showed him to his room. The first thing he did was to pull off his coat, roll it up with his hands, and fling it across the bed so violently it sent a pillow to the floor beyond. The next thing he did was to take a great pistol from his trousers pocket and slam it down on the dresser. After awhile he came rushing downstairs, as if his life depended on it, and as I stood at the foot of the stairs I said, "Now, you are taking breakfast with me?" "Oh, no," came the reply, "I promised Bishop [William] Lawrence I would breakfast with him—and good gracious! (clapping his right hand to his side) I've forgotten my gun!" Now he knew that it was against the law in Massachusetts to carry that pistol, and yet he carried it. Very lawless; a very lawless mind![21]

Shortly after the speech at Harvard, Roosevelt took up his summer residence at Oyster Bay, which he preferred to Washington. From there he continued to perform his presidential duties, most notably through his mediation of the peace talks between Japan and Russia. Yet his mind occasionally turned to football. In August, he wrote to Eliot about his son Ted, who was preparing for his freshman year at Harvard. "He is not an athlete of the first or even the second caliber; but I suppose he will try for the freshman eleven this fall, with the hope of becoming a substitute or something of that kind."[22]

. . . .

A MONTH LATER, still at Oyster Bay, Roosevelt received a letter from Endicott Peabody, an old friend from college who had worked with Walter Camp on the committee that had produced *Football Facts and Figures*. Peabody was a cousin of Roosevelt's first wife. He had served as an usher at the wedding. Following graduation, he had gone to seminary and traveled to Tombstone, Arizona, to oversee the construction of an Episcopal church. An athletic man, he started a baseball team in the shadow of the O.K. Corral. After six months in the West, he returned to Massachusetts, where he founded Groton School for Boys with the help of J. P. Morgan and others. Peabody rooted his academy in the principles of Muscular Christianity. For nearly sixty years, the man who became known as "the Rector" would serve as Groton's headmaster, educating children from many of the country's wealthiest families. Roosevelt sent his own boys there. They despised it, but their father was oblivious to their sentiments. Roosevelt held his friend in high esteem, especially on questions having to do with education.[23]

Peabody's three-page letter arrived about two weeks after Russia and Japan had signed their armistice agreement. "At a time when your powers are being tried to the utmost, I hesitate to do anything to add to your burden," said the note. Yet their mutual love of athletics compelled him to write. "The teaching of football at the universities is dishonest," he wrote. It encouraged trickery and cheating and therefore threatened to instill the wrong lessons. "You and I believe in the game, and in its beneficial effects upon boys and young men when it is carried on fairly," he wrote. Then Peabody urged Roosevelt to spark "a complete revolution" by summoning the coaches of Harvard, Princeton, and Yale "and persuade them to undertake to teach men to play football honestly." Roosevelt was in a unique position to improve the game: "You are the one man, so far as I know, who could accomplish this without much effort."[24] Roosevelt responded immediately: "I agree with you absolutely," he wrote.[25]

Roosevelt left Oyster Bay on Saturday, September 30 and returned to Washington. Planning the football summit became one of his first orders of business. He wrote to Walter Camp, inviting him to the White House for a meeting on Monday, October 9. He had known Camp from their earlier correspondence, which eventually led Roosevelt to invite Camp to visit Oyster Bay in 1901.[26] Yet the letter to Yale's coach was formal. "I want to talk over certain football matters with you, and I very earnestly hope that you will be able to come."[27] He requested that Camp bring another man from Yale and added that he was also inviting Edwin H. Nichols and William T. Reid of Harvard as well as John B. Fine and Arthur T. Hildebrand of Princeton. The note was short, both in length and on details. The recipients would have surmised that Roosevelt did not mean to discuss rosters or punting techniques, but the president's language nevertheless was vague.

All week long, the president stayed busy. In and out of cabinet meetings, he discussed railroad rates, postal appointments, and Chinese immigration. Yet football weighed on his mind, in part because of Ted's desire to go out for the first-year team at Harvard. "Ted is too small to make the freshman eleven, but I suppose he will try for it," wrote the president to a friend.[28] In a note to Ted, he praised his son's willingness to show "that in athletics you mean business up to the extent of your capacity."[29] Yet his language was unusually guarded. Roosevelt did not want to place too much pressure on Ted, who faced enough difficulties on campus simply by being his son. An early version of the paparazzi stalked him from the moment he set foot in Cambridge. "I am inclined to tell him, if he sees any man taking a photograph of him, to run up and smash the camera," wrote the president.[30] In time, Ted made the freshman team, to his father's pleasant surprise.

The week progressed with meetings on everything from

meatpacking to the Panama Canal. Football almost certainly came up on Thursday, when Roosevelt played tennis with Robert Bacon, his old friend from Harvard—the football star who had become his assistant secretary of state, serving under John Hay, the secretary of state who originally had come to the capital with Abraham Lincoln. ("Unless the Secretary has real reasons to keep you between 4 & 6, I guess I'll make it a 'command' for tennis between those hours!" wrote Roosevelt to Bacon that morning.)[31] On Friday, Roosevelt asked George Gray, a federal judge who had served as a Democratic senator from Delaware, to join the football summit. In doing so, Roosevelt revealed more about his intentions than he had to Camp and the others. "I want to take up the football situation and try to get the game played on a thoroughly clean basis," he wrote.[32] (Gray did not attend.) Roosevelt continued to work through Saturday. On Sunday, he wrote a few letters but otherwise took the day off. He and Edith went for a long ride around Washington.

Roosevelt's typical day at the White House started with breakfast around eight-thirty in the morning. Then the president focused on correspondence for an hour or two, until callers began to arrive for their appointments. On October 9, Roosevelt wrote to son Kermit at Groton: "Today I see the football men of Harvard, Yale, and Princeton, to try to get them to come to a gentleman's agreement not to have mucker play." He went on to note that Kermit's younger brothers, ages eleven and seven, had different feelings about the game. "Archie is playing football with much zeal. Quentin as yet does not care for any sport in which he is likely to get hurt."[33] Meetings consumed the rest of his morning, followed by a reception for the justices of the Supreme Court. At 1:30 P.M., Roosevelt entered the White House dining room for his meal with the football men.

Roosevelt probably took an immediate interest in Reid, Harvard's twenty-six-year-old coach, hired earlier in the year. Roosevelt was a loyal Harvard man, and he would have wanted to size up the new coach, whose seven-thousand-dollar salary was considerably higher than any professor's and almost as much as Eliot's. Reid was the son of a onetime president of the University of California, in Berkeley. His father had gone on to run a preparatory school south of San Francisco. When Camp had surveyed players and educators about football in the 1890s, the elder Reid wrote back, recommending that the sport be "modified or replaced by one less violent."[34] Camp did not publish this statement in *Football Facts and Figures* and he almost certainly did not make the connection between that response, which was one of many, and the young Harvard coach. Yet Reid was no stranger to Camp. Seven years earlier, as a Harvard sophomore, Reid had scored two touchdowns against Yale, giving Harvard a rare victory over its rival. Reid had become an instant star, with his picture printed in *Harper's Weekly*. As a coach, he was equally determined. "I don't see how a man can help feeling that hardly anything is more important than to beat Yale," he wrote in his diary.[35] Although Reid had spent the morning of the football summit climbing to the top of the Washington Monument, tourism was not the only item on his agenda. He also reviewed scouting reports on Yale's defense, for a game that was still more than seven weeks in the future.

At lunch, Roosevelt sat beside Camp. The other men arranged themselves around the table. Roosevelt had hoped that William Howard Taft would attend. At the time, Taft was the secretary of war. Eventually he would succeed Roosevelt as president. He was also an alumnus of Yale, and Roosevelt thought that his presence would balance his own Harvard loyalties. But Taft was not available. In his place came Elihu Root, the secretary of state, who had attended Hamilton College. In addition to the college men Roosevelt had specifically invited, Camp brought along John E. Owsley, who helped coach Yale's team.

Roosevelt opened the conversation. "Football is on trial," he said. "Because I believe in the game, I want to do all I can to save it. And so I have called you all down here to see whether you won't all agree to abide by both the letter and spirit of the rules, for that will help."[36] He probably repeated some of what he had said at his class reunion a few months earlier. Then he provided examples of what he considered crooked play by Harvard, Princeton, and Yale in previous seasons. He discussed the case of a team's coach urging his players to commit fouls when the referees could not see them.[37] Roosevelt said that just as cheating at cards was disgraceful, so was cheating at football. Both deserved punishment. He insisted that players and coaches must conduct themselves honorably, rather than with an eye toward securing an unfair advantage.[38] Roosevelt said he "deplored" the current state of affairs and "wanted to see if there was not some way in which the feeling between the colleges could be improved and the training of the players made more effective in the right way."[39]

The men from Princeton and Yale became defensive, refusing to confess any unfair play on the part of their teams. Camp, according to Reid, "was very slippery and did not allow himself to be pinned down to anything."[40] At some point, the conversation probably turned toward concrete steps that the colleges might take to reduce injuries and the game's overall violence. They almost certainly discussed proposals to create more open play. Many ideas were in circulation, discussed by players as they walked on campus and debated by sports columnists in newspapers. Camp supported a rule that would increase the distance necessary for a first down from five yards to ten—a change he had not been able to push through his rules committee. For several years, John Heisman had lobbied for the introduction of the forward pass, which he had seen performed illegally in 1895. Camp strongly opposed this idea.

No transcript of Roosevelt's conversation with the football men exists. What is known about it must be gleaned from a handful of sources, such as Reid's personal diary, plus reasonable speculation.

The meeting suffered no leaks to the press, either. The participants most likely understood that they were not to discuss the specifics of the meeting with journalists. A few hours before their lunch, in fact, Roosevelt had penned a note to Gifford Pinchot, his chief of the forest service. The president expressed frustration that details from a private meeting had found their way into the press. He called it a "gross impropriety" and announced a desire to identify the informant.[41]

At the time, Roosevelt was making famous the notion of the "bully pulpit"—another term he coined, which refers to how a president can use rhetoric to move national opinion. His speech at Harvard was an example of this. His approach with Camp and the others was different. It involved quiet persuasion rather than public bombast. It was closer in spirit to a saying that Roosevelt also popularized: "Speak softly and carry a big stick." In the closed confines of the White House, Roosevelt did not threaten his guests or their sport in any way. Yet it would have been impossible for Camp and the others to come away without a sense that Roosevelt expected them to take steps to improve football. Otherwise, they risked losing it—not because Roosevelt would ban it, which he had no authority and even less desire to do, but because they would have abandoned their most important ally in the fight against the prohibitionists.

The meeting lasted about two hours, with one interruption when the president had to attend to other matters. It concluded on the porch. Toward the end, Roosevelt made a request. He asked his guests to issue a joint statement about their intentions. Camp drafted it after leaving the White House, and the others approved it on their train ride north. That evening in New York, Camp wrote to Roosevelt: "I take pleasure in sending you herewith the results of the little meeting you were good enough to bring about today." He asked for Roosevelt to review the statement and said it would not be released without the president's approval. The statement was signed by all six football men:

At a meeting with the President of the United States it was agreed that we consider an honorable obligation existed to carry out in letter and in spirit the rules of the game of football relating to roughness, holding, and foul play and the active coaches of our Universities being present with us pledge themselves to so regard it and to do their utmost to carry out these obligations.[42]

The statement reached Roosevelt on Wednesday. The president immediately sent a Western Union telegram to Camp: "Most heartily approve of memorandum," he wrote. "Hope you will make memorandum public at once exactly in form you have sent it to me and with the signatures."[43] Camp's words soon made their way into the press. Roosevelt followed his telegram to Camp with a short letter. "I cannot tell you how pleased I am at the way you have taken hold. Now that the matter is in your hands I am more than content to abide by whatever you do."[44]

IN TRUTH, THE football coaches' statement did not say much. Roosevelt would have recognized this. Yet it expressed a commitment to fair play—one that Roosevelt could expect them to uphold. They were not making a general and unenforceable pledge to the public, but rather a personal commitment to the president of the United States.

Separately, Roosevelt forwarded a letter to Camp. It came from Spencer Borden, the head of the Fall River Bleachery in Massachusetts. Borden had read a newspaper article on the football summit and decided to write to the president directly. He had a strong connection to the game. Two of his sons had played for Harvard teams and his son-in-law was Bernie Trafford, who had participated in the first flying-wedge momentum play in 1892.

"A simple change in the rules would open up the whole game," wrote Borden. "Make it necessary to gain 10 yards in 3 downs, allow the forward pass, and mass plays where brute force alone counts would be abolished."[45] Roosevelt did not say so, but in passing on Borden's letter, he clearly wanted Camp to consider these ideas. Camp, however, showed little interest. He wrote back to Roosevelt, repeating that he favored only the ten-yard rule. Camp argued that the other proposals would not yield the results that reformers sought.[46] Roosevelt did not reply.

The press had some fun with Roosevelt's efforts. "Having ended the war in the Far East [and] grappled with the railroad rate question," quipped the *New York Times*, "President Roosevelt today took up another question of vital interest to the American people. He started a campaign for reform in football."[47] As Roosevelt was about to learn, reforming football would prove just as tricky, in its way, as bringing peace to Japan and Russia.

In the immediate aftermath of the football summit, Roosevelt thought he had done what he could for the game. "Just at present I do not see what else to say or do in the matter," he wrote to Nicholas Murray Butler, the president of Columbia.[48] Butler was a critic of football. Roosevelt knew this, which is why he tried to assure Butler that he was taking steps to reform the sport. Yet he was almost certainly unaware of how committed Butler was to eliminating football at Columbia. In a letter to Eliot, Butler suggested that he was eager to prohibit the game. "The difficulty in the way of such a course is primarily the fact that Columbia is not one of the institutions whose football teams are usually successful in their more important games, and that it might seem more or less presumptuous for an institution whose students are distinctly in the second rank of football teams to go so far."[49] Without saying so directly, Butler was telling Eliot that the prohibition of football would require Harvard's leadership.

. . . .

THE WEEK AFTER the football summit, Roosevelt embarked on a swing through the southern states. He left by train and returned by ship, with stops in Richmond, Virginia; Tuskegee, Alabama; and New Orleans. It took his mind off football for a while. Upon his return to Washington, however, he received a note from Ted, asking about a visit. "Of course we should be overjoyed to see you," replied Roosevelt, "but I don't want you to leave if it is to interfere with your football. . . . You must not lose the chance of getting into the Yale game."[50] A few days later, Roosevelt wrote again to his son, repeating the hope that Ted would play against Yale. He also expressed fatherly concern: "Though I would not have you fail to play, I sympathize with mother in being glad that after next Saturday your playing will be through." Ted had a history of getting hurt in football games. At Groton, he once broke his collarbone but refused to leave the field until the game was over. Roosevelt was both proud of his boy for exhibiting toughness and worried that he was getting knocked around by bigger students.[51]

As the Roosevelts pondered the Yale game, Eliot plotted to make sure it would be one of the last games of football that Harvard ever played. At least that was what Bill Reid thought. In an unpublished, handwritten manuscript now in the Harvard archives, Reid described how his friend Herbert White had learned that Eliot had persuaded one of Harvard's governing boards—either the overseers or the corporation, he was not sure which—to cast a "secret" vote to abolish football at the school.[52] Apparently the vote was kept from public view with the intention of making it known after the 1905 season. There is in fact no documentary evidence that either board took this step.[53] This means that Reid's claim cannot be confirmed, though it does not necessarily mean he was mistaken. Whatever the truth, Reid believed that White's report was accurate and that the threat to football was real. So he responded accordingly.

White brought the alarming news to Reid on November 3, at ten o'clock in the evening. They huddled with two colleagues, assistant coaches Bill Lewis and Bert Waters. Lewis was the black player who had starred for Harvard in the early 1890s; Waters was the man accused of poking his finger in the eye of a Yale player in 1894, which contributed to the temporary suspension of the annual Harvard-Yale game. The four men decided to take immediate action, traveling downtown to the office of the *Boston Globe*, where they met with night editor Billy Sullivan, a Harvard graduate whom Reid described as "a sports enthusiast, and a clear thinker." The group determined that Reid would write a public letter to the president of the Harvard Graduates' Athletic Association, "stating that the game was dangerous and that many changes should be made in the rules." Sullivan dug out a copy of Eliot's previous criticisms, including, presumably, his remarks on "The Evils of Football" (which the *Globe* had printed earlier in the year). Reid and his conspirators then wrote the letter, taking account of Eliot's objections and even trying to mimic his language. When it was ready, Sullivan prepared it for the next edition of the *Globe* and also sent copies to other newspapers in Boston, New York, and Philadelphia. The next day, the letter appeared in print around the country.[54] "I have become convinced that the game as it is played today has fundamental faults which cannot be removed by any mere technical revision of the rules," wrote Reid. "There is a distinct advantage to be gained from brutality and evasion of the rules. . . . I have come to believe that the game ought to be radically changed." Reid did not mention specifics, only that he would "put a higher premium on skill [and] make mere weight and strength of less value [in order to] produce a more scientific and interesting sport."[55]

The letter attracted wide notice because Reid was a football man who believed in the game, not a lifelong critic who failed to see its value. Reid came in for heavy criticism, especially because Harvard was about to play its two biggest games of the season, first against Penn and then against Yale. "Many thought that it was cry baby stuff and that it was in poor taste on my part to have written it at that particular time," observed Reid. "Through it all the five of us kept our mouths shut as to the reason behind the letter, because we weren't supposed to know about [the secret vote] and could not risk having anyone know why the letter was really written." Their hope was that Reid's letter would cause Eliot's scheme to "backfire."[56]

The letter "burst like a bombshell on the scene," according to Reid. The coach speculated on how the letter would have empowered football's supporters on the Harvard board, even though they had just been outvoted: "Here is Reid," he imagined them saying, "coming out and demanding the very changes that will satisfy President Eliot's objections—all without knowledge on his part of our impending action. Why not defer publishing the vote until we see what his committee accomplishes?" Reid believed that the letter bought him time. "Our ruse worked," he concluded.[57]

Yet new challenges loomed. The first test arrived a week later, during the game against Penn in Philadelphia on November 11. The night before, after Harvard had practiced, Penn tried to give itself a literal home-field advantage by soaking its football turf with water. The next day, its players put on shoes with oversized cleats. This helped them gain traction in the mud. Harvard's angry players had to make do with their ordinary shoes—and all they could manage was a loss, by a score of 12–6. Reid considered Penn's behavior an act of unsportsmanlike treachery. Two decades would pass before the schools played football again. Something else caught the attention of the press, however: Harvard's Bartol Parker slugged Penn's center. The referee ejected Parker, who claimed in futility that he had been hit first. As Parker stepped off the field, Reid asked him what had happened. "The Penn player hit me in the balls, not once but several times," replied Parker. "When the Penn center did it again I socked him."[58]

When Roosevelt learned of the fight—all he knew was that Parker had been tossed from the game—he summoned Reid to the White House. Reid attended a lunch that included Mrs. Roosevelt, Robert Bacon, German ambassador Baron Speck von Sternberg, and several others. After the meal, Roosevelt turned to von Sternberg. "Will you please go out on the porch for a few minutes? There are cigars and liqueurs there and make yourself at home. I want to have a talk with Mr. Reid." The president and the coach then walked from the dining room to Roosevelt's office. As they paced down the hallway, Roosevelt put his hands behind his back and spoke: "After the agreement we made here earlier [i.e., the statement that Camp had drafted and Reid had signed], it doesn't look too well to have Harvard the first college to break that agreement, so I thought I'd ask you down and find out how it happened." Reid said that he was grateful for a chance to explain. He recounted the incident, including the hit below the belt. When he was done, Roosevelt said nothing. The silence made Reid uneasy, so he broke it. "Mr. President, what would you have done under similar circumstances?" he asked. Roosevelt gritted his teeth and replied: "It wouldn't be good policy for me to state." This exchange, according to Reid, "closed the incident."[59]

MEANWHILE, THE FOOTBALL season continued. The freshman game between Ted's Harvard team and Yale took place on November 18. Ted weighed only about 130 pounds. He was small, but wiry and energetic. A writer for the *New York World* called him "a chip off the old block" who "worked like a demon."[60] Yet he could do nothing to prevent Yale from beating Harvard thoroughly. To add injury to insult, he was battered personally. His father must have loved the way Ted shrugged it off in a letter: "I was not seriously hurt at all. Just shaken up and bruised. I broke my nose." Several reports in the press suggested that Yale had gone after Ted because of his size. Ted called this "all bosh" and asked his parents to consider the source: "Of course I knew all the rotten talk would come out in the papers, but it could not be helped." Ted insisted that Yale had played "a clean, straight game." There were no hard feelings between the rivals, and the two teams went out for drinks together that evening.[61]

A week later, Harvard and Yale's varsity teams met in Cambridge, playing in front of forty-three thousand fans. Never before had so many people attended a football game. As usual, Yale won, but Harvard put up a tough fight. The final score was 6–0, and many fans felt the result could have gone either way. "The game was marked by clean, healthy football," commented the *New York Times*. The newspaper credited "the earnest words of President Roosevelt in behalf of cleaner sport and the general feeling that brutality must be eliminated."[62] Roosevelt was satisfied by what he read. "It seems to me," he wrote, "that this year Harvard, Yale, and Princeton have played absolutely straight and clean games."[63]

Before long, however, Roosevelt learned about an incident that had enraged Reid. In the first half, Harvard's Francis Burr called for a fair catch. Rather than let him have it, Yale's James Quill drove his fist into Burr's face, smashing his nose. Burr fell down, half conscious. The crowd hissed its disapproval, and a prominent booster urged Reid to remove his men from the field. Reid kept his team in the game but was astonished when the referee, Paul Dashiell, did not disqualify Quill. Years later, Reid commented that "the picture of Quill hitting Burr was indelibly etched in my memory."[64] He thought that the failure to call a penalty on Quill may have been the decisive factor in Harvard's loss. When the game was over, an irate Reid told Dashiell that he would never again preside over a Harvard game. Dashiell was probably the best-known referee in the country as well as a member of the football rules committee headed by Camp. Yet Reid's vow turned out to be true: Dashiell was done as a referee of games that included Harvard.

Once more, Roosevelt asked Reid to come to Washington. Dashiell was on the faculty of the U.S. Naval Academy, an institution over which Roosevelt had direct control. As fate would have it, he was up for a new appointment, making him especially vulnerable to Roosevelt's whims. When Dashiell learned that Reid was going to visit the White House, he begged the coach not to ruin "the ambition of his life."[65] Reid replied that he would convey the facts of the case. In Washington, Reid offered a blunt opinion of Dashiell's failure to make a necessary call. "I don't know whether that kind of man is fit to teach the boys at Annapolis," said Roosevelt.[66] Later, the president asked Dashiell to explain the Burr-Quill incident. The referee, now deeply worried, apologized profusely in a letter. "I regret the injury that it has done to the game, now in so critical a condition," he wrote.[67] The real purpose of Dashiell's letter—the pleading between the lines—was to preserve his livelihood as a professor. Six months would go by before Roosevelt approved his promotion. In the meantime, Roosevelt counted on him to work with Reid and support the reform of football.[68]

THE BURR-QUILL CONTROVERSY may have taken place in the most anticipated game of the season, but it was hardly the worst case of violence to take place on a football field that day. Teams from a pair of smaller schools, Union College and New York University, squared off in the Bronx. At one point, Union's Harold Moore, a sophomore, wrapped his arms around an NYU ball carrier. As the two men fell to the ground, another player from Union joined the tackle. His knee apparently struck Moore in the head. Moore lost consciousness. Doctors from both teams ran onto the field. A spectator drove Moore to Fordham Hospital, but it did no good. Four hours later, he was dead from a cerebral hemorrhage.[69]

NYU chancellor Henry MacCracken described the fatality as an accident: "a simple collision of one member of the New York University team with the opposing force."[70] Yet he also saw Moore's death as possibly preventable. His initial move was to stoke the anti-football movement. An ordained Presbyterian minister, he would play a leading role in creating the conditions for football's forthcoming transformation.

On the night Moore died, MacCracken cabled Eliot and urged him to convene a conference of college leaders "to undertake the reform or abolition of football."[71] He believed that the prestige of Harvard and Eliot was essential to success. At the same time, he understood the powerful sway of alumni—MacCracken was an accomplished fund-raiser who had secured financial contributions to NYU from the likes of Jay Gould. The death of Moore had taken place on Ohio Field, so named because the men who had paid for its construction were donors from Ohio. MacCracken had solicited their gifts. Presumably they would not be enthusiastic about football's prohibition. He may have mentioned the word *abolition* in his message to Eliot, but he was probably more in favor of a meaningful reform than an outright ban.

The *Nation* applauded MacCracken in one of its most vehement editorials yet. Football was "evil" and "a grave menace." It did not deserve a correction, even one whose "inspiration is from the White House." The sport, it concluded, must be eliminated once and for all. The publication trumpeted a quote from Shailer Mathews, the dean of the divinity school at the University of Chicago: "Football today is a social obsession—a boy-killing, education prostituting, gladiatorial sport." The magazine also demanded specific action: "A few schools and small colleges have abolished football, but its death-blow must come from such an institution as Harvard or Columbia."[72]

Columbia obliged. Over Thanksgiving weekend, while most of its students were away, the school abandoned its football program. The administration blasted Walter Camp's rules committee as "self-perpetuating, irresponsible, impervious to public opinion, and culpable in refusing to heed the increasingly dangerous character of the game."[73] Union College, reeling from Moore's death, followed Columbia's example. So did Northwestern. On the west coast, California and Stanford moved to replace football with rugby. The president of the University of Chicago, William Harper, wrote to Roosevelt and asked him to impose regulations on football. Roosevelt refused, but also tried to steer a middle course—he did not want Chicago to quit the game as well. "I am not," he wrote back, "undertaking the regulation of football. . . . I believe in the game and want to keep it, and I think much of the outburst about it hysterical; but on the other hand I think it cannot be kept unless there is a very resolute effort made to cut out the abuses."[74] Meanwhile, in public view, Roosevelt continued to play the part of a football fan. On December 2, he traveled to Princeton and had lunch with Woodrow Wilson, who had become president of the university. Then the two men watched the Army and Navy game together. Roosevelt came away pleased: "I saw West Point and Annapolis play and admired the way in which the umpire and the referee did their duty," he wrote.[75]

A day after responding to Chicago's Harper, Roosevelt tried to engage Eliot. He wrote to his old nemesis, encouraging him to join a productive reform effort, perhaps involving the selection of referees. The letter was typed, but included a handwritten postscript: "Don't you think there is a certain amount of hysteria in the present excitement about football?"[76] Eliot, of course, did not think that better referees would improve the sport—and he probably took exception to Roosevelt's use of the word *hysteria*. His only proposal, offered privately in a letter to Roosevelt rather than in a public forum where it might have made a difference, was to suggest that "intercollegiate football should be prohibited for a time."[77] Roosevelt wanted nothing to do with it. "I do not agree with you that the game should be stopped," he wrote back. Then he scolded Eliot for his role in the controversy: "I further think that one reason why [football's abuses] are not remedied is that so many of our people whose voices would be potent in reforming the game, try to abolish it instead."[78]

Eliot's reluctance to cooperate with Roosevelt is understandable. His refusal to heed the call of MacCracken and the *Nation*, however, was stranger. He questioned whether a special conference on football could accomplish anything. College presidents, he said, "certainly cannot reform football, and I doubt if by themselves they can abolish it."[79] Reform was impossible, he believed, because it would mean working with the rules committee dominated by Walter Camp—a man whom he despised. In Eliot's view, Camp was "directly responsible for the degradation and ruin of the game." He was "deficient in moral sensibility—a trouble not likely to be cured at his age."[80]

When it came to higher education, Eliot was a true visionary. In this case, however, his vision failed him. If he had answered MacCracken's plea, the history of football might have taken a different route. Eliot possibly could have delivered a lethal blow to its status as an intercollegiate sport. His assumption that there was no way to work around Camp was wrong. Roosevelt, Reid, and Mac-Cracken were about to prove it.

In the wake of Eliot's rebuff, MacCracken jumped into action. If Harvard would not sponsor a conference, then he himself would put one on at NYU. This was far from ideal, but it was also better than nothing. He sent out nineteen invitations to schools that had played football for at least a decade. Representatives from thirteen showed up on December 8. None of the participants came from the three major programs that Roosevelt had gathered at the White House. Yet their ranks were not without prestige. They included Columbia, which was a second-rate football school but a first-rate university, and Rutgers, which in 1869 had played in what is recognized as the first intercollegiate football game.

The meeting began with a bang, as Columbia proposed that "the present game of football as played under existing rules be abolished."[81] Five colleges voted in favor: Columbia, NYU, Rochester, Stevens Institute, and Union. Eight preferred an attempt to reform the sport and opposed the measure: Fordham, Haverford, Lafayette, Rutgers, Swarthmore, Syracuse, Wesleyan, and the U.S. Military Academy at West Point. So the reformers prevailed, barely. If only two of them had switched sides, football might have suffered a ruinous setback. The conference adjourned without making any specific recommendations on what reform would mean. Yet the colleges did agree to meet again at the end of the month, after inviting more schools to join them. They felt that they had built momentum and meant to take advantage of it.

Over the next few weeks, several factions fought to control the future of football. MacCracken hoped his conference would supplant Camp's committee. "It is the Russian people against the Russian grand dukes," said NYU's chancellor, in a reference to the revolution then erupting on the other side of the world.[82] Camp wanted to protect the authority of the governing body that he had dominated for a generation. He supported only incremental reform, and probably would have been satisfied if his committee had approved a single rule change, the one involving three downs and ten yards. In the past, Camp usually got his way. This time, however, things would be different.

REID'S PUBLIC LETTER pledging the reform of football may have been a ploy written under the duress of a perceived emergency, but it was more than an empty gesture. Reid made good on its central promise and consulted with Harvard's athletic committee. They prepared a large slate of rule changes. They also made plans to get them past Camp's committee, whose membership including both Reid and Dashiell. Working with Dashiell, whom Roosevelt had made newly sensitive to the cause of football reform, Reid managed to keep the committee from taking any action. "Have hands full to prevent abolition of game here [at Harvard]," he cabled Camp on December 19.[83] He managed to prevent Camp's committee from taking any action before December 28.

This was the same day that MacCracken had scheduled his own meeting. Harvard, Princeton, and Yale continued to stay away, but what MacCracken lacked in quality he made up for in quantity: Representatives from sixty-eight institutions attended. Most of his delegates came from small schools in the Northeast, but several traveled great distances, hailing from Colorado College, the University of Minnesota, and the University of Texas. Over the course of nine hours, MacCracken's upstart organization voted to establish its own committee on football rules and to seek a merger with Camp's group. If this proved impossible, the committee would establish a separate set of rules that would make football a more open game and cut down on its violence.[84]

This corresponded perfectly with the aims of Roosevelt and Reid. Harvard's athletic committee already had told Reid to seek a compromise. It demanded that both groups accept a series of rule changes, including Camp's proposal for first downs but also much more. If this was not possible, Harvard would discontinue its football program. "There will be no football at Harvard," warned Reid. "If Harvard throws out the game, many other colleges will follow Harvard's lead, and an important blow will be dealt to the game."[85]

For some, this would have been just fine. John Owsley, the Yale coach who had attended the meeting at the White House with Camp, wanted Yale to break with Harvard anyway. "I am very anxious to see Yale drop Harvard quietly in football," he wrote to Camp. "It is no pleasure for us at least not for me to have beaten Harvard and to afterwards hear the lies and whining of their players and some of their graduates."[86] He proposed scrapping the annual Harvard-Yale game and hosting a western team, by which he probably meant Chicago or Michigan.

Yet this was not realistic. Harvard and Yale were the biggest rivals in the country. Football had challenges—but none that eliminating its marquee event would solve. No record of Camp's reply to Owsley exists. The father of American football almost certainly understood the value of keeping Harvard in the sport. The equation was simple: Yale wanted to preserve football and football needed Harvard to keep playing. Camp knew he would have to compromise.

As Reid deployed both persuasion and threat to bring the rule-making bodies together, he enjoyed Roosevelt's hidden support. "If I can," said Roosevelt, "quietly and without appearing in print help I shall be glad to do so."[87] He pressured Dashiell to support Reid's maneuvering.[88] He also encouraged General Albert L. Mills, the superintendent at West Point—and a man who was required to answer to the commander in chief—to get behind reform.[89]

On January 12, 1906, Reid quit Camp's rules committee and joined the new group. After some initial wrangling, in which Camp tried to preserve his authority, the two bodies agreed to merge. They appointed officers, with Reid winding up as secretary, an influential post. Camp was an ordinary member of the panel, just a single voice among fourteen. He quickly realized that he had been outmaneuvered. He did not like it, but there was no alternative. The new organization called itself the Intercollegiate Athletic Association of the United States. Within a few years, it would rechristen itself as the National Collegiate Athletic Association, or NCAA. In the weeks ahead, it would transform football, setting the sport on an irreversible course toward its modern form.

Chapter Ten

THE AIR WAR

W hen Army kicked off to Notre Dame at three o'clock in the afternoon on November 1, 1913, none of the five thousand spectators who had gathered for the game at West Point anticipated what they were about to see. Most of them expected Army to roll over its unknown opponent from somewhere west of Ohio. The headline in the *New York Times* that morning captured the general sentiment: "Army Wants Big Score." The subhead declared that the cadets were "Confident of Victory."[1]

Army certainly had high hopes. It had already tallied four wins under its first-year coach, Lieutenant Charles Daly, a former Harvard football standout. There was talk of an undefeated season. A few people close to the program were disappointed that a knee injury would keep a promising young back named Dwight Eisenhower from taking the field, but they felt good about Daly and the success he had already achieved—the next year, in fact, Army would win a national championship. Amid these accomplishments and ambitions, the game against Notre Dame in 1913 was almost an afterthought. Army had not played a non-eastern college in more than a decade. It had agreed to host Notre Dame largely because its schedule had a hole to fill and the little Catholic school was available to fill it.[2]

The game started routinely, as two unfamiliar opponents began to test each other. Army kicked off. Notre Dame tried to rush the ball, gained no ground, and punted. The teams fought for field position. Notre Dame turned over the ball twice on fumbles, but Army failed to capitalize. Daly and his players came to understand that they were not playing pushovers. Even so, their kicking game appeared to be superior. They may have figured that over time they would wear down their opponents and win their fifth game of the season.

Toward the end of the first quarter, however, Notre Dame finally began to move the ball. Its running backs powered their way to Army's 25-yard line. On the next play, quarterback Gus Dorais faked a handoff and dropped back to pass. He put the ball in the air. It spiraled toward Knute Rockne, who sprinted down the left side of the field, wide open. Rockne kept his stride, letting the ball drop over his shoulder and into his hands. A few steps later, he was in the end zone for a touchdown. The pass and catch were flawless. The crowd was stunned. The fans—virtually all of them cheering for West Point—had not seen anything like it before.

Soon enough, they would witness it again. Notre Dame launched football's first grand air war, mixing its running game with a passing attack that West Point did not expect and hardly knew how to defend. By the time it was over, Dorais had thrown seventeen passes. He completed fourteen, including two for touchdowns. Notre Dame had gained 243 yards by passing the ball.[3] The final score signaled a blowout: Notre Dame 35, Army 13. "The Westerners flashed the most sensational football that has been seen in the East this year," gushed the *New York Times*. "The Army players were hopelessly confused and chagrined before Notre Dame's great playing, and their style of old-fashioned close line-smashing play was no match for the spectacular and highly perfected attack of the Indiana collegians."[4] Eisenhower watched from the sidelines. "Everything has gone wrong," he wrote to his girlfriend. "The football team . . . got beaten most gloriously by Notre Dame."[5]

On that day, Notre Dame revolutionized the sport of football. It was by no means the first team to use the forward pass. But it was the first team to take full advantage of the rule changes that went into effect following the controversial 1905 season—and, perhaps more important, the first team to put them on vivid display for a large audience of easterners who had become accustomed to a certain way of playing football. At the time, Roosevelt was touring South America, preparing for his celebrated journey of exploration to the River of Doubt in the unmapped heart of the Amazon. Yet his friend Leonard Wood, who had become U.S. Army chief of staff, saw Notre Dame's spectacle in person—and was "shocked" by the result.[6] The longed-for open game finally had arrived.

Notre Dame's upset of Army would go down in college football lore as one of the greatest games ever played. In addition to proving the potential of a concentrated pass attack, it secured Notre Dame's place in the public mind as a force in football as well as football's place in Notre Dame's own campus culture. The achievement sprang from many sources, such as the school's deep belief in the value of football. In the early part of the century, Notre Dame president John Cavanaugh said that it was better for young men to play football and suffer "a broken collar bone occasionally than to see them dedicated to croquet."[7] The success of the pass also owed a great deal to the innovative thinking of first-year coach Jesse Harper, who had experimented with passing as a coach at Wabash College and relished the opportunity to perform on a bigger stage. When Harper first met Dorais and Rockne in the spring of 1913, he impressed upon them the importance of practice, and urged them to work on the art of passing the ball to a moving receiver and catching it with soft hands. He gave them a few balls and told them to get busy. The two players spent their summer busing tables and emptying trash cans at a hotel in Cedar Point, Ohio, on the shores of Lake Erie. When they had free time, they tossed the ball back and forth, trying to master their technique.[8]

THE REAL STORY of Notre Dame's success, however, began years earlier, when Theodore Roosevelt and his allies orchestrated the merger of Walter Camp's existing rules committee with the new one created by Henry MacCracken's upstart group. Once it happened, Roosevelt pulled back from his advocacy of reform. He wanted the football men to do their work without political interference. He hoped to spur reform, not micromanage the details of football's rulebook. The president considered himself a casual fan of the sport, not an expert who knew its intricacies. He also probably understood that genuine improvements to the game would have to come from the willing adaptations of its participants rather than White House decrees. And although he often reveled in publicity and was a skillful manipulator of his image, he did not want Americans to see him as football's puppeteer. In a letter to Paul Dashiell, Roosevelt urged his recipient to support unspecified "radical innovations" and "radical changes" to the rules—and then instructed Dashiell not to allow the letter's publication.[9] The existence of this directive raises the interesting but unanswerable question of whether Roosevelt's involvement in football reform was even greater than the surviving historical record suggests.

The rule changes approved in the early months of 1906 were indeed radical. They marked football's final break from its rugby origins. Rather than tinkering their way through another off-season, as Camp's rules committee had done for a number of years, the reformers agreed to the game's extreme makeover, along the lines of what Reid and Harvard had insisted upon. They increased the yardage necessary to gain a first down from five to ten. This innovation—the only one that Camp strongly supported—was probably the subject of more discussion than any other. It was indeed important in reestablishing football as a game that featured high-speed end runs rather than a long series of battering-ram line plunges. Yet it was just the first step.

The reformers went on to approve a series of other changes with the express purpose of cutting down on injuries and foul play. They created a neutral zone at the line of scrimmage, which opened a passage between the offensive and defensive lines before the snap. This provided referees with a clear view of a previously hidden space, where players often had slugged each other without repercussion. They limited the number of players who could line up in the backfield to five, in an effort to lessen the effectiveness of momentum plays. They also reduced the length of the game from seventy to sixty minutes (to cut down on fatigue-related injuries), added a referee (to bring an extra pair of eyes to the officiating), and prohibited hurdling (to prevent head and neck injuries when players boosted ballcarriers into the air in desperate bids to gain a couple of yards). They defined unsportsmanlike conduct and personal fouls as significant infractions that would lead to penalties marked in yards as well as automatic expulsions from games.

These were sweeping revisions. Yet they would not have the transformative effect of the most important change of all: the advent of the forward pass. Up to this point, football was a game of running and kicking, not throwing. When teams tried to advance the ball, their plays usually involved handoffs or underhanded, lateral tosses. They simply were not allowed to fling the ball downfield to receivers. This was illegal, and it worked only when referees failed to see what had happened, as in the case of the game John Heisman had witnessed years earlier.

At first, the authors of the forward pass simply wanted to create a new tool for opening the game. Yet they seemed to sense the potential power of the pass to change the fundamentals of the sport. As a result, they imposed strong disincentives on its use. If no player touched a passed ball before it hit the ground, the incompletion resulted not in a loss of down but in a loss of possession—a punishment so severe that it made passing a high-risk option. Other restrictions also limited the effectiveness of the pass. The ball had to cross the line of scrimmage at least five yards away from its snap. Only players who lined up at the extreme ends of the offensive line could catch it, which meant that teams never had more than two eligible receivers on the field. Moreover, a pass could not cross the goal line for a touchdown. Violations of these rules resulted in turnovers, too. To top it off, the ball was still shaped like a watermelon. It was hard to throw well. Because of these restrictions, the forward pass was almost stillborn.

Camp probably had a hand in this. He continued to believe that the forward pass represented a corruption of the sport. Yet he lacked the clout to keep it out of the game entirely and probably did not even try, given that Harvard had made its introduction a nonnegotiable demand. He no longer dominated the sport's legislating body, but he remained a prestigious figure who sincerely believed passing would do nothing to lessen football's injuries. He feared that as receivers streaked across the field, they risked colliding into each other and defenders at full speed. The new committee had appointed Camp editor of football's rulebook, and he almost certainly used this position to limit the effectiveness of passing. Yet the concept gained a toehold.

Harvard's demands provided the catalyst for the forward pass and football's other changes, but Charles W. Eliot remained aloof. He did not participate in any of the new debates surrounding the game and how it should be played in the future. As arguments over the new rules raged, he repeated his shopworn opinions. "The American game of football as now played is wholly unfit for colleges and schools," he wrote. "It is childish to suppose that the athletic authorities which have permitted football to become a brutal, cheating, demoralizing game can be trusted to reform it."[10]

At the University of Wisconsin, frontier historian Frederick Jackson Turner railed against football, calling for its prohibition or at least its suspension, and tried to mobilize administrators and professors against it. On the night of March 27, when a rumor hit campus that football would be banned, hundreds of students took to the streets, chanting "Death to the faculty!" They surrounded Turner's home. The professor faced them on his porch. "When can we have football?" shouted a student. "When you can have a clean game," he yelled back. Turner tried to engage the young men, but they replied with catcalls. Later in the evening, they built a bonfire. The fire department showed up as the mob tried to burn three professors in effigy. The firefighters managed to save the last one. It was labeled "Prof. Turner."[11]

As the 1906 season approached, many coaches and teams did not know what to make of football's rule changes. In September, more than a hundred schools sent representatives to New York for special instruction. Many were skeptical, fearing that the game would become worse rather than better. But Harvard coach Bill Reid insisted that the future of football was at stake. "We have endeavored to reform the game in earnest and adopt measures which will prevent the continuance of the old grinding game," he said. "If the game does not stand the test it will be rooted out completely at Harvard and elsewhere."[12]

When the games finally got under way, teams struggled to achieve ten yards for a first down rather than five. They also experimented with the pass, trying to figure out the strengths and weaknesses of football's new offensive weapon. Many concluded that the risks outweighed the benefits, but most seemed to dabble in it. In the Harvard-Yale game, Yale quarterback Paul Veeder threw the ball to Clarence Alcott, in a play that set up the game-winning touchdown. The result—yet another triumph for Yale—had the ironic effect of costing Reid his job as Harvard's coach. He retired from the sport and became a businessman.[13]

Most fans seemed to approve of the changes. So did many football skeptics. Although one report showed that eleven players died on the gridiron in 1906, including three in college games, this was a statistical improvement from a year earlier.[14] More important, the game was perceived as safer: There were no high-profile deaths or controversies, as with Harold Moore of Union College or the Burr-Quill incident in the Harvard-Yale game. Even Eliot admitted progress, however grudgingly. "The game of foot-ball was somewhat improved by the new rules extorted from its creators and managers by the pressure of public opinion," he wrote in his annual report. It was "more interesting to watch" and there were "fewer opportunities for foul play and brutality." Despite these concessions, Eliot continued to view football as a blot on American life: "The spirit of the game, however, remains essentially the same. . . . It therefore remains an undesirable game for gentlemen to play." Harvard's president used his report to take a swipe at two other emerging pastimes: "An extreme recklessness remains a grave objection to the game of foot-ball, and it also makes basket-ball and hockey, as developed in recent years, undesirable games."[15]

The most important fact about the next few seasons is that football continued to be played. Columbia and Northwestern maintained their bans, as did California and Stanford. Yet Harvard stayed in the game. It even beat Yale in 1908, providing a much-needed morale boost to long-suffering alumni. At Wisconsin, Turner pressed for prohibition but ultimately suggested a compromise that allowed the school to keep a shortened schedule against minor opponents. The plan backfired because Wisconsin started to win football games. This success generated new levels of enthusiasm for the sport, eventually leading to its full restoration. In time, even the schools that quit football completely returned to the fold.

The hue and cry over football's brutality diminished. The movement to abolish the sport lost momentum, partly because it lacked leadership but mostly because the post-1905 rules produced their intended effect. The sport's popularity continued to grow, fueled by the rise of outstanding coaches and teams in the Midwest and South. At the University of Michigan, Fielding Yost earned a national reputation for his "point-a-minute" squads, enjoyed eight undefeated seasons, and established the school's fight-song boast as "the champions of the West." Amos Alonzo Stagg, the Yale star, abandoned a career in the ministry and became involved with the YMCA, where he played in the first game of basketball organized by James Naismith. He went on to become football coach at the University of Chicago, winning 255 games over a forty-year span at the school. In the South, John Heisman turned Georgia Tech into a perennial powerhouse, a feat that paved the way for Heisman to become the namesake of college football's best-known award. Glenn "Pop" Warner may have been the era's most inventive coach, developing the screen pass, the reverse, and the three-point crouch for linemen. He is also credited with the hidden-ball play, in which a player would stuff the ball beneath the shirt of a teammate, sowing confusion among defenders. (It was subsequently made illegal.) Warner coached at several schools, including Cornell and Georgia, but he made his deepest mark at the Carlisle Indian Industrial School, a now-defunct boarding school in Pennsylvania. He turned it into a national contender, thanks in part to the athletic prowess of future Olympian Jim Thorpe.

. . . .

ROOSEVELT NEVER AGAIN would involve himself in football as he did in 1905, but he remained a devoted fan, especially of Harvard. On February 23, 1907, he spoke his last important words on football and the value of sport, at the Harvard Union:

> As I emphatically disbelieve in seeing Harvard or any other college turn out mollycoddles instead of vigorous men, I may add that I do not in the least object to a sport because it is rough. Rowing, baseball, lacrosse, track and field games, hockey, football are all of them good. Moreover, it is to my mind simple nonsense, a mere confession of weakness, to desire to abolish a game because tendencies show themselves, or practices grow up, which prove that the game ought to be reformed. Take football, for instance. The preparatory schools are able to keep football clean and to develop the right spirit in the players without the slightest necessity ever arising to so much as consider the question of abolishing it. There is no excuse whatever for colleges failing to show the same capacity, and there is no real need for considering the question of the abolition of the game. If necessary, let the College authorities interfere to stop any excess or perversion, making their interference as little officious as possible, and yet as rigorous as is necessary to achieve the end. But there is no justification for stopping a thoroughly manly sport because it is sometimes abused, when the experience of every good preparatory school shows that the abuse is in no shape necessarily attendant upon the game.[16]

At a cabinet meeting later that year, Roosevelt's interior secretary, James Garfield (who shared a name with his presidential father), teased his boss about Harvard's football team. Garfield suggested that instead of playing Yale, perhaps Harvard should take on Vassar, which was then a women's college. "The subject of football has been too sore for me to discuss with Harvard and Yale members of the Cabinet," wrote Roosevelt. "I behaved with what dignity I could under distressing circumstances!"[17] The next week, Yale beat Harvard 12–0 in Boston.

AFTER SEVERAL YEARS of relative peace, football suffered a setback in 1909—and the prohibitionists mounted a final effort to do away with the sport. In a game against Villanova, Navy quarterback Edwin Wilson went down with an injury that left him paralyzed. (During the off-season, he died.) Two weeks later, Harvard played Army. It kept pounding the ball at Army's left tackle, Eugene Byrne. He was so banged up that a referee urged Army's coach to send in a substitute. But Byrne stayed in the game. A few minutes later, he was knocked unconscious. He died during the night—and his death became the subject of extensive treatment in east coast newspapers. Army canceled the rest of its season. The next month, University of Virginia halfback Archer Christian fell during a game against Georgetown, in Washington, D.C. He slipped into a coma and died of a brain hemorrhage early the next morning. His death also made the front pages. The *New York Times* called for the immediate suspension of football "before the next boy is killed."[18]

These injuries and fatalities were sensationalized, but the renewed case against football was not merely anecdotal. The *Chicago Tribune* counted thirty-one deaths related to football from the start of the 1908 football season to the summer of 1909, mostly at the prep level. Here was empirical evidence suggesting that the game had slipped back into the violent ways of its recent past.[19] Eliot, who had just retired from Harvard, wrote to Virginia's president, Edwin Alderman, and encouraged him to speak out against football. "Men are killed and wounded" in many sports, he said, but football was unique because its risks were "deliberately planned and deliberately maintained."[20]

Alderman faced additional pressure from an unlikely source: a seventy-six-year-old Confederate. John Singleton Mosby had attended the University of Virginia until he shot a fellow student in 1853. He served a prison sentence and eventually earned a law degree. When the Civil War broke out, he fought as a Confederate cavalry leader and became famous for his plumed hat, red cape, and daring raids. As an old man, he had gone on to work in Roosevelt's Department of Justice—and now he was ready for a new battle. Following Christian's death at Georgetown, he spoke out publicly against football. Mosby had not played sports as a boy and saw no reason why anyone else should enjoy them now. "I had no taste for athletics and have never seen a ball game," he wrote. Football was no better than cockfighting, he said, and professors who approved of it were "accessories" to the death of Christian.[21]

Despite these appeals, Alderman refused to attack football. He had supported the game in the past and resolved to support it during its new crisis. Following his school's gridiron tragedy, he praised the sport for how it encouraged "the use of self-denial, self-restraint, of resoluteness, of patience, of well-ordered attention, of loyalty to a cause, of a distinct form of unselfishness."[22] Yet he also demanded reform. In speeches before the Intercollegiate Athletic Association, Alderman did not spell out particular demands. He simply said that the game's rule makers should address the dangers of football.

Another great debate ensued. It lasted for several months and involved a wide range of opinions. Camp remained opposed to the forward pass and had lobbied against it even in his fiction, such as the 1909 novel *Jack Hall at Yale*.[23] He had several allies on the rulemaking body who also wanted to repeal the pass. Other members wanted to modify the rules of tackling. One suggested eliminating the neutral zone. Another said that ballcarriers were safer back in the days when their teammates could push or pull them through piles of opponents. For months they argued over proposals and counterproposals. They considered rule changes offered on their own merits and in packages cobbled together with an eye toward building a coalition of support. Ultimately, they required seven men to put themselves on the line of scrimmage, banned the pushing and pulling of ballcarriers, and permitted only a single player in the offensive backfield to go in motion before the snap of the ball. At one point they voted to confine the forward pass to behind the line of scrimmage, in a decision that technically would not have eliminated passing but would have rendered it virtually harmless. Later on, they thought better and restored the pass. Then they removed a few of its limitations, most notably by forbidding defenders from interfering with receivers before they caught the ball. Yet they also imposed a new restriction, too: A pass could not travel more than twenty yards before it was caught. When their work was done, Camp refused to put his name on the final product. The pressure of his job at the New Haven Clock Company had kept him away from several meetings, which made him less involved in the revisions than he had been in earlier years. Yet he also grew disenchanted with the direction that football was taking.

Most fans took a different view. During the 1910 season, just days after winning election as governor of New Jersey, Woodrow Wilson saw fit to comment on trends in the game. "The new game of football seems far more enjoyable than the old," he said in a pep talk to Princeton's team. "The new rules are doing much to bring football to a high level as a sport, for its brutal features are being done away with and better elements retained. The absence of grinding mass plays makes the game vastly more interesting to the spectators and at the same time it is rendered more desirable for the participants. The opportunity for unsportsmanlike play is greatly reduced and hence it is now a game in which gentlemen can successfully engage." He said that he would attend the team's game the following Saturday, and he predicted its victory. (Yale, in fact, defeated Princeton.) The excitement of the moment soon got the best of him: Wilson also likened football's changes to "the earlier ideals of America, when honor and courage were exalted above success."[24] Whatever they represented, the new rules solved the sport's immediate problem. Football fatalities and serious injuries dropped dramatically in 1910. None had the prominence of the deaths involving Navy, Army, and Virginia players.[25]

MORE CHANGES FOLLOWED and many of them prepared the way for Notre Dame to unleash the pass in 1913. The Intercollegiate Athletic Association switched its name to the National Collegiate Athletic Association (NCAA). Following the 1911 season, the rules committee increased the value of a touchdown to six points. Field goals fell from four points to three. The restrictions on passing had loosened in recent years—teams no longer lost possession for throwing incompletions—and now they continued to disappear. Passes could fly more than twenty yards and cross the goal line for touchdowns. The shape of the ball changed, too. It was made longer and more aerodynamic, which improved the ability of quarterbacks to fling it. Finally, the NCAA created the fourth down. Teams gained a fourth try to earn a first down, rather than having to stop at three. With these changes, football took the final steps toward assuming its modern shape.

Knute Rockne once described football before the period of changes that began after the 1905 season as a "modified shambles."[26] It would take several years of experimentation and adjustment before football was ready for the revolution that Rockne helped inaugurate. Notre Dame's astonishing defeat of Army in 1913 closed football's first long chapter. Following a period of profound crisis, in which the fate of the game occasionally appeared in doubt, the aerial combination of Gus Dorais and Rockne provided the sport with its very own Frank Merriwell ending.

It was a beginning, too. During the First World War, which erupted the next summer, soldiers could look up from their muddy trenches and see something wholly new in the history of armed conflict: airplanes. War will always find a role for infantries and football will always have its ground game—but airpower changed the way wars are fought and the adoption of the forward pass transformed the way football is played.

Theodore Roosevelt missed much of this. During the crisis of 1909, he was out of the country, having left shortly after the inauguration of William Howard Taft. He went hunting in Africa, collected his Nobel Peace Prize in Europe, and remained abroad for more than a year. When Notre Dame beat Army, he was trekking through South America on a trip that would keep him away until the spring of 1914. In between, he made a new bid for the White House as the presidential nominee of the Progressive Party—popularly known as the Bull Moose Party because Roosevelt liked to say he was "as fit as a bull moose." In the election of 1912, Roosevelt finished behind Wilson the Democrat and ahead of Taft the Republican. He never again ran for public office.

Roosevelt's youngest son, Quentin, volunteered for duty in the First World War. Perhaps entertaining visions of his father's battlefield success, he became a fighter pilot, training and serving with American ace Eddie Rickenbacker. Flying over France in 1918, Quentin was killed in the air. His plane crashed behind German lines. The former president announced that he was "glad that [Quentin] got to the front and had a chance to render some service to his country, and show the stuff that was in him." He grieved the loss of his son but also invoked the words that he had once applied to himself, referring to Quentin's "crowded hour . . . his day of honor and triumph."[27]

. . . .

AS THE FORWARD pass won a permanent place in the rules of football, Walter Camp began to edge away from the game, though he remained an advisor to Yale's team. He had built a large personal fortune through the clock company. During the First World War, as questions of national readiness took hold, he enjoyed a kind of second career as a promoter for physical fitness. In conjunction with the navy, he developed the "Daily Dozen," a calisthenics routine. Camp said he came up with the idea from watching a tiger at a zoo go through what appeared to be a set of stretching exercises. The result may have been Camp's single most popular piece of writing, with the possible exception of his All-America football lists. At one point, he worked in Washington, D.C., and led a morning exercise regimen for a number of top federal officials, including members of Wilson's cabinet and a thirty-five-year-old assistant secretary of the navy named Franklin D. Roosevelt.[28] "I find that this job of running the Navy Department all alone means about fourteen hours a day if one is to do it well," wrote the young Roosevelt, a cousin of the former president. "But those exercises . . . have made the fourteen hours possible."[29] Camp made his peace with the forward pass, though he remained capable of grousing that it was turning the sport into "nothing but outdoor basketball."[30] He died in 1925, while attending a football rules meeting in New York City.

Camp's older brother-in-law, William Graham Sumner, had died earlier, in 1910. His last great work was *Folkways*, a massive book on social customs. One section referred to sports as "a sort of mimic warfare."[31] Charles W. Eliot almost certainly would have agreed with that assessment, especially as it applied to football. After the 1909 season, when Eliot tried unsuccessfully to pass the baton of football prohibition to the president of the University of Virginia, Eliot had little to say about the game. He retired as

Harvard's president earlier that year, finishing a career in which he did more to shape higher education in the United States than any single person before or since. He lived until 1926, dying at the age of ninety-two—a long life made possible by his own commitment to personal fitness. His crusade against football was perhaps his most conspicuous professional failure, though it would be wrong to suggest that he had no influence on the sport. Without the pressure he applied, with the relentlessness of a football team that always runs the ball, the sport might have felt considerably less pressure to reform itself. "Is not the most effective mode of making people think to get them involved in controversy?" he asked in 1920.[32] If Eliot had kept his opinions about football to himself, the controversy surrounding football might not have erupted the way it did. Roosevelt possibly would have remained on the sidelines—and left football to an uncertain future.

ROOSEVELT DIED IN 1919, at the age of sixty. Through the force of his personality, he altered the nature of the presidency in many ways—and not least through his advocacy of the strenuous life, which he defined in both word and deed. He had once worried that Americans would not accept a sporting president. In part because of his example, Americans came to expect their presidents to engage in a certain amount of sport, whether it involved throwing out the first pitch on baseball's opening day or golfing for recreation. A number of Roosevelt's successors played football growing up—most notably Gerald Ford, who starred as a center at the University of Michigan in the 1930s and turned down a possible professional career in order to attend law school.

By the end of the 20th century, long after Roosevelt's death, football had become his country's national game—a distinctive creation of Americans and more popular than any other athletic pastime. As with any great success story, many people could take credit for the sport's achievements. Bill Reid, the man who coached Harvard during football's most tumultuous episode, never doubted the importance of what Roosevelt did for the game in 1905 and 1906. "Except for this chain of events there might now be no such thing as American football as we know it," he wrote many years later. "You asked me whether President Theodore Roosevelt helped save the game. I can tell you that he did."[33]

In 1905, Roosevelt invited the coaches of Harvard, Yale, and Princeton to the White House. "Football is on trial," he told them. "Because I believe in the game, I want to do all I can to save it." (*Courtesy The Library of Congress*)

APPENDIX: DEATHS AND SERIOUS INJURIES IN FOOTBALL, 1905-16

Year	Deaths/Total	Deaths/College	Injuries/Total	Injuries/College
1905	18	3	159	88
1906	11	3	104	54
1907	11	2	98	51
1908	13	6	84	33
1909	26	10	69	38
1910	14	5	40	17
1911	14	3	56	36
1912	10*	0*	26	17
1913	14	3	56	36
1914	12	2	n.a.	n.a.
1915	n.a.	n.a.	n.a.	n.a.
1916	16	3	n.a.	n.a.

n.a. = not available

* Plus one injury later resulting in death.

Source: John S. Watterson, "The Gridiron Crisis of 1905: Was It Really a Crisis?," *Journal of Sport History* (Summer 2000), p. 294; figures derived from *New York Times* and *Chicago Tribune*.

Acknowledgments

My friend Arthur Herman once said that authors write the books they want to read but can't find. That certainly describes the origins of this one. The idea for *The Big Scrum* came to me in 2001, after stumbling across a brief reference to the number of football players who had died on the field around the turn of the century. I wanted to learn more. Instead of locating a standard reference work that would answer my questions, I found a trail of footnotes—and discovered an amazing story that needed to be told.

For years, *The Big Scrum* gestated. Friends listened to me describe its story. I'm indebted to many for their assistance and encouragement—too many to name here, though I want to single out a few who made an important difference: Mark Bauerlein, David Bernstein, Richard Brookhiser, Kim Dennis, Brian Domitrovic, Arthur Herman, Mike Long, Rich Lowry, Mark Molesky, Wilfred McClay, Jesse Naiman, Nick Schulz, Elise Viebeck, and Michael Warren.

It took the prompting of my attentive agent, Michael Carlisle, to turn my notes into a formal proposal. It took the guidance of my brilliant editor, Adam Bellow, to turn my proposal into a manuscript. It took the financial support of a generous philanthropy, the Earhart Foundation, to support my research. I'm grateful to all.

My family has lived with this book almost as much as I have. My wife, Amy, not only has put up with a husband who is often lost in thought about what the next chapter should say, but has embraced the sometimes uncertain life of a writer. When I started thinking about *The Big Scrum* almost a decade ago, two of our children had been born and the third was on the way. His arrival, we often point out, forced us to switch from man-to-man coverage to a zone defense. These three kids, to whom this book is dedicated, bring joy and satisfaction to our home even as they've transformed it—or perhaps *because* they've transformed it—into our own big scrum.

Notes

CHAPTER 1: THE KILLING FIELDS

1. TR to Martha Bulloch Roosevelt, November 19, 1876, in *The Letters of Theodore Roosevelt: The Years of Preparation, 1868–1898*, ed. Elting E. Morison (Cambridge, Mass.: Harvard University Press, 1951), p. 20.

2. Ibid.

3. Parke H. Davis, *Football: The American Intercollegiate Game* (New York: Charles Scribner's Sons, 1911), pp. 251–52; "Glorious Victory for Yale," *Morning Journal and Courier* (New Haven, Conn.), Nov. 20, 1876, p. 2; "Foot Ball: The Yales Defeat the Harvards and Princeton Defeats Columbia," *Boston Daily Globe*, November 20, 1876, p. 3.

4. Bernard M. Corbett and Paul Simpson, *The Only Game That Matters: The Harvard/Yale Rivalry* (New York: Crown, 2004), p. 127.

5. Guy Maxton Lewis, "The American Intercollegiate Football Spectacle, 1896–1917" (Ph.D. diss., University of Maryland, 1965), p. 29.

6. Allison Danzig, *The History of American Football: Its Great Teams, Players, and Coaches* (Englewood Cliffs, N.J.: Prentice-Hall, 1956), p. 12.

7. Tim Cohane, *The Yale Football Story* (New York: G. P. Putnam's Sons, 1951), p. 23.

8. Richard P. Borkowski, "The Life and Contributions of Walter Camp to American Football" (Ph.D. diss., Temple University, 1979), p. 40.

9. Ibid., pp. 40–41.

10. "Foot Ball: The Yales Defeat the Harvards and Princeton Defeats Columbia," *Boston Daily Globe*, November 20, 1876, p. 3.

11. TR to Martha Bulloch Roosevelt, November 19, 1876, in *The Letters of Theodore Roosevelt: The Years of Preparation, 1868–1898*, p. 20.

12. Foster Rhea Dulles, *A History of Recreation: America Learns to Play*, 2nd ed. (New York: Appleton-Century-Crofts, 1965), pp. 198–99.

13. Frederick Rudolph, *The American College and University: A History* (New York: Knopf, 1962), pp. 373–74.

14. Edmund Morris, *The Rise of Theodore Roosevelt*, rev. ed. (New York: Modern Library, 2001), pp. 55–56.

15. John Higham, *Writing American History: Essays on Modern Scholarship* (Bloomington: Indiana University Press, 1970), p. 84.

16. "Foot-ball at New Haven," *New York Times*, November 19, 1876, p. 7.

17. "Intercollegiate Foot-ball: Princeton Defeats Columbia in Three Straight Games—Three of the Players Receive Injuries," *New York Times*, November 19, 1876, p. 5; Frank Presbrey and James Hugh Moffat, eds., *Athletics at Princeton: A History* (New York: Frank Presbrey, 1901), p. 282.

18. John S. Watterson, "The Gridiron Crisis of 1905: Was It Really a Crisis?," *Journal of Sport History* (Summer 2000), p. 294.

19. "The Athletic Craze," *Nation*, December 7, 1893.

20. Caspar Whitney, "The Sportsman's View-Point," *Outing*, January 1903.

21. "Football," *New York Times*, November 10, 1897.

22. "Two Curable Evils," *New York Times*, November 23, 1897.

23. One common legend says that Roosevelt threatened to abolish football after seeing a picture of a bloodied Swarthmore player, Bob Maxwell. John S. Watterson traces this error to a 1944 sports encyclopedia. See Watterson, "The Gridiron Crisis of 1905," pp. 291–98.

24. Theodore Roosevelt, "The Strenuous Life," *Letters and Speeches*, ed. Louis Auchincloss (New York: Library of America, 2004), p. 755.

25. "Pres. Roosevelt on Play and Work," *Harvard Graduates Magazine*, June 1907, pp. 779–80; "Pres. Roosevelt's Address," *Harvard Crimson*, February 25, 1907.

26. Scott Ganz and Kevin Hassett, "Little League, Huge Effect," *American*, May/June 2008, pp. 64–67.

27. Sean Gregory, "The Problem With Football," *Time*, February 8, 2010, pp. 36–42.

28. Alan Schwarz, "Dementia Risk Seen in Players in N.F.L. Study," *New York Times*, September 30, 2009.

29. Malcolm Gladwell, "Offensive Play," *New Yorker*, October 19, 2009.

30. Alan Schwarz, "N.F.L.'s Dementia Study Has Flaws, Experts Say," *New York Times*, October 27, 2009.

CHAPTER 2: CREATION STORIES

1. Carleton Putnam, *Theodore Roosevelt: The Formative Years, 1858–1886* (New York: Charles Scribner's Sons, 1958), p. 23.

2. Ibid., p. 26.

3. Theodore Roosevelt, *An Autobiography* (New York: Library of America, 2004), p. 266.
4. Morris, *The Rise of Theodore Roosevelt*, pp. 11–12.
5. Putnam, *Theodore Roosevelt*, p. 63.
6. William Roscoe Thayer, *Theodore Roosevelt: An Intimate Biography* (Boston: Houghton Mifflin, 1919), pp. 10–11.
7. Corinne Roosevelt Robinson, *My Brother Theodore Roosevelt* (New York: Charles Scribner's Sons, 1921), p. 50.
8. John Wood, "Helped Build Up Roosevelt's Muscle, Back in the 70's," *New York World*, January 24, 1904, p. 5.
9. Ibid.
10. Robinson, *My Brother Theodore Roosevelt*, pp. 50–51.
11. Putnam, *Theodore Roosevelt*, p. 27.
12. Jacob A. Riis, *Theodore Roosevelt: The Citizen* (New York: Outlook, 1904), pp. 7–8.
13. Hermann Hagedorn, *The Boys' Life of Theodore Roosevelt* (New York: Harper & Brothers, 1918), pp. 20–21.
14. Roosevelt, *Autobiography*, pp. 267–68.
15. Ibid., pp. 269–70.
16. Hagedorn, *The Boys' Life of Theodore Roosevelt*, p. 39.
17. Theodore Roosevelt, "What We Can Expect of the American Boy," *St. Nicholas*, May 1900, pp. 571–74. The other book was *Story of a Bad Boy*, by Nelson Aldrich.
18. Harry Potter should tip his hat to Tom Brown. Both *Tom Brown's Schooldays* and *Harry Potter and the Sorcerer's Stone* tell of an eleven-year-old boy who leaves home for a boarding school. Whereas J. K. Rowling wrote a fantasy in which the hero plays a team sport that involves flying broomsticks, its nineteenth-century antecedent aimed for realism and its protagonist plays football or rugby. *Harry Potter and the Sorceror's Stone*, in fact, is a kind of hybrid of *Tom Brown's Schooldays* and *The Lord of the Rings*, by J. R. R. Tolkien.
19. Thomas Hughes, *Harvard Advocate Supplement*, October 14, 1870, p. 1.
20. Two other children also predeceased Hughes; one who outlived him, daughter Lily, went down with *Titanic* in 1912.
21. "Thomas Hughes," *Oxford Dictionary of National Biography*, vol. 28, p. 681.
22. Hughes, *Tom Brown's Schooldays*, pp. 73–74.
23. Ibid., p. 89.
24. Ibid., pp. 98–99.
25. Ibid., pp. 105–6.
26. The quote may be apocryphal. See Paul F. Boller, Jr., and John George, *They Never Said It: A Book of Fake Quotes, Misquotes, and Misleading Attributions* (New York: Oxford University Press, 1989), pp. 130–31. If Wellington did not actually speak these words, they still came to capture a popular sentiment around the time Hughes wrote.

27. K. G. Sheard, "Ellis, William Webb," *Oxford Dictionary of National Biography*, vol. 18, pp. 272–73.

28. Davis, *Football*, p. 3.

29. Athenaeus, *The Deipnosophists, or Banquet of the Learned*, vol. 1 (London: Henry G. Bohn, 1854), pp. 23–24, http://digital.library.wisc.edu/1711.dl/Literature .DeipnoSub.

30. Galen, *Selected Words*, ed. P. N. Singer (Oxford: Oxford University Press, 1997), pp. 299–304.

31. Theodore Roosevelt, "A Journey in Central Brazil," *Geographical Journal*, February 1915, p. 100. See also Candice Millard, *The River of Doubt: Theodore Roosevelt's Darkest Journey* (New York: Broadway, 2005), p. 101.

32. *King Lear*, 1.4.74.

33. *The Comedy of Errors*, 2.1.355.

34. Montague Shearman, *Athletics and Football* (London: Longmans, Green, 1887), pp. 291–92. Scott also has a line about football in his long poem *The Lay of the Last Minstrel* (1805): "Some drive the jolly bowl about / With dice and drafts some chase the day / And some with many a merry shout / In riot, revelry, and rout / Pursue the football play."

35. William Safire, *Safire's Political Dictionary*, updated ed. (New York: Oxford University Press, 2008), p. 555.

36. Hughes, *Tom Brown's Schooldays*, pp. 282–83. "Spiritual wickedness in high places" alludes to Ephesians 6:12: "For we wrestle not against flesh and blood, but against principalities, against powers, against the rulers of the darkness of this world, against spiritual wickedness in high places." See Hughes, *Tom Brown's Schooldays*, p. 403 n. 282.

37. Nick J. Watson, Stuart Weir, and Stephen Friend, "The Development of Muscular Christianity in Victorian Britain and Beyond," *Journal of Religion and Society* 7 (2005).

38. Margaret McGehee, "A Castle in the Wilderness: Rugby Colony, Tennessee, 1880–1887," *Journal of East Tennessee History* (1998), pp. 62–89.

39. Hughes, *Tom Brown's Schooldays*, pp. 1–2.

40. Henry Adams, *The Education of Henry Adams* (Boston: Houghton Mifflin, 1973), p. 38. Adams does allow that in their free time, "boys could skate and swim . . . they played a rudimentary game of baseball, football, and hockey."

41. John R. Betts, "Mind and Body in Early American Thought," *Journal of American History* 54, no. 4 (March 1968), pp. 787–805; Dulles, *A History of Recreation*, pp. 158–59; H. W. Brands, *The First American: The Life and Times of Benjamin Franklin* (New York: Doubleday, 2000), p. 196.

42. Margaret Farrand Thorp, *Charles Kingsley, 1819–1875* (Princeton, N.J.: Princeton University Press, 1937), p. 172.

43. Clifford Putney, *Muscular Christianity: Manhood and Sports in Protestant America, 1880–1920* (Cambridge, Mass.: Harvard University Press, 2001), pp. 11–15.

44. Douglas Brinkley, *The Wilderness Warrior: Theodore Roosevelt and the Crusade for America* (New York: HarperCollins, 2009), p. 24.

45. Betts, "Mind and Body in Early American Thought," p. 797.

46. Putney, *Muscular Christianity*, pp. 20–21.

47. Dulles, *A History of Recreation*, pp. 183–84.

48. Brenda Wineapple, *White Heat: The Friendship of Emily Dickinson and Thomas Wentworth Higginson* (New York: Knopf, 2008), p. 19.

49. Guy Lewis, "The Muscular Christianity Movement," *Journal of Health, Physical Education, and Recreation* (May 1966), p. 28.

50. Wineapple, *White Heat*, p. 94.

51. Tilden G. Edelstein, "Thomas Wentworth Higginson," *American National Biography*, vol. 10, pp. 757–60; Stephen B. Oates, *To Purge This Land With Blood: A Biography of John Brown* (New York: Harper & Row, 1970), pp. 189–91, 315–16; Evan Carton, *Patriotic Treason: John Brown and the Soul of America* (Lincoln: University of Nebraska Press, 2009), p. 324–26.

52. Thomas Wentworth Higginson, "Saints and Their Bodies," *Atlantic Monthly*, March 1858, pp. 582–95.

53. Ronald A. Smith, *Sports & Freedom: The Rise of Big-Time College Athletics* (New York: Oxford University Press, 1988), p. 55.

54. Putney, *Muscular Christianity*, pp. 22, 64–65.

55. Dulles, *A History of Recreation*, pp. 182–96; Donald J. Mrozek, *Sport and the American Mentality, 1880–1910* (Knoxville: University of Tennessee Press, 1983), p. 74; John Rickards Betts, "The Technological Revolution and the Rise of Sport, 1850–1900," *Mississippi Valley Historical Review* 40, no. 2 (September 1953), pp. 231–56; Gerald F. Roberts, "The Strenuous Life: The Cult of Manliness in the Era of Theodore Roosevelt" (Ph.D. diss., Michigan State University, 1970), p. 17.

56. Putney, *Muscular Christianity*, pp. 69–72.

57. Robinson, *My Brother Theodore Roosevelt*, p. 50.

58. Roosevelt, *Autobiography*, p. 294.

CHAPTER 3: GAME TIME

1. Roosevelt, *Autobiography*, p. 280.

2. Hagedorn, *The Boys' Life of Theodore Roosevelt*, pp. 39–40.

3. Roosevelt, *Autobiography*, p. 281.

4. Ibid., p. 271.

5. Edmund Morris, *Theodore Rex* (New York: Random House, 2001), pp. 172–74.

6. Thayer, *Theodore Roosevelt*, pp. 8–9; Hagedorn, *The Boys' Life of Theodore Roosevelt*, p. 45.

7. Roosevelt, *Autobiography*, p. 270. Bell is also briefly discussed in Richard Rhodes, *John James Audubon: The Making of an American* (New York: Knopf, 2004), pp. 419, 423, 427–28.

8. Kathleen Dalton, *Theodore Roosevelt: A Strenuous Life* (New York: Random House, 2002), p. 53.

9. Roosevelt, *Autobiography*, pp. 270–71.

10. Iain Manson, *The Lion and the Eagle* (London: SportsBooks, 2008).

11. Roosevelt, *Autobiography*, p. 281.

12. Putnam, *Theodore Roosevelt*, p. 85.

13. Robinson, *My Brother Theodore Roosvelt*, p. 55.

14. Putnam, *Theodore Roosevelt*, p. 89 n. 13.

15. Ibid., p. 92.

16. Robinson, *My Brother Theodore Roosvelt*, pp. 56–57.

17. David McCullough, *Mornings on Horseback* (New York: Simon & Schuster, 1981), p. 125. McCullough calls this "one of the rare observations on the children written by somebody outside the family."

18. Morris, *The Rise of Theodore Roosevelt*, p. 41.

19. Robinson, *My Brother Theodore Roosevelt*, pp. 64–65.

20. Sam Spirn, "A Scientific Sport Fit for Gentlemen: Why Rugby Supplanted Soccer in the Early History of American Football, 1860–1877" (honors thesis, Harvard University, 2003), p. 44.

21. Danzig, *The History of American Football*, p. 7; Mark F. Bernstein, *Football: The Ivy League Origins of an American Obsession* (Philadelphia: University of Pennsylvania Press, 2001), p. 5.

22. Spirn, "A Scientific Sport Fit for Gentlemen," p. 41.

23. Danzig, *The History of American Football*, p. 7; Bernstein, *Football*, pp. 6–8.

24. Danzig, *Oh, How They Played the Game* (New York: Macmillan, 1971), p. 4.

25. Herbert in Danzig, *Oh, How They Played the Game*, p. 5.

26. Davis, *Football*, p. 49.

27. Ibid., p. 50.

28. Danzig, *Oh, How They Played the Game*, p. 8.

29. Sam Spirn, "A Scientific Sport Fit for Gentlemen," pp. 69–70.

30. Morris, *The Rise of Theodore Roosevelt*, p. 42.

31. TR to Theodore Roosevelt, Sr., June 15, 1873, in *The Letters of Theodore Roosevelt: The Years of Preparation, 1868–1898*, pp. 8–9.

32. Putnam, *Theodore Roosevelt*, p. 111 n. 25.

33. TR to Theodore Roosevelt, Sr., June 15, 1873, in *The Letters of Theodore Roosevelt: The Years of Preparation, 1868–1898*, pp. 8–9.

34. Putnam, *Theodore Roosevelt*, p. 111.

35. Ibid., p. 112. Emphasis in original.

36. TR to Theodore Roosevelt, Sr., June 29, 1873, in *The Letters of Theodore Roosevelt: The Years of Preparation, 1868–1898*, pp. 10–11.

37. Morris, *The Rise of Theodore Roosevelt*, p. 51.

38. TR to Anna Minckwitz Fisher, February 5, 1876, in *The Letters of Theodore Roosevelt: The Years of Preparation, 1868–1898*, p. 14.

39. Morris, *The Rise of Theodore Roosevelt*, p. 51.

CHAPTER 4: CAMP DAYS

1. Thomas G. Bergin, *The Game: The Harvard-Yale Football Rivalry, 1875–1983* (New Haven, Conn.: Yale University Press, 1984), p. 16.
2. Borkowski, "The Life and Contributions of Walter Camp to American Football," pp. 2–3.
3. Ibid., p. 12.
4. Ibid., p. 7.
5. Walter Camp Papers, Reel 47, Yale University, New Haven, Conn.; Borkowski, "The Life and Contributions of Walter Camp to American Football," pp. 10–12.
6. Borkowski, "The Life and Contributions of Walter Camp to American Football," pp. 29–30.
7. Walter Camp Papers, Reel 47.
8. Ibid.; Borkowski, "The Life and Contributions of Walter Camp to American Football," pp. 46–48, 52.
9. Danzig, *The History of American Football*, p. 12.
10. Borkowski, "The Life and Contributions of Walter Camp to American Football," p. 41.
11. Harford Powel, Jr., *Walter Camp: The Father of American Football* (Boston: Little, Brown, 1926), p. 20.
12. Walter Camp Papers, Reel 47.
13. Borkowski, "The Life and Contributions of Walter Camp to American Football," p. 45.
14. Corbett and Simpson, *The Only Game That Matters*, pp. 128–29.
15. Borkowski, "The Life and Contributions of Walter Camp to American Football," pp. 43–44; Powel, *Walter Camp*, p. 28.
16. Borkowski, "The Life and Contributions of Walter Camp to American Football," p. 32.
17. Powel, *Walter Camp*, p. 30.
18. Borkowski, "The Life and Contributions of Walter Camp to American Football," p. 53.
19. John Sayle Watterson, *College Football: History, Spectacle, Controversy* (Baltimore: Johns Hopkins University Press, 2000), p. 24.
20. David McCullough, *Brave Companions: Portraits in History* (New York: Simon & Schuster, 1992), p. 75.
21. Allen P. Splete and Marilyn D. Splete, eds., *Frederic Remington: Selected Letters* (New York: Abbeville, 1988), p. 23.
22. Cohane, *The Yale Football Story*, pp. 354–60.
23. *Papers of Woodrow Wilson*, vol. 1, *1856–1880*, ed. Arthur S. Link (Princeton, N.J.: Princeton University Press, 1966), p. 405.
24. Henry Wilkinson Bragdon, *Woodrow Wilson: The Academic Years* (Cambridge, Mass.: Harvard University Press, 1967), pp. 39–41; Parke H. Davis, "What

Woodrow Wilson Did for American Foot-Ball," *St. Nicholas*, November 1912; Stephen R. Dujack, "The Man Who Made the World Safe for Football," *Washington Post*, September 7, 1986, p. C1.

25. Danzig, *The History of American Football*, p. 10.

26. Davis, *Football*, p. 72.

27. Ibid., pp. 73, 85. Rudolph, *The American College and University*, p. 385.

28. Davis, *Football*, p. 468.

29. Davis, *Football*, p. 469.

30. Borkowski, "The Life and Contributions of Walter Camp to American Football," p. 64–65.

31. Davis, *Football*, pp. 71, 78.

32. Ibid., p. 81.

33. Ibid., p. 83; Arthur Lubow, *The Reporter Who Would Be King: A Biography of Richard Harding Davis* (New York: Charles Scribner's Sons, 1992), p. 21.

34. Danzig, *The History of American Football*, p. 16.

35. Borkowski, "The Life and Contributions of Walter Camp to American Football," p. 222.

36. Walter Camp Papers, Reel 47.

37. Ibid., p. 68.

38. Walter Camp, "Youth the Time for Physical Development," Walter Camp Papers, Reel 44.

39. "Followed a False Clue," *New York Times*, March 6, 1887.

40. Walter Camp Papers, Reel 44.

41. "George Condit Smith Married," *New York Times*, October 26, 1887.

42. Walter Camp to William Graham Sumner, August 30, 1886, Walter Camp Papers, Reel 16.

43. Diary entry dated January 15, 1880, Walter Camp Papers, Reel 47.

44. Harris E. Starr, *William Graham Sumner* (New York: Henry Holt, 1925), p. 20.

45. Ibid., p. 21.

46. Ibid., p. 31.

47. Ibid., p. 518.

48. A. G. Keller, *Reminiscences (Mainly Personal) of William Graham Sumner* (New Haven, Conn.: Yale University Press, 1933), p. 68.

49. Amos Alonzo Stagg with Wesley Winans Stout, *Touchdown!* (New York: Longmans, Green, 1927), p. 111.

50. Borkowski, "The Life and Contributions of Walter Camp to American Football," p. 105.

51. Ibid., p. 188.

52. Keller, *Reminiscences*, p. 68.

CHAPTER 5: THE CAPACITY TO INFLICT PAIN

1. Owen Wister, *Roosevelt: The Story of a Friendship, 1880–1919* (New York: Macmillan, 1930), p. 5.

2. Morris, *The Rise of Theodore Roosevelt*, pp. 58–59; Putnam, *Theodore Roosevelt*, p. 179.

3. Theodore Roosevelt, *Diaries of Boyhood and Youth* (New York: Charles Scribner's Sons, 1928), pp. 363–64. See also Watterson, *The Games Presidents Play*, pp. 38–39.

4. Morris, *The Rise of Theodore Roosevelt*, pp. 58–59.

5. Ibid., pp. 73–74, 94.

6. McCullough, *Mornings on Horseback*, p. 223.

7. Wister, *Roosevelt*, pp. 4–5.

8. Morris, *The Rise of Theodore Roosevelt*, p. 91.

9. Putnam, *Theodore Roosevelt*, p. 198 n. 2.

10. Hagedorn, *The Boys' Life of Theodore Roosevelt*, p. 64.

11. Henry James, *Charles W. Eliot: President of Harvard University, 1869–1909* (Boston and New York: Houghton Mifflin, 1930), vol. 1, p. 14.

12. Alar Lipping, "Charles W. Eliot's Views on Education, Physical Education, and Intercollegiate Athletics" (Ph.D. diss., Ohio State University, 1980).

13. James, *Charles W. Eliot*, vol. 1, pp. 38–39.

14. Lipping, "Charles W. Eliot's Views on Education," p. 30.

15. Ibid., p. 31.

16. Ibid., p. 34; James, *Charles W. Eliot*, vol. 1, p. 55.

17. Lipping, "Charles W. Eliot's Views on Education," p. 169.

18. Ibid., p. 171.

19. Ibid., p. 170.

20. Charles W. Eliot, "Old and New," *Harvard Graduates Magazine*, March 1900, p. 465.

21. James, *Charles W. Eliot*, vol. 1, pp. 80–81.

22. Ibid., vol. 1, p. 90.

23. Ibid., vol. 1, p. 107 n. 1.

24. Ibid., vol. 1, p. 78.

25. Lipping, "Charles W. Eliot's Views on Education," p. 73.

26. James, *Charles W. Eliot*, vol. 1, p. 321.

27. Donald Fleming, "Harvard's Golden Age?," in *Glimpses of the Harvard Past*, ed. Bernard Bailyn, Donald Fleming, Oscar Handlin, and Stephan Thernstrom (Cambridge, Mass.: Harvard University Press, 1986), p. 77.

28. Lipping, "Charles W. Eliot's Views on Education," p. 98.

29. James, *Charles W. Eliot*, vol. 1, pp. 308–9.

30. Ibid., vol. 1, p. 310.

31. Ibid., vol. 1, p. 134. On another occasion, Eliot commented: "I hate Catholicism as I do poison, and all the pomp and power of the Church is depressing and mortifying to me." See ibid., vol. 1, p. 141.

32. Ibid., vol. 1, p. 313.

33. Ibid., vol. 2, p. 31.

34. Ibid., vol. 2, p. 60.

35. Lipping, "Charles W. Eliot's Views on Education," p. 189.

36. Ibid., p. 242.

37. Ibid., p. 175.

38. Ibid., p. 251.

39. James, *Charles W. Eliot*, vol. 2, p. 69.

40. Ibid., vol. 2, p. 70.

41. Davis, *Football*, p. 9.

42. Ibid., p. 18.

43. Kim Townsend, *Manhood at Harvard: William James and Others* (New York: Norton, 1996), p. 101.

44. Lipping, "Charles W. Eliot's Views on Education," p. 257.

45. John Stuart Martin, "Walter Camp and His Gridiron Game," *American Heritage*, October 1961, p. 51.

46. Watterson, *College Football*, p. 24.

47. Lipping, "Charles W. Eliot's Views on Education," p. 266.

48. "The Documents on the Football Question," *Harvard Graduates Magazine*, June 1895, p. 521.

49. Ronald A. Smith, *Pay for Play: A History of Big-Time College Athletic Reform* (Urbana: University of Illinois Press, 2010), pp. 27–28.

50. Stagg, *Touchdown!*, pp. 93–94.

51. Lipping, "Charles W. Eliot's Views on Education," pp. 200–1.

52. McCullough, *Mornings on Horseback*, p. 214.

CHAPTER 6: THE VIRILE VIRTUES

1. Watterson, *The Games Presidents Play: Sports and the Presidency* (Baltimore: Johns Hopkins University Press, 2006), p. 65.

2. Morris, *The Rise of Theodore Roosevelt*, pp. 100, 804 n. 120.

3. Dalton, *Theodore Roosevelt*, p. 79.

4. TR to Corinne Roosevelt, August 24, 1881, in Peter Collier with David Horowitz, *The Roosevelts: An American Saga* (New York: Simon & Schuster, 1994), p. 58.

5. TR to Anna Roosevelt, August 5, 1881, in *The Letters of Theodore Roosevelt: The Years of Preparation, 1868–1898*, pp. 49–50.

6. Morris, *The Rise of Theodore Roosevelt*, p. 134.

7. Ibid., p. 149.

8. Ibid., p. 168.

9. Dalton, *Theodore Roosevelt*, p. 82.

10. Roosevelt, *Autobiography*, p. 295.

11. McCullough, *Mornings on Horseback*, p. 277.

12. Ibid., p. 287.

13. Hermann Hagedorn, *Roosevelt in the Bad Lands* (Boston and New York: Houghton Mifflin, 1921), p. 466.

14. Ibid., p. x.

15. Collier, *The Roosevelts*, p. 65.
16. McCullough, *Mornings on Horseback*, pp. 328–29.
17. Ibid., p. 338; Morris, *The Rise of Theodore Roosevelt*, p. 207.
18. Morris, *The Rise of Theodore Roosevelt*, p. 280.
19. Roosevelt, *Autobiography*, pp. 377–78.
20. Morris, *The Rise of Theodore Roosevelt*, p. 273.
21. McCullough, *Mornings on Horseback*, p. 341.
22. Morris, *The Rise of Theodore Roosevelt*, p. 336.
23. Theodore Roosevelt, "Value of an Athletic Training," *Harper's Weekly*, December 23, 1893, p. 1236.
24. Ibid.
25. The author of the *Evening Sun* article was probably Richard Harding Davis. See Lubow, *The Reporter Who Would Be King*, p. 77. For attendance figures, see Lewis, "The American Intercollegiate Football Spectacle," pp. 40, 46, 55, 75.
26. Lewis, "The American Intercollegiate Football Spectacle," pp. 148–49.
27. George H. Nash, *The Life of Herbert Hoover: The Engineer, 1874–1914* (New York: Norton, 1983), pp. 29–30, 593–94 n. 32.
28. Davis, *Football*, p. 93; Lewis, p. 177.
29. Lewis, "The American Intercollegiate Football Spectacle," pp. 149–59.
30. Richard Harding Davis, "A Day with the Yale Team," *Harper's Weekly*, November 18, 1893, p. 1110.
31. Lewis, "The American Intercollegiate Football Spectacle," pp. 44, 111, 118; Lubow, *The Reporter Who Would Be King*, p. 130.
32. Alexander Leitch, *A Princeton Companion* (Princeton, N.J.: Princeton University Press, 1978), http://etcweb.princeton.edu/CampusWWW/Companion/poe_brothers.html.
33. Edgar A. Poe, "Foot-ball," *Harper's Young People*, November 25, 1890, p. 62.
34. Lewis, "The American Intercollegiate Football Spectacle," pp. 128–29.
35. Poe, "Foot-ball," p. 63.
36. Davis, *Football*, p. 83.
37. Lewis, "The American Intercollegiate Football Spectacle," p. 46.
38. W. A. M. Burden to William T. Reid, August 31, 1899, Harvard University archives, HUD 8010, 1899 folder.
39. Borkowski, "The Life and Contributions of Walter Camp to American Football," p. 91.
40. Scott A. McQuilkin and Ronald A. Smith, "The Rise and Fall of the Flying Wedge: Football's Most Controversial Play," *Journal of Sports History* (Spring 1993), p. 60.
41. Stagg, *Touchdown!*, p. 183.
42. "Change the Football Rules," *New York Times*, December 2, 1893.
43. Ibid.
44. Watterson, *College Football*, pp. 48–49.
45. Smith, *Sports & Freedom*, p. 93.
46. Roosevelt, "Value of an Athletic Training."

CHAPTER 7: LET THEM BE MEN FIRST

1. Watterson, *College Football*, p. 17.
2. Ibid., p. 15.
3. Cohane, *The Yale Football Story*, p. 90.
4. Watterson, *College Football*, p. 16.
5. Ibid., p. 16.
6. "Yale Again Triumphant," *New York Times*, November 25, 1894.
7. Watterson, *College Football*, p. 16.
8. TR to Henry Childs Merwin, December 18, 1894, in *The Letters of Theodore Roosevelt: The Years of Preparation, 1868–1898*, p. 412.
9. President Eliot's Report, *Harvard Graduates Magazine*, March 1894, pp. 378–83.
10. Bragdon, *Woodrow Wilson*, pp. 172–73; Dujack, "The Man Who Made the World Safe for Football." This account of Wilson's cheering may be apocryphal. See Bragdon, *Woodrow Wilson*, p. 439 n. 25.
11. *The Papers of Woodrow Wilson*, vol. 8, *1892–1894*, ed. Arthur S. Link (Princeton, N.J.: Princeton University Press, 1970), pp. 45, 47–48; Bragdon, *Woodrow Wilson*, pp. 298, 463 n. 29; Watterson, *College Football*, p. 26.
12. *The Papers of Woodrow Wilson*, vol. 8, ed. Link, pp. 449–50.
13. Ibid., vol. 8, pp. 482–84; "Football or No Football: The Question Discussed by Profs. Wilson and Wilder," *New York Times*, February 18, 1894; Bragdon, *Woodrow Wilson*, pp. 212–13.
14. Ibid. See also "Dr. Burt G. Wilder Dies," *Cornell Alumni News*, January 29, 1925, pp. 223–24.
15. Roberts, *The Strenuous Life*, p. 90.
16. Watterson, *College Football*, pp. 29–30; "Strangled by Chlorine Gas," *New York Times*, February 21, 1894; "The Poisoning at Cornell," *New York Times*, February 22, 1894.
17. Watterson, *College Football*, p. 30.
18. Richard F. Hixson, "Godkin, Edwin Lawrence," *Dictionary of American National Biography*, vol. 9, pp. 152–54.
19. "The New Football," *Nation*, November 29, 1894, pp. 399–400.
20. Morris, *The Rise of Theodore Roosevelt*, p. 353.
21. Ibid., p. 272.
22. William M. Armstrong, *E. L. Godkin: A Biography* (Albany: State University of New York Press, 1978), p. 245 n. 43.
23. Roosevelt, *Autobiography*, p. 457.
24. Roosevelt, "Value of an Athletic Training."
25. Walter Camp, *Football Facts and Figures* (New York: Harper & Brothers, 1894).
26. Ibid., p. 14.
27. The historian Ronald A. Smith has argued that Camp was "selective" in determining what information to include and what to leave out. He did not, for instance, pass on the fact that 20 percent of former football players reported permanent injuries. See Smith, *Sports & Freedom*, pp. 92–93.

28. This reply does not appear in *Football Facts and Figures*, but Poe's form, filled out by his brother John P. Poe, Jr., plus the forms of other respondents, may be found in the Walter Camp Papers, Reels 28 and 29.

29. Camp, *Football Facts and Figures*, p. 180.

30. Ibid., p. 29.

31. President Eliot's Report, *Harvard Graduates Magazine*, March 1895, p. 369.

32. Ibid.

33. "The Documents on the Football Question," *Harvard Graduates Magazine*, June 1895, p. 524.

34. Camp, *Football Facts and Figures*, pp. 15–16.

35. Ibid., p. 526.

36. Wister, p. 39.

37. Morris, *The Rise of Theodore Roosevelt*, p. 439.

38. Wister, *Roosevelt*, p. 6.

39. TR to Walter Camp, March 11, 1895, in Walter Camp Papers, Reel 15.

40. Charles Francis Adams to Walter Camp, January 23, 1895. Walter Camp Papers, Reel 1.

41. TR to Walter Camp, September 17, 1895, in Walter Camp Papers, Reel 15.

42. Walter Camp and Lorin F. Deland, *Football* (Boston: Houghton Mifflin, 1896). See also Borkowski, "The Life and Contributions of Walter Camp to American Football," pp. 167–69.

43. "Athletic Agreement with Yale," *Harvard Graduates Magazine*, March 1897, p. 418; "Football," *Harvard Graduates Magazine*, December 1897, p. 258.

44. Wiley Lee Umphlett, *Creating the Big Game: John W. Heisman and the Invention of American Football* (Westport, Conn.: Greenwood, 1992), pp. 51–52.

CHAPTER 8: ROUGH RIDING

1. George Magruder Battey, Jr., *A History of Rome and Floyd County*, vol. 1 (Atlanta: Webb & Vary, 1922), pp. 343–52.

2. Ibid., p. 349.

3. Ibid.

4. Ibid., p. 351.

5. Bill Reid, *Big-Time Football at Harvard, 1905: The Diary of Coach Bill Reid*, Ronald A. Smith, ed., (Urbana, Ill.: University of Illinois Press, 1994), p. xviii n. 3.

6. Roberts, *The Strenuous Life*, pp. 89–90.

7. Henry F. Pringle, *Theodore Roosevelt: A Biography* (New York: Harcourt, 1956), p. 116.

8. Perhaps apocryphal. See Watterson, *The Games Presidents Play*, p. 33.

9. Pringle, *Theodore Roosevelt*, p. 117.

10. Safire, *Safire's Political Dictionary*, p. 527.

11. Warren Zimmermann, *First Great Triumph: How Five Americans Made Their Country a World Power* (New York: Farrar, Straus, & Giroux, 2002), pp. 330–31.

12. Ibid.
13. TR to Henry Cabot Lodge, April 29, 1896, in *The Letters of Theodore Roosevelt: The Years of Preparation, 1868–1898*, pp. 535–36.
14. "President Eliot's Report," *Harvard Graduates Magazine*, March 1897, p. 363.
15. Watterson, *College Football*, pp. 56–57.
16. Jack McCallum, *Leonard Wood: Rough Rider, Surgeon, Architect of American Imperialism* (New York: New York University Press, 2006), pp. 49–50; Joseph Hamblen Sears, *The Career of Leonard Wood* (New York: D. Appleton, 1919), p. 58; Watterson, *College Football*, pp. 46–47.
17. McCallum, *Leonard Wood*.
18. Smith, *Sports & Freedom*, p. 98.
19. Thorstein Veblen, *The Theory of the Leisure Class: An Economic Study of Institutions* (New York: Funk & Wagnalls, 1967), p. 204.
20. Lewis became a friend of Roosevelt's. He spent a night at Sagamore Hill in August 1900; in 1903, Roosevelt appointed him assistant U.S. attorney for Boston. See Evan J. Albright, "William Henry Lewis," *Harvard Magazine*, November–December 2005, pp. 44–45.
21. Lubow, *The Reporter Who Would Be King*, pp. 26–27; Lewis, "The American Intercollegiate Football Spectacle," p. 127.
22. Robert H. Boyle, *Sport: Mirror of American Life* (Boston: Little, Brown, 1963), pp. 264–65.
23. Gary Scharnhorst, "Patten, Gilbert," *American National Biography*, vol. 17, pp. 126–128; Stewart H. Holbrook, "Frank Merriwell at Yale Again and Again and Again," *American Heritage*, June 1961.
24. Stephen Crane, *The Red Badge of Courage* (New York: Dell, 1960), p. 153.
25. Roberts, *The Strenuous Life*, p. 86.
26. Richard Posner, *The Essential Holmes: Selections from the Letters, Speeches, Judicial Opinions, and Other Writings of Oliver Wendell Holmes Jr.* (Chicago: University of Chicago Press, 1992), pp. 87, 91–92.
27. Albert W. Alschuler, *Law without Values: The Life, Work, and Legacy of Justice Holmes* (Chicago: University of Chicago Press, 2000), p. 48.
28. Ibid., p. 225 n. 73.
29. Henry Cabot Lodge, *Speeches and Addresses, 1884–1909* (Boston: Houghton Mifflin, 1909), pp. 292–93.
30. Morris, *The Rise of Theodore Roosevelt*, p. 627.
31. McCullough, *Brave Companions*, p. 80.
32. He spelled it "Elliott," which was the spelling of his brother's first name. TR to Eliot, April 7, 1898. The same misspelling may be found in a pair of letters sent several months later: TR to Eliot, July 27, 1898 (written in Cuba) and September 6, 1898. Additional correspondence on the canceled speech appears in TR to Eliot, November 11, 15, and 19, 1897, Theodore Roosevelt Papers, Library of Congress, Washington, D.C.

33. Morris, *The Rise of Theodore Roosevelt*, p. 633.
34. Theodore Roosevelt, *The Rough Riders* (New York: Library of America, 2004), p. 12.
35. Ibid., p. 14.
36. Sears, *The Career of Leonard Wood*, p. 58.
37. Roosevelt, *The Rough Riders*, pp. 18–20, 27.
38. Ibid., p. 103.
39. Roberts, *The Strenuous Life*, p. 217.
40. McCullough, *Brave Companions*, p. 81.
41. Roosevelt, *The Rough Riders*, p. 167.
42. Roberts, *The Strenuous Life*, pp. 102–3.
43. Ibid., p. 86.
44. Camp and Deland, *Football*, p. 278.
45. William Graham Sumner, *Essays of William Graham Sumner*, vol. 2, ed. Albert Galloway Keller and Maurice R. Davie (New Haven, Conn.: Yale University Press, 1934), p. 303.
46. "President Eliot's Report for 1897–98," *Harvard Graduates Magazine*, March 1899, p. 384.
47. Roosevelt, *Autobiography*, p. 305.
48. Ibid., p. 306.
49. Theodore Roosevelt, "What We Can Expect of the American Boy," *St. Nicholas*, May 1900, pp. 571–74; Theodore Roosevelt, *The Strenuous Life: Essays and Addresses* (New York: Century, 1902), pp. 155–64.

CHAPTER 9: FOOTBALL IS A FIGHT

1. Reid, *Big-Time Football at Harvard, 1905*, p. 74 n. 67; Watterson, *College Football*, pp. 67–68.
2. Henry Beach Needham, "The College Athlete, Part 2: His Amateur Code," *McClure's Magazine*, July 1905, pp. 260–73. See also Needham, "The College Athlete, Part 1: How Commercialism Is Making Him Professional," *McClure's Magazine*, June 1905, pp. 115–28.
3. Pringle, *Theodore Roosevelt*, p. 258.
4. Alfred Henry Lewis, ed., *A Compilation of the Messages and Speeches of Theodore Roosevelt, 1901–1905* (Washington, D.C.: Bureau of National Literature and Art, 1906), p. 644.
5. Joseph Bucklin Bishop, ed., *Theodore Roosevelt's Letters to His Children* (New York: Charles Scribner's Sons, 1919), pp. 62–63.
6. Pringle, *Theodore Roosevelt*, p. 158.
7. Ibid., p. 173.
8. TR to Henry Beech Needham, July 19, 1905, TR Papers.
9. Morris, *Theodore Rex*, p. 696, note to p. 376.
10. Henry Beach Needham, "Theodore Roosevelt—An Outdoor Man," *McClure's Magazine*, January 1906, p. 231.

11. Pringle, *Theodore Roosevelt*, p. 345.
12. Watterson, *College Football*, p. 60.
13. Ibid., p. 62.
14. Charles W. Eliot, "The Evils of Football," *Harvard Graduates Magazine*, March 1905, pp. 383–87.
15. "Experts Cannot See It That Way," *Boston Globe*, February 3, 1905.
16. "Game Needs No Defence," *Boston Globe*, February 3, 1905.
17. TR to Edward Deshon Brandegee, March 7, 1906, in *The Letters of Theodore Roosevelt: The Big Stick, 1905–1907*, ed. Elting E. Morison (Cambridge, Mass.: Harvard University Press, 1954), pp. 172–73.
18. Lester, *Stagg's University*, p. 240 n. 30.
19. Lipping, "Charles Eliot's Views on Education," p. 141.
20. Charles W. Eliot to Edward L. Godkin, January 26, 1900, Charles W. Eliot Papers, Harvard University, Cambridge, Mass., Box 41.
21. James, *Charles W. Eliot*, vol. 2, p. 159.
22. TR to Charles W. Eliot, August 16, 1905, TR Papers. The letter is typed, but the words "or even the second" are a handwritten addition.
23. Putney, *Muscular Christianity*, pp. 107–8.
24. Endicott Peabody to TR, September 16, 1905, TR Papers.
25. TR to Endicott Peabody, September 19, 1905, TR Papers.
26. TR to Walter Camp, September 7, 1901, Walter Camp Papers.
27. TR to Walter Camp, October 2, 1905, Walter Camp Papers.
28. TR to A. B. Colton, October 2, 1905, TR Papers.
29. TR to Ted Roosevelt, October 10, 1905, TR Papers.
30. TR to Charles W. Eliot, September 29, 1905, in *The Letters of Theodore Roosevelt: The Big Stick, 1905–1907*, p. 42.
31. TR to Robert Bacon, October 5, 1905, TR Papers.
32. TR to George Gray, October 6, 1905, in *The Letters of Theodore Roosevelt: The Big Stick, 1905–1907*, p. 46.
33. TR to Kermit Roosevelt, October 9, 1905, TR Papers.
34. Smith, *Sports & Freedom*, p. 93.
35. Reid, *Big-Time Football at Harvard, 1905*, p. 301.
36. Reid handwritten manuscript, William T. Reid Papers, Harvard University, Cambridge, Mass., HUD 8010, "Correspondence" folder. Reid wrote the document in pencil. An unnamed editor made several alterations, though it is possible to discern Reid's original wording. The pages have no date, but Reid probably wrote them in 1948, because an internal reference says "1905 was forty-three years ago." See also H. F. Manchester, "Reveals How College Football Was Saved in 1905," *Boston Herald*, October 17, 1926, p. E7.
37. Reid, *Big-Time Football at Harvard, 1905*, pp. 193–94.
38. TR to Irving Putnam, October 14, 1905, TR Papers.
39. Reid, *Big-Time Football at Harvard, 1905*, p. 194.
40. Ibid.

41. TR to Gifford Pinchot, October 9, 1905, TR Papers.

42. Walter Camp to TR, October 9, 1905, Walter Camp Papers.

43. TR to Walter Camp, October 11, 1905, TR Papers.

44. TR to Walter Camp, October 11, 1905, TR Papers.

45. Spencer Borden to TR, October 10, 1905, Walter Camp Papers.

46. Walter Camp to TR, October 13, 1905, Walter Camp Papers.

47. "Roosevelt Campaign for Football Reform," *New York Times*, October 10, 1905.

48. TR to Nicholas Murray Butler, October 11, 1905, TR Papers.

49. Nicholas Murray Butler to Charles W. Eliot, November 3, 1905, Charles W. Eliot Papers, Box 31.

50. Lewis, "The American Intercollegiate Football Spectacle," p. 231.

51. H. Paul Jeffers, *Theodore Roosevelt Jr.: The Life of a War Hero* (Novato, Calif.: Presidio, 2002), pp. 42–43.

52. Reid ms., pp. 2–3.

53. Ronald A. Smith, "Harvard and Columbia and a Reconsideration of the 1905–06 Football Crisis," *Journal of Sports History* (Winter 1981), p. 18 n. 40.

54. Reid ms., pp. 3–4.

55. "Reid Condemns Football," *Harvard Graduates Magazine*, December 1905, p. 300.

56. Reid ms., pp. 4–5.

57. Ibid., p. 5.

58. Ibid., p. 19. In the document, the line "in the balls" is scratched out and edited as "in the groin." See also Smith, *Sports & Freedom*, p. 196; Reid, *Big-Time Football at Harvard, 1905*, pp. 275–77.

59. Reid ms., pp. 20–21. Reid does not provide a date for the lunch, but it probably occurred on November 27, 1905. Mark Twain also may have attended the lunch, though Reid does not mention his presence.

60. Jeffers, *Theodore Roosevelt Jr.*, pp. 57–58.

61. TR to Walter Camp, November 24, 1905, in *The Letters of Theodore Roosevelt: The Big Stick, 1905–1907*, pp. 93–94.

62. "President Eliot Not There," *New York Times*, November 26, 1905; "Yale Downs Harvard By Only Six Points," *New York Times*, November 26, 1905.

63. Lewis, "The American Intercollegiate Football Spectacle," p. 234.

64. Reid ms., p. 14.

65. Ibid., p. 13.

66. Ibid., p. 14. This quote is scratched out by the document's editor and changed to "I'll have to give this matter further thought." On the back of the page, the editor comments, "My quote of Teddy's tones it down so that no offense could possibly be taken."

67. Paul J. Dashiell to TR, December 7, 1905, Charles W. Eliot Papers, Box 118.

68. Smith, *Sports & Freedom*, p. 197.

69. Watterson, *College Football*, p. 72.

70. "Half Back Moore Buried," *New York Times*, November 29, 1905.
71. Henry M. MacCracken to Charles W. Eliot, November 25, 1905, Charles W. Eliot Papers, Box 101.
72. "Football Reform By Abolition," *Nation*, November 30, 1905, pp. 437–38.
73. "President Issues Letter: Give Reasons for Abolishing the Game at Columbia," *Columbia Spectator*, December 4, 1905.
74. TR to William R. Harper, December 4, 1905, TR Papers.
75. TR to Paul J. Dashiell, December 5, 1905, TR Papers.
76. TR to Charles W. Eliot, December 5, 1905, TR Papers.
77. James, *Charles W. Eliot*, vol. 2, p. 157.
78. TR to Charles W. Eliot, December 21, 1905, TR Papers.
79. Smith, *Sports & Freedom*, pp. 198–99.
80. Ibid., p. 200.
81. Ibid.
82. Ibid., p. 201.
83. William T. Reid to Walter Camp, December 19, 1905, Walter Camp Papers.
84. Smith, p. 202; Watterson, *College Football*, pp. 77–78.
85. Smith, p. 204.
86. John E. Owsley to Walter Camp, December 16, 1905, Walter Camp Papers, Reel 13.
87. Lewis, "The American Intercollegiate Football Spectacle," p. 246.
88. Lewis, "The American Intercollegiate Football Spectacle," p. 247.
89. TR to A. L. Mills, January 10, 1906, TR Papers.

CHAPTER 10: THE AIR WAR
1. "Army Wants Big Score," *New York Times*, November 1, 1913.
2. Murray Sperber, *Shake Down the Thunder: The Creation of Notre Dame Football* (Bloomington: Indiana University Press, 1993), p. 38. See also Frank P. Maggio, *Notre Dame and the Game That Changed Football* (New York: Carroll & Graf, 2007), pp. 97–122.
3. Philip L. Brooks, *Forward Pass: The Play That Saved Football* (Yardley, Pa.: Westholme, 2008), p. 206.
4. "Notre Dame's Open Play Amazes Army," *New York Times*, November 2, 1913.
5. Stephen E. Ambrose, *Eisenhower: Soldier, General of the Army, President-Elect, 1890–1952*, vol. 1 (New York: Simon & Schuster, 1983), p. 50.
6. Ibid.
7. Smith, *Sports & Freedom*, p. 97.
8. Brooks, *Forward Pass*, pp. 171–74.
9. TR to Paul J. Dashiell, January 10, 1906, TR Papers.
10. Charles W. Eliot, "Topics from the President's Report," *Harvard Graduates Magazine*, March 1906, pp. 405–6.
11. Ray Allen Billington, *Frederick Jackson Turner: Historian, Scholar, Teacher* (New York: Oxford University Press, 1973), p. 273.
12. "Football Differences," *New York Times*, September 30, 1906. See also Watterson, *College Football*, p. 105.

13. Watterson, *College Football*, p. 107; Bergin, *The Game*, pp. 92–93.

14. Watterson, *College Football*, p. 108.

15. Charles W. Eliot, *Reports of the President and the Treasurer of Harvard College 1905–06* (Cambridge, Mass.: Harvard University, 1907), pp. 43–44. In 1908, W. H. Roberts wrote to Eliot and asked for an opinion on whether children should play football and basketball during morning recess. "The excitement of such violent games is unwholesome for children in the middle of the morning session," replied Eliot. "I ought to add that, in my opinion, neither of these games is fit for general use in schools and colleges."

16. "Pres. Roosevelt on Play and Work," *Harvard Graduates Magazine*, June 1907, pp. 779–80; "Pres. Roosevelt's Address," *Harvard Crimson*, February 25, 1907.

17. TR to Ralph Delahaye Paine, November 19, 1907, in *The Letters of Theodore Roosevelt: The Big Stick, 1905–1907*, p. 853.

18. Watterson, *College Football*, pp. 111–12.

19. Borkowski, "The Life and Contributions of Walter Camp to American Football," p. 218.

20. Watterson, *College Football*, p. 114.

21. James A. Ramage, *Gray Ghost: The Life of Col. John Singleton Mosby* (Lexington: University Press of Kentucky, 1999), pp. 329–30.

22. Watterson, *College Football*, pp. 114–15.

23. Borkowski, "The Life and Contributions of Walter Camp to American Football," p. 208.

24. *The Papers of Woodrow Wilson*, vol. 22, *1910–1911*, ed. Arthur S. Link (Princeton, N.J.: Princeton University Press, 1976), pp. 4–5.

25. Watterson, *College Football*, p. 130.

26. Lester, *Stagg's University*, p. 74.

27. H. Paul Jeffers, *Ace of Aces: The Life of Capt. Eddie Rickenbacker* (New York: Ballantine, 2003), pp. 125–28.

28. Borkowski, "The Life and Contributions of Walter Camp to American Football," pp. 246–47.

29. FDR to Walter Camp, March 24, 1919, Walter Camp Papers.

30. Borkowski, "The Life and Contributions of Walter Camp to American Football," p. 279.

31. William Graham Sumner, *Folkways: A Study of the Sociological Importance of Usages, Manners, Customs, Mores, and Morals* (Boston: Ginn, 1906), p. 639.

32. James, *Charles W. Eliot*, vol. 2, p. 285.

33. Reid ms., p. 18.

Index